The Big Book of What, How, and Why

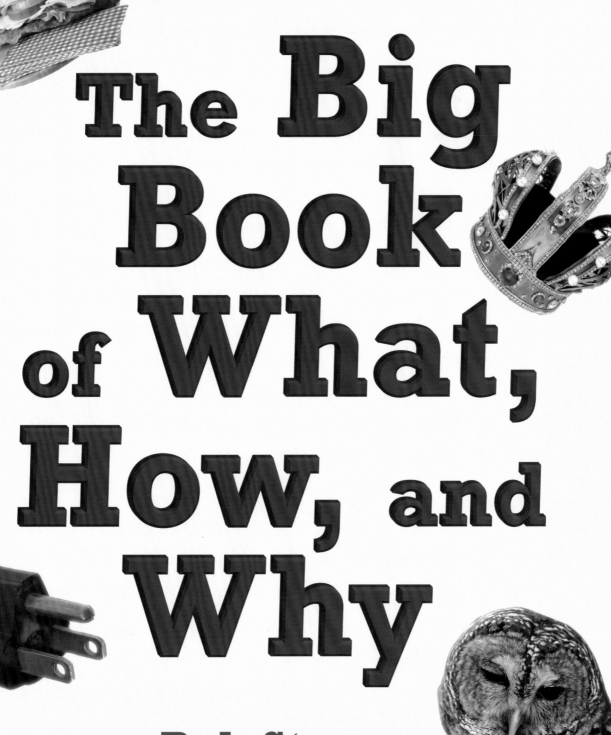

The Big Book of What, How, and Why

Bob Strauss

Main Street
A division of Sterling Publishing Co., Inc.
New York

Library of Congress Cataloging-in-Publication Data
available on request

2   4   6   8   10   9   7   5   3

Published by Sterling Publishing Co., Inc.
387 Park Avenue South, New York, NY 10016
© 2005 by Sterling Publishing Co., Inc.
Distributed in Canada by Sterling Publishing
c/o Canadian Manda Group, 165 Dufferin Street
Toronto, Ontario, Canada M6K 3H6
Distributed in the United Kingdom by GMC Distribution Services,
Castle Place, 166 High Street, Lewes, East Sussex, England BN7 1XU
Distributed in Australia by Capricorn Link (Australia) Pty. Ltd.
P.O. Box 704, Windsor, NSW 2756, Australia

Sterling ISBN-13: 978-1-4027-2900-3
ISBN-10: 1-4027-2900-6

Edited by Cassandra Case
Production Design by StarGraphics Studio

Photographs and images licensed from JUPITERIMAGES; Dynamic Graphics;
Anglo-Australian Observatory/David Malin Images (Photo of *Proxima Centauri* on page 276);
NASA/Jon Morse (Photo of *Eta Carinae* on page 277).

For information about custom editions, special sales, premium and
corporate purchases, please contact Sterling Special Sales
Department at 800-805-5489 or specialsales@sterlingpub.com.

Contents

Introduction 9

Section 1 ANIMAL KINGDOM 11

Section 2 **CIVILIZATION** 75

Communication

History

Man-Made

Recreation

Systems

Section 3 HUMAN BODY 147

Section 4 **SCIENCES** 213

Introduction

Have you ever wondered why bird's eggs aren't perfectly round? Or why a bolt of lightning isn't laser-beam straight, but broken up into short, jagged chunks? These are the kinds of questions you'll find answered here, along with over a thousand others, on topics ranging from neutron stars to ice-cream sundaes to the French Revolution.

In writing this book, I tried to be mindful of the kinds of questions kids ask every day—not just the common ones, like "Why is the sky blue?" or "How does popcorn pop?", but the uncommon ones as well, like "Why do stop signs have eight sides?" and "Why is it so hard to swat a fly?" Many of the questions in *The Big Book of What, How, and Why* were solicited from actual, everyday, real-life kids, and the answers are written in a fun, breezy, informative way that real-life kids can easily understand.

I've also been very careful to provide 100 percent, rock-solid answers only when 100 percent, rock-solid information is available. In my experience, too many books of this type skip over those all-important "buts," "excepts," and "unlesses." So when I tackle a question like, "What was the world's largest dinosaur?", I make clear that my answer is based on the best knowledge available today—and that that answer may change as scientists make new discoveries. And when I wander into a thicket like, "What's the difference between a fruit and a vegetable?", I make clear to kids that many of the experts are as confused as they are!

On a related note, you won't (I hope!) find any urban myths propagated on these pages. For example, it's long been accepted as common knowledge that the Great Wall of China is the only man-made structure visible from outer space. Well, it turns out that this isn't quite true, as I state in my answer. I've tried to provide similar no-nonsense replies to questions like "What is the Bermuda Triangle?" and "How did the Egyptians build the pyramids?" I feel it's important that kids learn to think logically about the world, so every question in this book has a logical answer.

Since I know that kids have short attention spans (or at least shorter attention spans than their parents would like!), I've thrown the occasional curve ball into my answers, just to keep them on their toes. So when I describe a tangelo as a "cross between a tangerine and a buffalo" or say that bears prepare for hibernation by eating the occasional camper, don't worry—that's just the prelude to the real explanation!

—*Bob Strauss*

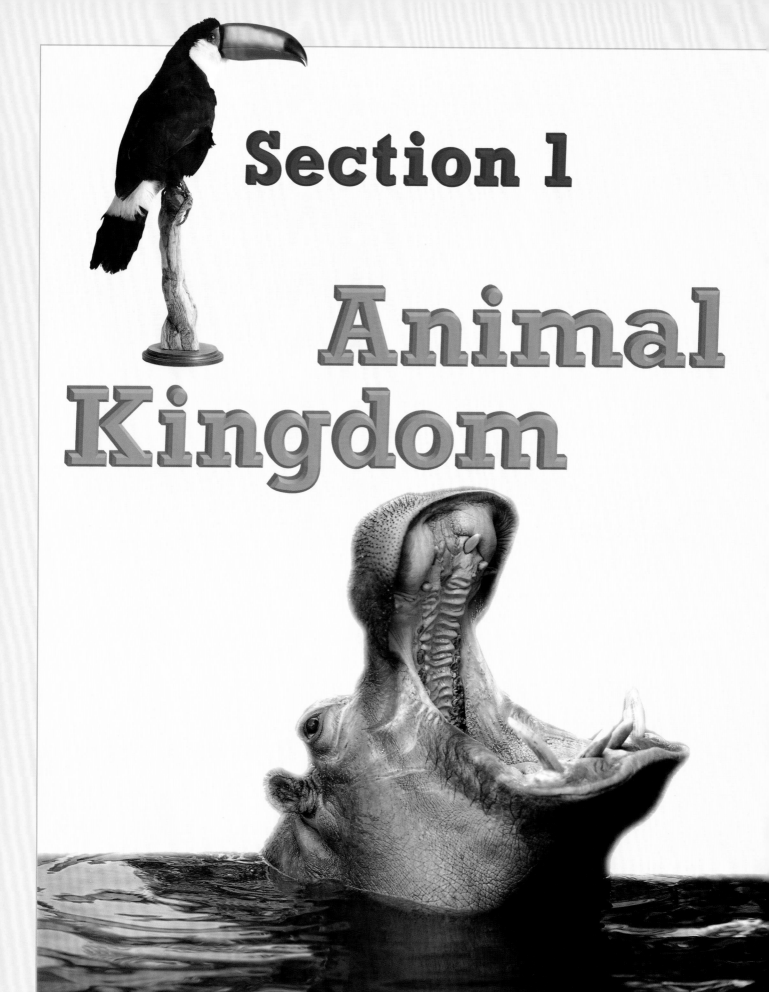

Section 1

Animal Kingdom

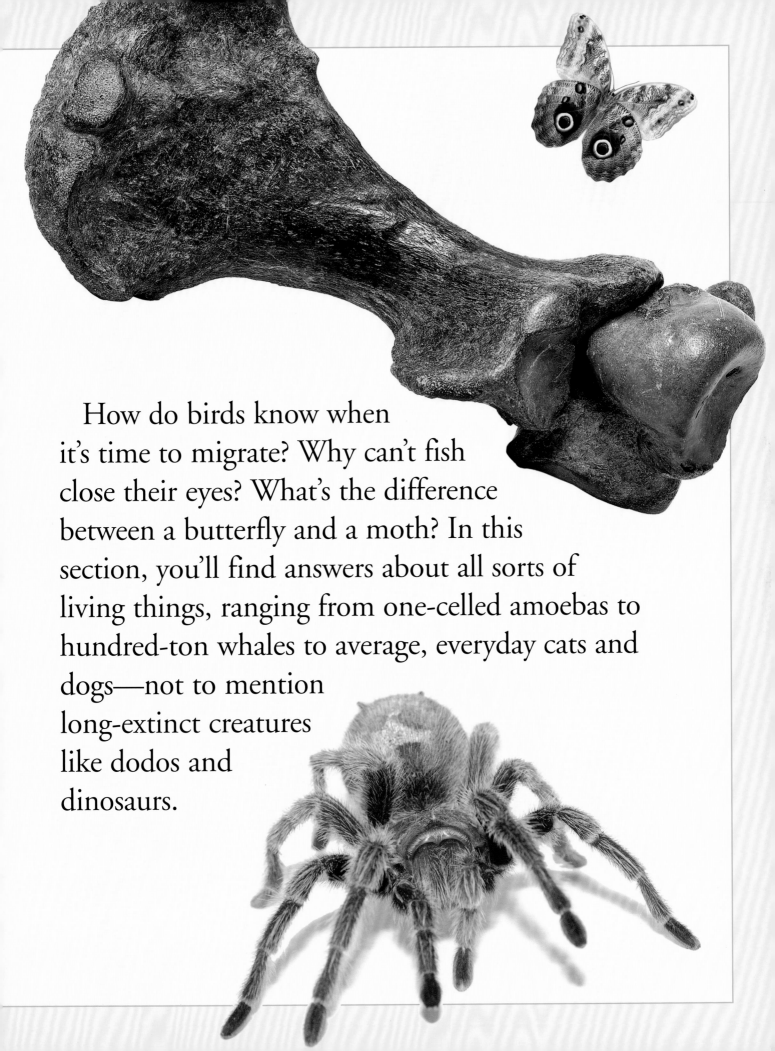

How do birds know when it's time to migrate? Why can't fish close their eyes? What's the difference between a butterfly and a moth? In this section, you'll find answers about all sorts of living things, ranging from one-celled amoebas to hundred-ton whales to average, everyday cats and dogs—not to mention long-extinct creatures like dodos and dinosaurs.

HOW do baby birds eat?

Since baby birds can't eat solid food, the mother bird chews up the food first, then regurgitates it into her young ones' eager beaks. Doves handle this process a bit differently: the mother dove chews the food, opens her mouth wide, and lets her baby birds stick their heads in and chow down.

WHY do you never see baby pigeons?

This is one of those riddles that has baffled city-dwellers for decades. The answer is that baby pigeons stay in the nest for an unusually long time—practically until they're adults! By the way, the reason pigeons like to nest in tall buildings (and on the top of statues) is that they're descended from cliff-dwelling birds native to Asia.

HOW do birds learn to fly?

Baby birds (or "fledglings," as they're sometimes called) don't need to be instructed how to fly, but they do sometimes need to be encouraged by their parents. Like all animals, birds are born with hard-wired instincts, one of which is to hop out of the nest (or be pushed out by its mom) and start to fly when the time is right—usually a couple of weeks after it's hatched from its egg.

WHY do birds sing?

As with so much behavior in the animal kingdom, the main reasons male birds sing (and males do practically all of the singing!) is to attract females and warn competing males to stay away. Because they're constantly competing with each other for mates, the male birds of some species have developed some very elaborate melodies.

Generally, the kind of song a bird has is determined by its environment. In the forest and jungle—where sounds are absorbed by leaves and trees—birds have short, repetitious songs, while birds that fly over open, flat areas produce buzzing bursts of sound that carry over long distances. If there's a lot of noise in the area (say, because of a nearby waterfall), the result is a high, piercing warble.

By the way, most birds aren't born knowing their tunes—they have to learn how to sing from their parents, the same way humans do!

WHY aren't eggs perfectly round?

An egg acquires its oval shape as it's pushed through the mother bird's narrow oviduct while its shell is still relatively soft. And it's a good thing that most bird eggs are oval-shaped, rather than round—a perfectly spherical egg would roll out of a nest too easily, while an oval egg's "wobble" keeps it from straying too far too fast.

You may wonder: Why aren't eggs shaped like cubes, so they stay put once and for all? Well, not only would a square egg be painful, if not impossible, to lay, but its perfectly flat sides and corners would be too susceptible to outside damage. A curved shell has a certain amount of surface tension that makes it slightly easier to break from the inside than the outside so the hatchling inside can break out with a minimum of effort. If you were hatching out of an egg, wouldn't you rather the shell were thin and crumbly, rather than as tough as, say, a coconut?

WHY do eggs have yolks?

The yolk (yellow part) of an egg is where a baby chick develops after the egg is fertilized; that's why it's rich in protein and other nutrients. As tasty as it is, the albumin (white part) of the egg mainly serves as a shock absorber, to protect the yolk and the developing chicken inside from accidental bumps or jostles.

WHAT keeps birds from falling out of trees when they sleep?

When a bird lands on a tree branch, it "locks" its sharp claws in place with the help of special tendons in its legs. Securely attached, the bird can safely grab a few ZZZ's without fear of plummeting to the ground.

WHY do birds have feathers?

All things being equal, you'd think the average bird would be happier with warm, thick fur than with a silly bunch of feathers. But all things aren't equal: unlike fur, feathers are aerodynamic, providing the lift a bird needs to take off and stay in the air. And, though they may not look it, water-repellent feathers covering cozy down can be just as warm as any animal's pelt.

WHY do birds fly in V formation?

This was a mystery for a long time, but scientists finally figured out that it helps the birds save energy. As the V-shaped flock of birds slices through the air, this reduces wind resistance for the birds in the rear, allowing them to stop flapping their wings occasionally and simply glide (studies have found that the heart rates of flocking pelicans are lower than when these big birds fly solo). This is the same "slipstream" principle that allows a racing car to cut down on fuel consumption by closely following the car in front.

Besides conserving energy—which is crucial for larger birds that migrate for thousands of miles at a stretch—flying in V formation provides another advantage: it keeps the flock close together. This makes it easier for birds to communicate with one another and to change direction on short notice.

WHY do geese honk when they fly in formation?

Geese don't only make a racket when they fly overhead: these are among the most talkative of all birds, even when they're standing still. That said, scientists believe geese "honk" in flight in order to keep track of each other and encourage lagging birds to keep up with the flock.

WHY do birds fly into windows?

If a bird slams into a window once, it's probably because it was completely fooled (even unwary people will occasionally bump into a clear plane of glass). But if it bumps into the window repeatedly, that means it's being fooled by its own reflection, which it thinks is another bird that it's trying to attack.

HOW high can birds fly?

Although some birds occasionally venture higher, the avian altitude champ is the bar-headed goose, which regularly flies over the Himalayan mountains (including Everest, the tallest mountain in the world) during its annual migration. That's a height of over five miles, comparable to a cruising passenger jet.

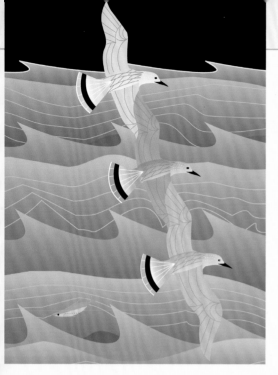

HOW do birds know when it's time to migrate?

As winter approaches in the northern hemisphere, the days become shorter and shorter. In birds (and in all migrating animals, for that matter), the reduced exposure to sunlight triggers the brain's pituitary gland to secrete hormones that stimulate the creatures' appetite. Over the course of a few weeks, the birds "plump up"—that is, accumulate fat stores under their skin that can be used during the impending journey.

Now that the birds are ready, all they need is a cue from the environment. A sudden drop in temperature, or an unsuccessful day searching for food, will convince at least a few birds that it's time to get going. This behavior triggers similar behavior in the rest of the flock, and before you know it, a huge swarm of birds is on the wing and heading south.

WHY do birds fly south in the winter?

Birds fly south for two reasons: first, because they need to be light enough to fly, they don't tolerate cold weather as well as other animals, and second, food is more plentiful in warmer climates.

WHAT is the farthest a bird can migrate?

Every year, arctic terns flock from Maine to Africa, then all the way to Antarctica. That's a round trip of over 20,000 miles, or more than six times the distance from New York to California!

HOW do birds find their nests?

Like many animals, birds have a natural "homing" ability that enables them to find their way back to their nests from hundreds of miles away. Scientists aren't quite sure how they manage this, but it's possible that birds have a memory for landmarks like mountains and rivers, or even an inbuilt "compass" that allows them to navigate according to the earth's magnetic field (which may also be how they know to fly south in the winter).

WHAT do vultures eat?

Unlike owls or eagles that hunt—swooping down from the sky to carry off live mice or rabbits—vultures eat dead animals. Not only dead, but already rotting; they are nature's garbage men. These birds can occasionally be found in populated areas, but they're most common in the wide-open spaces of Africa and Asia, where they come in to clean up such things as dead wildebeest and zebra carcasses lying around after the lions have fed.

HOW long can a chicken survive without its head?

About as long as a person can, despite what you may have heard. Back in 1945, there was a famous story about a chicken named "Mike" that survived after two-thirds of his head was cut off (leaving part of his brain intact). However, there's no truth to the myth that a chicken can run around for weeks after having its head completely chopped off!

WHAT did birds evolve from?

As with so many species in the three-billion-year history of life on our planet, there was no one "aha!" moment when the first bird took wing. Scientists now believe that primitive birds evolved about a hundred million years ago from small, two-legged dinosaurs called "theropods," a theory that got a big boost when paleontologists dug up the fossils of two previously unknown feathered theropods—which may be the long-sought "missing link" between the two types of creatures.

As proof that evolution proceeds in fits and starts, these feathered theropods weren't the first (non-bug) flying creatures. The gigantic archeopteryx flourished about 150 million years ago, yet apparently represented an evolutionary dead end, never evolving into a true bird. The primitive birds that appeared about 50 million years later fared better, possibly because they benefited from the sudden extinction of the dinosaurs—which opened up plenty of room for new species.

WHAT is a kiwi?

Found only in New Zealand, the kiwi is a small, flightless bird with thin, stringy feathers that look like hair. It spends its nights poking through soil and leaf litter in search of tasty worms and grubs. Because New Zealand doesn't have any small land animals, such as squirrels or badgers, the kiwi filled this evolutionary niche.

WHY did dodos become extinct?

Dodos—squat, flightless birds weighing about 50 pounds—used to live on Mauritius, an isolated island in the Indian Ocean. Scientists believe these huge birds evolved from common pigeons, which landed on the island millions of years before and thrived in the absence of natural competition.

Because dodos had never encountered humans (or any large predators) before, they were completely unprepared when Portuguese settlers landed on Mauritius in 1505. The birds had no way to defend themselves from the hungry settlers, and were hunted to extinction in less than 200 years.

Since then, dodos have become the poster-birds for extinction (which is where the phrase "dead as a dodo" comes from). Sadly, this is a common result whenever human populations encounter large, gentle animals (like seals and bison) that have never needed to evolve any natural defenses.

WHY can't penguins fly?

In the south polar regions, where penguins live, there's not much food to be found on land. That's why penguins evolved to dive for fish—and part of what makes them such good divers is their thick, heavy bones (which act as "ballast" to keep them deep in the water). Since it's hard to get off the ground with all that extra weight, penguins gradually lost the ability to fly, though they still have tiny wings.

WHAT are emus?

Almost as big as their nearest relatives, ostriches, emus are gangly, flightless birds native to Australia. The most fascinating thing about emus is the way they hatch their young: the smaller males sit on the eggs, while the larger females defend the nests from intruders!

WHY are sailors superstitious about albatrosses?

Sighting an albatross—a large, flying bird similar to a seagull—has long been considered a good omen by sailors, because it means land can't be far away. There's also a tradition that killing an albatross brings bad luck, the subject of a famous poem by Samuel Taylor Coleridge called "The Rime of the Ancient Mariner."

HOW many kinds of parrot are there?

In ornithological terms, the word "parrot" is kind of like the word "dog," covering an amazingly diverse number of individual breeds. This extended family includes lovebirds, parakeets, macaws, and budgerigars (also known as "budgies"), just to name a few familiar examples.

Anatomically, all parrots have curved beaks, an erect posture, and four toes on each foot (two in the front and two in the back). These birds can be found in abundance in all the world's warmer climates, including Africa, India, and the Far East, though the largest and most colorful varieties (like macaws) are native to Central and South America. (Oddly, considering how popular they are as pets, no species of parrot is native to the U.S.)

Most parrots live for an unusually long time, making them the exception to the general rule that the smaller the animal, the shorter its life span. It is not unusual for a well-cared-for pet parrot to exceed 50 years of age—meaning these birds often outlive their owners!

WHY did they have canaries in coal mines?

Canaries are more sensitive to odorless and colorless gases than people are. If a canary in a coal mine became sick or started acting strangely, the miners knew they were being exposed to poisonous gases like carbon monoxide. Today, electronic detectors have done away with the need for using canaries.

WHAT is the difference between a cockatoo and a cockatiel?

These two names are often used indiscriminately, but bird owners know that a cockatoo (a close relative of the parrot) is a large bird with a movable headcrest, while a cockatiel is a smaller species of cockatoo, with a pointed yellow crest. The reason cockatoos and cockatiels make good pets is that they have relatively calm temperaments (in bird terms, at least), and bond closely with their owners when they're raised from fledglings.

WHY are bird cages covered with a blanket at night?

Some birds (like parrots) are extremely sensitive to light, because they evolved to live in dense jungles where not even the moon is visible at night. Even though your bedroom might be dark enough at night for your dog or cat to sleep, it's still too bright for the average parrot, so covering the cage with a blanket provides the absolute darkness the bird needs to catch a few Z's.

WHY are some pet birds illegal?

Some of the most colorful and sought-after birds (which live in the dense jungles of South America, among a few other places) also happen to be endangered. For this reason, it's illegal to remove individuals from the wild, though this hasn't prevented some shady people from selling these spectacular birds on the international "black market" for thousands of dollars apiece.

WHY aren't lovebirds sold in pairs?

As you can guess from their name, lovebirds are extremely affectionate—in fact, a male and female bird will mate for life (about 10 to 15 years). Although it's possible to buy paired lovebirds in a single cage, most experts recommend against this, because the birds will spend so much time being affectionate with each other that they'll barely pay any attention to you! Also, male and female lovebirds in close proximity have a habit of producing, well, lots and lots of baby lovebirds.

HOW do birds learn how to talk?

Certain kinds of birds, like mockingbirds, mynahs, and African Grey parrots, have evolved the ability to mimic the sounds made by other animals. It's not clear why this ability should be so important, but—as with most things in the animal kingdom—it probably has something to do with attracting mates.

Since a jungle bird can learn to imitate the howl of a monkey, it shouldn't come as a surprise that a caged pet bird can mimic the sound of human speech. Most birds pick up random bits of conversation (if they bother to talk at all!), but professional bird trainers can give a talented parrot an extensive "vocabulary" and train it to respond to certain cues. This way, it appears that the parrot is actually thinking about what it says—which it almost certainly isn't!

What makes a talking bird's ability even more amazing is that it can clearly reproduce human speech without the aid of a tongue or teeth. Instead, these birds have extremely complicated larynxes (voice boxes) that can "manufacture" all sorts of sounds.

WHAT is the world's biggest bird?

As you may have guessed, the ostrich—which can grow up to nine feet tall and weigh over three hundred pounds—is the biggest living thing with feathers. As for birds that actually know how to fly, the Kori Bustard of Africa weighs in at up to 50 pounds, and several species of birds (including the albatross) have wingspans of well over ten feet.

Although ostriches can't fly, that doesn't mean they can't get away quickly in an emergency. A full-grown ostrich can sprint close to 45 miles per hour in short bursts, and can keep up a comfortable pace of a little over 30 miles per hour. This big bird covers a lot of ground—each of its strides is 10 to 15 feet long!

One thing an ostrich doesn't do is bury its head in the sand. This myth may have started because a mother ostrich guarding her eggs will press flat against the ground to avoid detection. But an ostrich won't dig a hole in the sand and stick its head inside, or even stick its head in an already-dug hole if it finds one.

WHY do owls have big eyes?

Despite the legends, owls don't have big eyes because they're smart—they have big eyes because they hunt by night, and big peepers see better in dim light than do small ones (by gathering in more light). By the way, an owl's eyes are so big that they can't rotate in their sockets; the bird has to move its entire head if it wants to look in a different direction!

WHAT bird has the biggest nest?

Yes, it's the bald eagle, but honorable mention goes to the mallee of Australia. Mallee fowl lay their eggs in gigantic, sculpted mounds of dirt weighing thousands of pounds each.

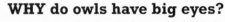

HOW did the bald eagle get its name?

Centuries ago, the word "bald" meant "white," not its modern meaning of "hairless." A bald eagle actually has as much "hair" (feathers, really!) on its head as other birds, although its white pate gives it a "bald-as-a-cue-ball" appearance to the birdwatcher.

Even though it's the official bird of the United States, for many years the bald eagle teetered on the brink of extinction (the species is still hunted illegally, which can result in heavy fines and even jail time). Thanks to protection efforts, the bald eagle population in the U.S. has rebounded to about 100,000, which is still far below its numbers a few centuries ago.

As befits their large size, bald eagles can build enormous nests: one specimen discovered in Florida in 1962 was ten feet deep, twenty feet wide, and weighed over two tons.

HOW fast is a road runner?

It's not quite as fast as its cartoon counterpart, but a real-life road runner can run as fast as 18 miles per hour—more than quick enough to elude most of its enemies or catch a tasty squirrel. Here's one more amazing road runner fact: it likes to hunt rattlesnakes!

WHY do flamingos stand on one leg?

Scientists don't know for certain, but they think a flamingo stands on one leg to conserve energy. By drawing one leg close up to its body, the flamingo keeps it warm, which enables the bird to burn less energy during cold weather. Because it spends so much time in the water, it's also possible that the flamingo stands on one leg just to give the other one a chance to dry out every now and then.

WHY do toucans have such big beaks?

A toucan's bright, prominent beak is almost as long as the rest of its body (it's not nearly as heavy, though, because it's mostly hollow and made of lightweight material). This oversized schnozz allows the bird to easily reach berries on nearby branches, and is also helpful for attracting mates.

HOW does a hummingbird hover?

In a way, hummingbirds have more in common with mosquitoes than with other birds. This gentle creature beats its wings tremendously fast—up to 80 times a second—in a slightly rotating motion, which allows it to stay in one place or move slowly forward, like a helicopter. Not surprisingly, a hummingbird has the most powerful breast muscles (relative to its size) of any bird.

HOW dangerous are piranhas?

Despite their fearsome reputation, piranha fish aren't quite as dangerous—at least to humans—as you might think. These toothy South American fish mostly feed on other fish and small insects, and occasionally will nibble on the carcass of a dead animal lying in the water. Still, you wouldn't want to stick your hand into a tank of piranhas.

HOW do jellyfish swim?

Much of the time, a jellyfish doesn't have to swim—it just hitches a ride with the nearest ocean current. But when it has to move, a jelly squeezes its body and ejects water from its underside, creating a small jet that propels it through the water. Some jellyfish also have tiny hairs on their bodies (called "cilia") that wriggle like tiny oars. The only things a jellyfish doesn't use to swim are its tentacles—those are strictly for catching food.

WHAT is the biggest shark?

The aptly named whale shark, a non-human-munching shark that feeds on tiny plankton, is even bigger than the Great White shark. It can grow up to 50 feet in length.

WHY do sharks attack people?

In fact, sharks have more reason to be afraid of people than people have to be afraid of sharks. In the sea, a shark reigns supreme, but sportsmen with fast boats and harpoons can capture and kill even a fearsome Great White shark that can span a whopping 35 feet from nose to tail. The Great White also has about 3,000 three-inch-long teeth arranged in rows, which are sharp as razors. The first couple of rows of teeth are used for ripping apart prey, while the rows in the rear can move forward as the front teeth break, die, or fall out.

What attracts sharks is movement, and humans, with their long, gangly legs and arms, make perfect bait. By the way, shark attacks are very rare, since most sharks congregate out in the ocean—far away from the shoreline and people out for a swim. In fact, many, many more sharks have been killed by people than vice-versa.

HOW fast can a shark swim?

The big blue shark can attain speeds of up to 25 miles per hour (that's pokey for land, but blazingly fast for water), while the smaller shortfin mako has been known to go as fast as 45 MPH.

HOW big is a giant squid?

Giant squids aren't quite as monstrous as they appear in science-fiction movies, but they are still pretty impressive: these rarely-seen creatures can grow to a length of about 60 yards, or three-fifths of a football field. Although there have been no authenticated instances of giant squids overturning boats—let alone eating a crew!—it's easy to see why these alien-looking ocean-dwellers have long inspired fear in sailors.

Compared to its enormous squid cousin, the Giant Pacific Octopus is a relative lightweight. This gentle creature rarely exceeds fifteen feet in length (including tentacles) and only weighs about a hundred pounds, though there have been reports of individuals two or three times as heavy. And unlike the giant squid, the giant octopus can be found in abundance everywhere from Alaska to northern California, where it's fished commercially by (presumably very strong!) sailors and sold as food.

HOW slippery is an eel?

So slippery you probably couldn't hold one in your hands for more than a few seconds. An eel's healthy coat of slime serves two purposes: it helps keep its skin moist, and it allows the eel to penetrate into narrow underwater nooks and crannies to hide from predators or search for food.

WHAT is a stingray?

As you can guess from its name, the stingray is a kind of ray (a wide, flat, boneless fish closely related to the shark) with poisonous spines on its tail that it uses to sting and paralyze other fish. Fortunately, stingrays are much smaller than nonstinging species like the Manta Ray—a gentle, large ray that can grow to be over 20 feet wide and weigh a few tons.

WHAT is a coelacanth?

This primitive fish, thought to be extinct for at least 70 million years, made a huge splash (so to speak) when a specimen was caught alive and well off the east coast of South Africa in 1938. Before this, the coelacanth had only been known from its numerous fossils.

Among paleontologists, the discovery of a live coelacanth (which has a three-lobed tail fin and thin, primitive scales) caused as much surprise as if a 40-foot-tall T. Rex had attacked New York. Despite an intensive search, a second coelacanth wasn't found until 14 years later, near the Comoros Islands. In 1997, scientists discovered another species of coelacanth off the waters of Indonesia.

The discovery of a live coelacanth has had repercussions far beyond the fish's importance: since ancient coelacanths lived at the same time as dinosaurs, finding a live fish opened the door to the possibility that somewhere, somehow, a small species of dinosaur has escaped extinction!

HOW high can a flying fish fly?

Flying fish don't really fly like birds do—they build up a head of steam underwater, jump out over the surface, and dive back in. The highest a fish can jump is only a few feet above the water, and it doesn't stay airborne for more than a few seconds. But a flying fish can cover a lot of distance in a single jump: up to 100 yards, or the length of a football field!

WHY do salmon swim upstream?

When it's time for them to spawn (that is, for the females to lay eggs and the males to fertilize them), salmon embark on the toughest migration in the animal kingdom. These fish lay their eggs inland, meaning they have to fight their way against river currents to make the trip. This involves leaping backward over small waterfalls, wriggling their way through tumbling rapids, and avoiding getting eaten by hungry bears!

HOW do fish breathe?

A fish uses its gills (which are kind of like underwater lungs) to extract the oxygen that is dissolved in water and disseminate it through its bloodstream. Like people, fish will suffocate if they can't get enough oxygen. Even when a fish is in the water, this can happen because of water pollution, oil spills or other natural disasters.

WHAT is a bottom feeder?

The bottom feeder is the low man on the fish totem-pole. Consisting of various species (among them the catfish), these creatures literally eat anything they find on the ocean floor—including plankton, algae, and the waste of other fish! Not surprisingly, the phrase "bottom-feeder" is also used to describe shady business people who will do anything to make a buck.

WHY do fish swim in schools?

Fish swim in schools for the same reason birds fly in V-shaped formations: to save energy. By swimming in schools, the fish become more "hydrodynamic" and can more easily take advantage of natural eddies in the current, allowing them to get where they're going without exhausting themselves.

WHY can't fish close their eyes?

Unlike, say, birds—which smack into rain, snow, and tiny grains of dust as they fly through the air—a fish swims in pretty much the same, unchanging environment all the time. This is the main reason these creatures never needed to evolve eyelids; the only protection they require is a clear, glassy layer over their eyes to ward off floating grains of sand.

However, just because fish can't close their eyes doesn't mean they can't sleep. Fish will rest occasionally in undersea cracks or crevices (which gives them protection from being caught unawares and eaten by bigger fish). Some ocean creatures, like sharks, need to swim all the time, and scientists haven't yet figured out how they catch their Z's (it may have something to do with "shutting down" one side of their brains at a time).

WHAT is the difference between a turtle and a tortoise?

Turtles and tortoises are both lizards, but with one big difference: turtles spend most of their time in the water, while tortoises are land animals. Not to confuse the issue, but tortoises and turtles are both different from terrapins, which live in both land and water!

HOW long can a giant tortoise live?

If you observe its behavior, a giant tortoise doesn't seem to do all that much, and what it does do, it does very slowly. But it's got a lot of time to do it in: these lumbering beasts have been known to live as long as 150 years, much longer than the longest-lived human being. The only animal that even comes close is the turkey buzzard, which can reach an old age of about 120 years.

WHAT is the difference between frogs and toads?

The best way to tell a frog from a toad is by its skin: a frog's skin is usually moist and slimy, while a toad's skin is dry and bumpy (which is why some people believe you can get warts from touching toads). Also, frogs spend most of their lives in the water, while toads venture out onto dry land every now and then.

WHAT are amphibians?

Amphibians are one of the five classes of vertebrates (that is, animals with backbones), the others being fish, birds, reptiles, and mammals. They're unique because their life cycles are equal parts wet and dry: amphibians lay their eggs in water, where the young develop before heading for land. Frogs, toads and salamanders are all amphibians, as are some weird wormlike creatures that live in tropical climates.

In historical terms, amphibians are important because they represent the stage of evolution when animals first ventured out of the sea and onto dry land. About 400 million years ago, amphibians were the first creatures to develop lungs (in addition to their preexisting gills), and shortly after that they began walking on land as a way to bridge the distance from one lake or mud puddle to the next.

WHAT is the difference between an alligator and a crocodile?

Not that you'd want to get a close look in the wild, but the best way to tell a crocodile from an alligator is by examining the shape of its head: the alligator has a round, blunt snout, while the crocodile's is more tapered and pointy. This is because a gator eats crunchier foods (like turtles), and needs stronger jaws to chew up its meals.

A full-grown alligator has the most powerful bite of any creature on earth: it can snap its jaws shut with a force of over 2,000 pounds, about the same as if someone dropped a car on you. While it's nearly impossible to unpry a gator's jaws once it's chomped down on something it wants to eat, it's relatively easy to hold them shut, which is how alligator trainers handle these ferocious beasts.

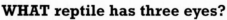

WHAT reptile has three eyes?

The tuatara, a large lizard native to New Zealand, has two normal eyes and a tiny, light-sensitive growth on top of its head that connects to the pineal gland in its brain. Some scientists believe this rudimentary eye regulates the tuatara's sleep cycle and triggers its annual hibernation.

WHAT is the world's biggest reptile?

It all depends on how you measure "big." Some giant turtles weigh over a thousand pounds, while a species of Australian crocodile can reach a length of over 20 feet. If we're just talking land lizards, though, the clear winner is the Komodo Dragon, which grows up to about 10 feet in length and weighs up to 300 pounds.

WHY does a starfish have five arms?

Starfish have radial symmetry, meaning they look the same no matter how you slice them down the middle (people, on the other hand, have bilateral symmetry—there's only one way to cut a person in half so that both sides match). It's unclear why starfish evolved this way, though the multiple arms may help to transfer food to its central mouth more quickly. (By the way, not all starfish have five arms—some species have dozens.)

Besides their unusual layout, starfish are notable for two other oddities. First, some species can quickly regenerate new arms when they're cut off, and conversely, a cut-off arm (if it contains a portion of the central disk) can grow into a completely new starfish. Second, a starfish can push its entire stomach out of its body—allowing it to engulf and digest organisms that would be way too big for it to swallow otherwise.

HOW do barnacles stick?

Barnacles don't spend their entire lives stuck to the keels of ships—when it's born, the barnacle flits through the sea like any other tiny creature. When it finds a good spot, it secretes a super-hard glue that fixes it there (head first!) until the end of its life. This glue is so strong and so waterproof that it's been studied in depth—and often imitated—by glue companies.

HOW much does a giant clam weigh?

A full-grown giant clam is over four feet wide and weighs about 500 pounds. These enormous creatures once had a fearsome reputation as man-eaters, until it was discovered that no people had ever been swallowed whole (or even injured) in a giant clam attack!

WHAT is the smallest animal?

This is a hard question to answer, since the word "animal" covers a lot of territory—ranging from bugs to mollusks to mammals. Some of the simplest animals, called protozoa, are also the smallest, including such tiny creatures as amoebas and algae. Bacteria are smaller than amoebas, but technically they're not animals at all.

That said, the very simplest animal is an organism called the trichoplax, a tiny marine animal consisting of only a few thousand cells. It is the most primitive multicelled animal yet discovered: it doesn't have any internal organs or nervous system, and basically looks like a giant amoeba. Trichoplaxes haven't been found in the wild; they were first discovered clinging to the sides of fish tanks.

WHAT are seashells made of?

Mollusks manufacture seashells of all shapes and sizes using a simple recipe: a little bit of a tough protein called conchiolin, and a whole lot of the mineral calcium carbonate (the main ingredient of limestone). Since shells are built to last, they remain scattered on beaches long after their soft, tiny inhabitants have passed away.

WHAT is seaweed?

It may look like a giant plant, but seaweed is something much, much weirder: a collection of giant-sized algae, single-celled organisms that float on or under the sea and turn sunlight into energy. Technically, seaweed isn't quite a plant, but it's not quite an animal either, or a fungus, for that matter. But some people (especially in the Far East) think it makes a tasty meal!

HOW small are microbes?

So small that you can't see them without a microscope—which is how they got their name. To put things in perspective, a single teaspoon of soil or seawater contains, in varying proportions, about a billion microbes, including viruses, plankton, and bacteria.

WHY do fiddler crabs have one big claw?

As with many seemingly useless animal features—like the peacock's tail and the proboscis monkey's nose—a male fiddler crab's oversized claw is primarily to attract females (though it does occasionally come in handy for fighting other male crabs). Why are female fiddler crabs attracted to giant claws? No one really knows!

WHY don't snakes chew their food?

A snake can't afford the luxury of a strong jawbone and a full set of teeth—imagine what a rattler would look like with a giant head and a long, skinny body! Instead, the snake's jaws are only loosely connected to its skull, so it can open its mouth incredibly wide and swallow its prey whole. At that point, its backward-pointing fangs keep the rabbit or mouse (if it's still alive) from trying to fight its way back out.

If this sounds like a painful way to eat dinner (not to mention a painful way to *be* dinner), keep in mind that a snake doesn't have to eat nearly as often as other animals do. Because they're cold-blooded—and don't use or produce as much energy as warm-blooded mammals—snakes can go for weeks without a meal. The biggest snakes, like boas and pythons, only chow down about once every two weeks, when they swallow some unfortunate animal whole.

WHY does a rattlesnake rattle its tail?

Many people believe rattlesnakes rattle right before they strike, which doesn't make much sense—why alert your prey and give it a chance to escape? The truth is, a rattler only rattles its tail when it's scared or trying to defend its territory. If that doesn't warn the intruder away, it may well go on the attack, which is probably how the myth of the pre-meal rattle began.

WHY don't snakes have legs?

We know for a fact that the long-gone ancestors of snakes had arms and legs; the question is why these limbs gradually disappeared in the course of evolution. Some scientists believe the absence of legs made it easier for snakes to burrow into small holes in the ground, while others think the change occurred when snakes still lived in water and long limbs were an impediment to gliding.

HOW does a snake move?

A snake's flexible backbone is surrounded by hundreds of muscles, which propel it forward in a slithering, side-to-side motion. It also has crosswise scales on its belly that act like treads to pull it forward. The "treads" of some species of snakes are strong enough to cling to bark and enable the snake to scale trees.

WHY do snakes shed their skin?

A snake's scales are tough, but not very flexible, so as the snake grows it has to periodically shed its skin and grow a new one (which is why young snakes shed more often than older snakes).

WHY do snakes have forked tongues?

It may look scary, but a snake's forked tongue is actually a sophisticated device for analyzing its environment. Every time the snake flicks its tongue, specialized cells capture chemicals from the air, which are then analyzed by plugging the forks into an organ inside the snake's mouth. This way, the snake can identify any tasty meals that happen to be cowering nearby.

HOW does snake venom work?

There are two main kinds of snake venom: neurotoxins, which shut down the nervous system, and hemotoxins, which poison the blood. Neurotoxins prevent nerve cells from conducting signals, making it difficult for the victim to breathe and eventually stopping his heart cold. Needless to say, the most dangerous snakes usually have neurotoxins in their venom.

HOW does a boa constrictor kill its prey?

Unlike other snakes, which kill their food with sharp fangs or venom (or both), the boa constrictor has evolved a neat trick: it grabs its prospective meal by the head, wraps its coils around its body, and squeezes tight. As the coils squeeze tighter, the victim is unable to breathe, and quickly suffocates.

HOW dangerous is a cobra?

Despite its reputation, the cobra isn't the world's most dangerous snake—with prompt, proper treatment, most people can recover from even a severe cobra bite. In fact, a cobra attack is a walk in the park compared to an encounter with a more exotic snake, like the black mamba of Africa or the Australian Taipan, whose chomps are nearly 100% fatal if they're not treated immediately with antivenin (a chemical that counteracts the snakes' poison).

Not only is the cobra a relative wimp venom-wise, but it has an unlikely natural enemy—the mongoose, a small, weasel-like creature that has perfected the art of cobra-fighting. Mongooses have thick hides, to protect them from cobra bites, and even if they happen to be struck, they have a natural resistance to cobra venom (though a mongoose can be killed by large amounts of venom, just like any other creature).

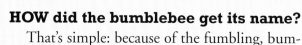

HOW do bees choose a queen?

Unlike real-life queens, queen bees don't inherit their titles. The queen of a hive is chosen at random, when worker bees zero in on a single egg and feed the larva inside something called "royal jelly" (which causes it to grow bigger than its companions). Basically, the queen bee's purpose in life is to lay lots and lots of eggs: over one thousand a day over the course of three years.

HOW did the bumblebee get its name?

That's simple: because of the fumbling, bumbling way this bug appears to fly. By the way, many years ago, some folks preferred the name "humblebee" to "bumblebee", observing how this gentle bug likes to stay out of the way of other creatures.

WHY do bees sting?

Unlike, say, spiders—which sting other bugs as a prelude to eating them—a bee's sting is strictly for defensive purposes (since it subsists on honey, not other insects). A bee will only sting if it is feeling threatened, so if you happen across a nervous-looking bee, walk (don't run!) calmly away.

HOW are ant colonies organized?

Ant colonies are dug underground by ants to live, store their food and stay safe from predators. There are some differences among species, but most ant colonies consist of three "castes," or social levels: winged females (or queens) capable of producing eggs; a few winged males, whose sole function is to impregnate the winged females; and a huge number of wingless, infertile females (the ordinary ants you see scurrying along the ground).

Ant colonies are ruled by a single queen—as they mature, the surplus queens take wing to start new colonies, where they can produce eggs for as long as 15 years. (The winged males aren't as lucky: they die shortly after leaving the parent colony.)

While most species of ant depend on wingless females to do all the work, "slave-making" ants use a different system: they raid the colonies of other species and carry off their developing eggs, which are hatched into a ready-made pool of slave labor.

HOW do bees make honey?

Most flowers produce nectar, the main ingredients of which are sugar and water. When a bee stops at a flower to collect nectar, the exchange benefits both parties: the bee, because it turns the nectar into honey (which it uses for food), and the flower, because tiny pieces of its pollen cling to the bee's body and wind up fertilizing other flowers.

After a bee has collected its nectar quotient for the day (by visiting up to a thousand flowers), it returns to the hive and passes its bounty on to a worker bee. The worker bee chews the nectar, and special enzymes in its saliva change the simple sugars of the nectar into the complex sugars of honey.

When it's done chewing, the worker bee deposits the resulting sugary syrup into the honeycomb. As its moisture slowly evaporates, the result is a pool of sweet, sticky honey.

HOW does an ant lift 50 times its own weight?

Ants are known to be champion weightlifters, but it's not because they have exceptionally strong muscles. Most of an ant's (or any insect's) strength has to do with its tiny size: because it occupies such a small volume, it can lift more in proportion to its weight. If an ant somehow grew to human size, it wouldn't be any stronger than we are!

HOW do ants communicate?

Like many insects, ants "speak" to each other by emitting chemicals (some species have special glands in their heads that secrete an "alarm chemical" in times of danger). Ants can also leave chemical trails with the bottoms of their abdomens, so when they discover a new source of food it can be tracked and located by the other ants in the colony.

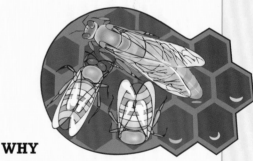

WHY do bugs have antennae?

A bug uses its antennae the same way we use our nose and ears, to detect smells, vibrations, and even tiny changes in air current. In some species (like ants) the antennae transmit chemical information, such as the detailed coordinates of a tasty pile of food.

HOW are beetles different from other bugs?

In terms of anatomy, the distinguishing feature of beetles is their hardened, shell-like forewings, called "elytra," which protect them from damage and allow them to burrow into otherwise inaccessible places. In a larger sense, though, what's most amazing about beetles is their sheer diversity.

Beetles account for 40% of all insect species, and are by far the single biggest class of animals on the entire planet. Scientists have classified over 350,000 species of beetle, ranging in size from less than a millimeter to over six inches, and they suspect there are hundreds of thousands of undiscovered varieties lurking in the deepest recesses of the rain forest.

By the way, the name "beetle" derives from the Old English phrase "little biter." Scientists know these bugs better by their Latin name, "coleoptera," meaning "shielded wings."

WHAT is a cicada?

This cricket-like insect is unusual for two reasons. First, the males produce a shrill, often deafening sound with drumlike organs on their abdomens called "tymbals." And second, cicada nymphs live underground, only burrowing their way out when they're fully grown. Some cicada species hide away like this for years, then emerge (all at the same time!) in huge, buzzing swarms.

HOW do insects breathe?

Unlike more advanced animals, which have lungs or gills, insects breathe by diffusion—oxygen seeps in through tiny openings in their bodies and circulates directly to their internal organs. This is the reason (no matter what you've seen in monster movies) that an insect can't grow to human size: its diffusion system wouldn't supply enough oxygen for the enormous bug's needs.

WHAT is the most disgusting bug?

The dung beetle would probably rank high on most people's lists. These insects subsist on dung, or animal droppings. Some species of dung beetle pack the dung of larger animals into a big ball, then happily roll it along the ground to store in their burrows.

WHAT is the world's biggest bug?

It all depends on your definition of the word "big." Some stick insects measure over a foot long, while a tarantula can grow big enough to kill a mouse. But scientists agree that the biggest flying bug is the aptly named goliath beetle, which weighs almost a quarter-pound (or as much as a hamburger!)

HOW do crickets chirp?

Crickets don't "chirp" the way birds do—in fact, they don't use their mouths at all. A cricket makes its characteristic sound by rubbing its upper wing against its lower wing, like a bow on a violin. By the way, only male crickets chirp, mostly to attract females, but sometimes to warn away other males.

HOW long do bugs live?

As a general rule, the smaller the animal, the shorter its life span. Insects are no exception: some species of bugs, like fruit flies, live for only a day or so; others, like dragonflies, can last for a few months; and one species of giant tarantula has been known to live for as long as fifteen years. Unlike people, though, bugs generally don't die of diseases—if they don't succumb to insecticide poisoning they usually just drop out of the sky when their time is up.

The accelerated life span of small insects makes them a valuable resource for scientists. For instance, biologists study heredity by breeding populations of fruit flies and seeing how mutations are passed down from one generation to the next. If these experiments were conducted on larger animals with longer life spans, such as mice, they would require months or years to produce results.

WHY do praying mantises pray?

A praying mantis doesn't really pray—it just holds its pincers in the "praying" position, the better to catch any unwary bugs as they zip past. Here's another weird praying mantis fact: a female mantis will sometimes kill and eat the male during the act of mating (which, come to think of it, is a good reason for males to start praying!).

HOW did butterflies get their name?

Have you ever thought that butterflies should be called "flutter-bys?" Some word experts believe they did have this name, many years ago, and it changed to "butter-fly" by accident. It's also possible that the name "butterfly" came about because people in the middle ages believed these insects stole milk and butter.

WHAT is the difference between a butterfly and a moth?

There are plenty of subtle differences between butterflies and moths, most of which only an entomologist (a scientist specializing in insects) would be likely to notice. For example, a butterfly's antennae are slender and straight, while a moth has shorter, hairier feelers. Also, a moth larva spins a soft cocoon around itself when it prepares to metamorphose, while a butterfly larva prepares for the change in a harder shell called a chrysalis.

For ordinary folks, though, there are two reliable ways to tell moths and butterflies apart. First, most moths are nocturnal (that is, they're only active at night), while butterflies only fly during the day. And second, butterflies have much more colorful wing patterns than moths, which usually sport dullish grey or brown wings (the exceptions are a few species of day-flying moths).

WHY are moths attracted to flame?

Like many creatures, moths aren't used to bright, man-made lights that are close by (as opposed to bright, natural lights, like the sun and full moon, that are far away). When a moth sees a flame, it becomes disoriented, and tries to steer away from it as if it's far in the distance. But because the light is actually close by, the moth winds up spiraling in closer and closer.

WHAT is the fastest insect?

The fastest insect known to exist is the sphinx moth, which can fly about 45 miles per hour (that's without any wind). By comparison, a plain old honey bee moseys along at a top speed of about 10 mph.

WHY do monarch butterflies migrate?

For the same reason birds do—to escape the winter chill of Canada for the warmer temperatures of Mexico and California. Monarchs aren't the only insect species that migrate, but with their million-strong swarms and large, bright-orange wings, they're definitely the most noticeable.

Up until the 1930's, no one knew exactly where the Monarch butterflies that descended annually on California originated. That changed when an enterprising scientist attached tiny tags to the butterflies' wings, then enlisted thousands of people across the country to do the same. As a result, one single butterfly was proven to have flown from Highland Creek, Ontario to San Luis Potosi, Mexico—a distance of almost 2,000 miles—in the space of four months.

By the way, monarch butterflies only make one round-trip in their lifetime: they usually die after returning to Canada to lay their eggs.

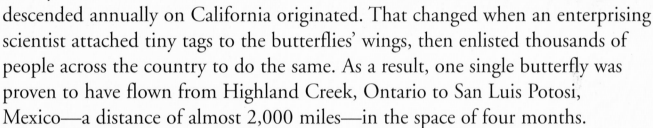

WHAT is a luna moth?

Found mostly in the eastern U.S., the luna moth is one of the largest flying bugs in the world, with a wing span of a little less than half a foot. As big as they are, though, these beautiful creatures are rarely seen in the wild, since they fly only at night and have an adult life span of one week. A fully grown luna moth won't even eat, since it only lives long enough to find a mate and reproduce.

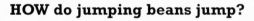

HOW do jumping beans jump?

A Mexican jumping bean doesn't jiggle around on its own. A species of moth lays an egg inside the bean, and after it hatches from the egg, the moth larva feasts on the bean's insides. When there's no more food left, the larva wriggles back and forth inside the hollow shell, so the bean appears to be "jumping" under its own power.

WHAT is the smallest butterfly?

The Western Pygmy Blue, found in the western U.S., measures only about half an inch from wingtip to wingtip. Since these tiny butterflies aren't very brightly colored, most folks don't even notice when a swarm passes by!

WHAT are ticks?

Unlike mosquitoes, which fly in for a quick bite and then buzz off, ticks attach themselves to skin for the long term and swell into reddish-black balls as they gorge on blood. Because some ticks carry disease, they should be removed as soon as they're found.

WHAT are lice?

Lice are tiny insects that survive by feeding on human blood. They usually set up shop on the scalp, not because hair keeps them warm, but because it protects them from being scratched away. As gross and itchy as they are, lice are basically harmless, but in conditions where lots of people are crowded together (like refugee camps) they've been known to spread disease.

WHY do fruit flies like fruit?

When a fruit is over-ripe, its outer layers start fermenting—that is, reacting with air and moisture to create sugar. This is a perfect place for fruit flies to lay their eggs, since the hatching larvae have a steady source of food.

HOW big is a locust swarm?

Like hurricanes, swarms of locusts come in all sizes, ranging from a few million to a few billion flying bugs. Whatever the size, it's best to stay out of the way: these swarms devour all the food in their path (only plants, not people) and cover several hundred miles a day. If you're a farmer about to bring in his crops, you can see why this might be a bit of a problem!

HOW do flies eat?

Flies can't eat solid food, so instead they vomit up a substance from their stomachs that dissolves food into a gooey mass. Then they suck the goo up with their tubelike tongues, just the way you drink a milkshake through a straw.

For this reason, you don't want to let flies land on your food—but you may have noticed that it is very hard to swat a fly. There are two reasons for this: First, the fly's compound eyes are very sensitive, making it hard to sneak up on. And second, the tiny bristles on the fly's body register slight changes in wind current, which are easily detected when you swing a rolled-up newspaper. That's why flyswatters have holes, to minimize air currents and catch the fly by surprise.

WHAT are termite mounds?

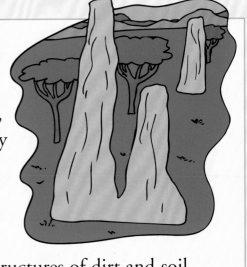

Most people think of termites as pesky insects that chew through wood, but in the southern part of Africa, they're responsible for the biggest structures built by any creature on earth, excluding humans.

The African mound-building termite (also known as *Macrotermes bellicosus*, which translates roughly as "giant warlike bug") erects irregular, twisted structures of dirt and soil that can reach twenty feet in height and a hundred feet in circumference. Inside the mounds are intricate networks of caves, tunnels, and ventilation shafts, which conduct air down to the underground "cellars" where the insects actually live.

In order to keep these mounds running smoothly, African termites have evolved the most intricate social structure of any insects. These miniature cities contain kings, queens, workers, soldiers, and "juveniles" (termite kids to you and me).

HOW can termites eat wood?

When a termite takes a bite out of your front porch, the specially adapted bacteria in its gut turn the wood's cellulose (the tough, stringy fibers that make it so hard) into sugars that the termite uses for energy. Without the help of these microbes, a termite would starve to death, no matter how much wood it ate.

HOW far can a flea jump?

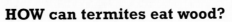

It's no wonder flea circuses were once a popular attraction. A flea can jump seven or eight inches into the air in a single leap, and over a foot horizontally. Considering that these pesky insects are only one or two millimeters long, that's the equivalent of a grown man jumping over 100 feet, or more than one-third of a football field.

HOW bad is a bedbug bite?

"Good night, sleep tight, don't let the bedbugs bite," your mom may sing as she puts you to bed. Well, odds are your room doesn't really have any bedbugs, but if it does, it's not a big deal: a bedbug bite is small and itchy, kind of like a mosquito bite. The bedbug itself is a tiny, reddish-brown insect that can be found pretty much all over the world.

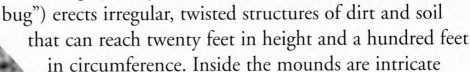

WHY do zebras have stripes?

This is one of those questions that seems obvious: after all, every kid is taught in school that a zebra's stripes are strictly for camouflage. For a long time, naturalists thought this, too, but they've recently discovered that not everything is as simple as it seems.

Scientists have discovered that an individual zebra's stripes are as distinctive as a human fingerprint—and that zebras have an innate ability to recognize these patterns. This helps a lost zebra identify the pack to which it belongs, and may even aid a mother zebra in recognizing her own children (and vice-versa).

As for camouflage, a zebra's stripes don't do it much good when it's standing all by itself. This adaptation works best when zebras run in packs: a prowling lion sees a big black-and-white blur, and may find it difficult to target individual members of the herd.

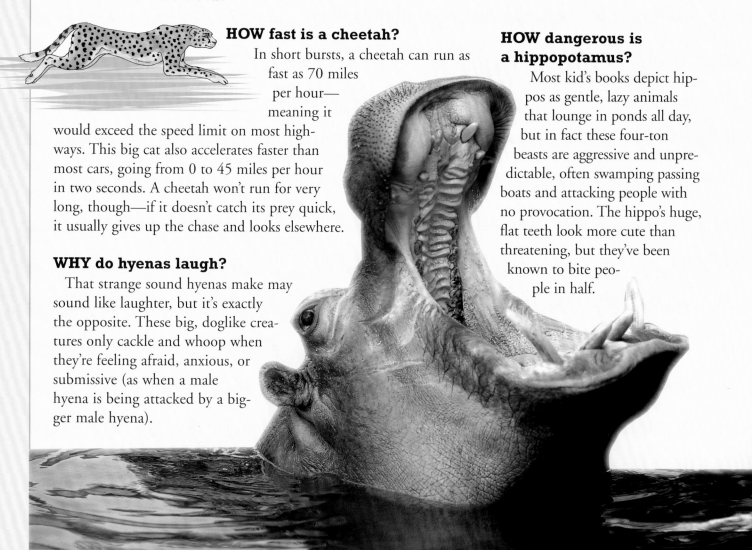

HOW fast is a cheetah?

In short bursts, a cheetah can run as fast as 70 miles per hour—meaning it would exceed the speed limit on most highways. This big cat also accelerates faster than most cars, going from 0 to 45 miles per hour in two seconds. A cheetah won't run for very long, though—if it doesn't catch its prey quick, it usually gives up the chase and looks elsewhere.

WHY do hyenas laugh?

That strange sound hyenas make may sound like laughter, but it's exactly the opposite. These big, doglike creatures only cackle and whoop when they're feeling afraid, anxious, or submissive (as when a male hyena is being attacked by a bigger male hyena).

HOW dangerous is a hippopotamus?

Most kid's books depict hippos as gentle, lazy animals that lounge in ponds all day, but in fact these four-ton beasts are aggressive and unpredictable, often swamping passing boats and attacking people with no provocation. The hippo's huge, flat teeth look more cute than threatening, but they've been known to bite people in half.

HOW big is an elephant?

Elephants are the world's largest land animals—full-grown adults weigh between four and five tons. Even baby elephants are enormous, weighing up to 300 pounds at the moment of birth. Not surprisingly, mother elephants are pregnant for almost two years, compared to nine months for human moms—it takes a long time for a baby elephant to grow in the womb!

An elephant also has very big ears. These act as a cooling mechanism—as blood pumps through its ears, the elephant fans them slowly, dissipating heat into the outside air and cooling its blood. This is why African elephants (which live in a hotter climate) have bigger ears than Asian elephants.

As you can imagine, to maintain their bulk, elephants have to eat all day, every day. Elephants in the wild plow through about 600 pounds of food each day, though elephants in zoos can get by with less. Fortunately for us and other animals, elephants are strict vegetarians, feasting on grass, leaves, and bark, among other tasty snacks.

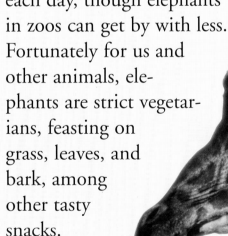

WHY do elephants have tusks?

Elephants are basically gentle creatures, so you might wonder why nature took the trouble to provide them with dangerous-looking tusks. These giant teeth are mostly used to dig up trees, but they also come in handy when a male elephant battles another male for territory, or defends its kids against encroaching lions or tigers.

WHY are elephants afraid of mice?

The fact is, most of the time elephants don't even notice mice: their eyesight is too poor and they're too high off the ground! There's a bit more truth, though, to the saying that "elephants never forget." Elephants do have good memories, and can remember the location of tasty trees and watering holes—but they don't necessarily have better memories than other animals, which also have to survive by their wits.

WHY do giraffes have long necks?

To survive in the wild, you have to go where the food is—and for giraffes, that food is way up in the sky, in the form of leaves hanging off the tops of trees. That's why giraffes have not only ten-foot-long necks, but eighteen-inch-long tongues. (Interestingly, despite its length, a giraffe's neck has no more vertebrae than any other mammal, including humans.)

WHY don't animals get colds?

Actually, animals do get colds, as you may know if you've ever had a sneezy cat or dog. The reason we don't perceive animals as getting sick the way we get sick is because they don't show symptoms the way we show symptoms—for example, a cow doesn't whine, blow into a handkerchief, or lie down and take a nap.

Just like people, animals can come down with potentially fatal illnesses. Although the viruses and bacteria that endanger the lives of horses or chickens generally don't affect people (and vice versa), there is a risk that a germ can mutate (that is, change its genetic composition) and become infectious to humans. Scientists believe this is how AIDS started, when a virus that affected only monkeys mutated suddenly and began infecting people.

WHY are some cave animals blind?

There's not much point in having eyes if you live your entire life in a pitch-black cave. Oddly enough, some cave-dwelling creatures (including species of lizards, insects, and fish) have visible, but nonworking, eyes, remnants of a time millions of years ago when their ancestors lived in the sunlight.

WHY are some animal's noses cold?

Many animals can sweat from only a few places on their bodies, including their paws and their noses. The main reason their noses are cold and wet is because they're loaded with sweat glands.

WHY don't some animals sleep at night?

Nocturnal animals sleep during the day and hunt or forage by night. Some creatures—such as rabbits and skunks—are nocturnal because it's easier for them to avoid predators at night. Others sleep during the day because they live in dry, sunny climates (such as deserts) where the days are too hot and it would be dangerous to be out and about.

HOW can animals hear sounds people can't?

Unlike people, animals can "point" their ears, allowing them to gather and amplify sounds more effectively. That's part of the reason they can hear high-pitched sounds, like dog whistles, that are well beyond the range of human hearing.

WHY do dogs smell bad when they get wet?

Unlike cats, dogs aren't particular about what they'll play with or roll around in, whether it's a filthy mud puddle or a rotting fish, and dogs don't clean themselves nearly as much as cats, either. A dog smells "doggy" when its fur is dry, too, but it's just not as noticeable. Your sweater will smell worse when it's wet, also.

WHY do animals see in black and white?

Since we can't get a dog or cat to tell us, we can't know for sure that they lack color vision. In fact, scientists now think that dogs, at least, can tell apart certain colors (like red and blue) that would be an indistinguishable grey if they had only black-and-white vision. Even some birds and fish appear to have a limited capacity for seeing in color.

WHY do dogs howl at the moon?

They don't—at least, not any more than they howl at an overcast sky. The main reason dogs (and wolves) howl is to communicate with other dogs and wolves. Because these creatures often communicate at night, and because they turn their snouts up when they howl, it looks like they're baying at the moon.

Another myth about dogs (which has been perpetrated by innumerable cartoons and movies) is that they hate cats. In fact, dogs don't naturally hate cats, or vice versa, at least not any more than dogs hate other dogs or cats hate other cats. Whenever two animal strangers meet, they are naturally cautious and ready to defend their turf. Many people have dogs and cats as pets in the same house, and everyone lives together quite happily!

HOW big is a gorilla?

Gorillas are big, but they're not King Kong big; males (which are much bigger than females) can grow to a size of about 600 pounds. Also, despite the way they're portrayed in movies, gorillas are basically gentle creatures that will rarely attack people. (A male gorilla will hoot and holler and thump his chest, but that's just his way of showing off!)

HOW strong is a monkey's tail?

Some monkeys have "prehensile" tails, meaning they can be manipulated like a finger to perform complicated tasks. Unlike most mammalian tails, the sensitive parts of prehensile tails have no hair, allowing the monkey to feel objects with its bare skin and get a better grip on tree branches.

Most of the time, a monkey uses its prehensile tail to hang down from tree branches while keeping its arms and legs free. This requires a lot of strength, which is why monkeys' tails have proportionately more muscles than the relatively useless tails of dogs or cats. For example, the howler monkey's tail is about as heavy as one of its legs, and contains a disproportionate amount of the creature's muscles.

Monkeys aren't the only animals with prehensile tails. Two other species with this handy adaptation are the prehensile-tailed porcupine and the prehensile-tailed skink (a kind of lizard).

WHY are rhesus monkeys important to science?

Rhesus monkeys—which are native to central and eastern Asia—are often used in medical research, for two reasons: first, they're easy to raise in captivity, and second, their blood types closely match those of humans (which is why one of the elements of human blood is called its "rhesus factor.") Thanks to stricter research guidelines, today's rhesus monkeys are treated much better than those of a few decades ago.

WHAT is the world's smallest monkey?

The tarsier, which lives in southeast Asia, is about the size of a rat, and much weirder looking—it has huge eyes, a long, hairless tail, and suction cups on the ends of its fingers and toes, which help it climb up vertical surfaces. It also spends its entire life in trees.

WHAT is the difference between monkeys and apes?

Both monkeys and apes (as well as human beings) belong to the order called "primates." Primates are defined as mammals with forward-facing eyes, long, flexible arms and legs, and fingers rather than claws. The primate order is divided into two suborders: "prosimians," in which are grouped the lower, less intelligent mammals (the big-eyed lemur is a good example), and "anthropoids," the more intelligent primates.

Here is where we get to the heart of the matter. The anthropoid suborder is further divided into three categories: monkeys, apes, and hominids (that is, humans). Monkeys are distinguished by their skeletal structure—which more closely resembles that of a cat or a dog than a human or an ape—their lower intelligence, and their long tails. Apes, by contrast, are more intelligent than monkeys, have no tails, and possess a body structure more closely resembling that of a human being.

HOW many words can a chimpanzee understand?

Over the past few decades, chimps have been taught to communicate using various kinds of sign language. A few famous chimps have managed to learn over 100 sign-language words, but there's disagreement among scientists as to whether they really understand these words the way humans do.

WHAT animals besides humans use tools?

This is a difficult question to answer, because the word "tool" can be defined in many ways. (For example, one species of vulture drops rocks on eggs to smash them open—is the bird using the rocks as a tool, or is it acting on instinct?) Pending more evidence, most scientists believe that only advanced primates (like chimpanzees) can use tools in the way that people do, such as long sticks or stacked boxes to reach distant objects.

WHY is the platypus the weirdest animal?

Everyone has his or her favorite bug-eyed critter, but if you ask most naturalists, they'll say the platypus takes the prize. This small, furry, seal-shaped animal (which is found only in Australia) has a soft, rubbery beak and webbed feet like a duck, and the males have a poisonous spur on their ankles that they use to ward off competing males and predators.

Its jigsaw-puzzle appearance isn't the only strange thing about the platypus—this is the only mammal that lays eggs instead of giving birth to live young. The young hatch out of the sticky, marble-sized eggs after only ten days, then crawl into an underground burrow where they develop for another four months. One last weird platypus fact: the mother platypus doesn't nurse its young with nipples, like other mammals, but seeps the milk directly out of glands in her stomach.

WHAT is a Tasmanian devil?

Found only on the island of Tasmania, off the coast of Australia, the Tasmanian devil is a dog-sized marsupial that you definitely wouldn't want to keep as a pet: it's loud, smelly, and voracious, with a mean disposition as well. And since you were about to ask, a real Tasmanian devil doesn't spin like its cartoon counterpart.

WHAT is a koala bear?

The koala is not really a bear—it's a marsupial that just looks like a stuffed teddy bear. But as cuddly as they look, koalas can have a mean disposition, especially during mating season when the males become territorial. Koalas eat only the bark and leaves of the eucalyptus tree, which has a very low nutritional value, so you don't see koalas hopping and bopping around; they enjoy nothing more than to curl up in a tree trunk and take a 20-hour nap. The only time they venture onto solid ground is when they decide to change homes and set out in search of another hospitable tree.

HOW high can a kangaroo jump?

When it's built up a full head of steam, a full-grown kangaroo can jump as high as 10 feet—enough to sail over the head of a professional basketball player.

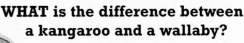

WHY does Australia have so many strange animals?

Although it's classified as a continent, Australia is still technically an island—a body of land surrounded by water (and lots of it!) on all sides. Because of this, Australian wildlife has been able to evolve in its own unique way over millions of years, without being "invaded" by foreign creatures (like mammals) that would take over its turf.

WHAT is the difference between a kangaroo and a wallaby?

Kangaroos and wallabies both belong to the "macropod" (big foot) family, which has about 30 species. Basically, the name "kangaroo" is applied to larger macropods, while smaller macropods are called "wallabies." If that's not confusing enough, macropods halfway in size between kangaroos and wallabies are called "wallaroos"!

HOW did the kangaroo get its name?

According to a famous story (which may or may not be true), hundreds of years ago a European settler asked an Australian native, "what is that animal?" The native answered "Kanga roo"—which meant "I don't understand the question" in his language.

WHY do kangaroos have pouches?

Kangaroos are marsupials—a strange kind of mammal (mostly native to Australia) whose young develop partly in the womb, but mostly inside a pouch on the female's stomach. When a baby kangaroo emerges from the womb—blind, barely an inch long and weighing about a tenth of an ounce—it makes the slow, arduous journey into its mother's pouch, where it stays put and develops for another eight months.

Despite what you've seen in cartoons, a kangaroo's pouch is strictly for incubating baby kangaroos—after the baby (called a joey) is done gestating, it doesn't climb back in for a ride whenever it wants. Nor will a female kangaroo store objects in her pouch like a purse. The kangaroo is the most famous marsupial, but other members of this group include wombats, koala bears, and Tasmanian devils.

WHY don't ducks get wet?

Like all birds that spend a lot of time in the water, ducks can't afford to let their feathers get soggy. If the down under their feathers got wet, they would get very cold. Also, having waterlogged feathers would make it difficult to fly away in an emergency. For this reason ducks secrete a special oil (from organs called "preen glands") and spread it constantly on their feathers. The oil waterproofs the feathers and keeps them dry and supple even during deep underwater dives.

Another adaptation that waterfowl—ducks, geese, swans, and the like—have in common is that they all have webbed feet, which help propel them through the water. (In fact, scuba divers wear flippers designed to be like webbed feet, because they work so well.) As useful as they are for swimming, though, webbed feet are very clunky on land, which is why ducks waddle when they walk.

WHY are cattle branded?

Cattle farmers need a way to identify their cows and bulls, in case one is stolen or accidentally wanders off. Branding cattle with a red-hot iron in a trademark shape sears the design into their hide so they will carry a permanent mark that can't easily be removed.

WHY do pigs roll in mud?

Pigs don't have a thick coat of fur like other animals, and their bare skin doesn't produce much sweat. The reason pigs roll in mud is simply to cool themselves down and protect their skin from the hot sun—not because they like to get dirty!

WHY do roosters crow at sunrise?

Like other male birds, roosters like to mark out their territory—their crows are a warning to other roosters to stay away. Roosters crow at all times of the day, not just sunrise, but because they crow so loud (and wake so many people up) they have earned a reputation as early risers.

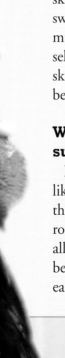

HOW many stomachs does a cow have?

Because its diet consists exclusively of grass—which is difficult to digest—a cow has not one, but four separate stomachs.

The first stomach, the rumen, stores the chewed grass, where it gradually softens as its tough, stringy cellulose is digested by microscopic organisms. (This first stomach is the reason grass-eating creatures—including cows, deer, and sheep—are called "ruminants.") Even these tiny microbes can't completely digest the cellulose, so the contents of the rumen are regurgitated into the cow's mouth, where it can chew and soften the cellulose even more by grinding it with its enormous flat teeth (this is the "cud" that a cow is constantly chewing).

After the cow swallows its cud, the other three stomachs—the reticulum, the omasum, and the abomasum—get to work, further breaking down the grass's proteins, extracting nutrients, and (in females) turning the digested grass into milk.

HOW much milk can a cow produce each day?

A healthy, well-fed cow can produce up to 10 gallons of milk every day, enough to meet the needs of a few dozen families. (You have to remember that baby cows are much bigger than baby humans, and need their mothers to produce a correspondingly large amount of milk.) To keep up this amazing pace, a cow needs to drink about 20 gallons of water every day, in addition to the grass it eats.

WHY do rabbits have big ears?

Rabbits don't have a lot in the way of natural defenses, so they depend on their sense of hearing to steer clear of predators (or kids who want to capture them and keep them as pets). A bunny's big, sensitive ears are good at picking up sounds, so it can keep its distance from the animals that make them.

HOW many eggs can a hen lay in her lifetime?

A hen who's on top of her game can lay about 300 eggs a year, which translates to a little less than one egg each day. But she can't keep up this pace for long, since the average chicken lives only a few years. It's the rare hen who can lay as many as a thousand eggs.

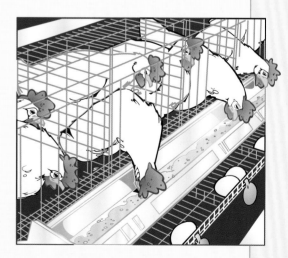

WHAT makes cats land on their feet?

Thanks to its finely tuned sense of balance, a cat has a special talent for telling which way is up. This, combined with its flexibility, allows the cat to turn itself around in midair during a fall, move its feet into the correct position, and come in for a soft landing. This trick doesn't always work, though. Like any other creature, a cat can be seriously hurt or even killed by a long fall, especially one of more than two stories.

WHY do cats have nine lives?

They don't, as you've probably figured out already. Because cats have excellent balance, usually land on their feet after a fall, and are able to wriggle their way out of tight spots, a tradition developed (probably in ancient Egypt) that they had multiple lives. But they only get one go-round, just like a dog, a gerbil, or a human being.

WHY do cats hate water?

Not all cats are hydrophobic—tigers, lions, and jaguars like to go swimming any chance they get. No one is sure why most house cats dislike water. It may have something to do with the way they maintain their fur—cats never clean themselves with water, but always use their own tongues. Also, cats hate surprises, so they're not particularly fond of sudden baths or getting zapped by their owners with a water gun.

WHY can't you teach a cat tricks?

Actually, it is possible to teach a cat tricks—it's just so frustrating that most people give up! Unlike dogs, cats don't respond well to commands, and they're not inclined to try to impress their owners.

The trick to teaching a cat tricks is to wait until just before dinnertime. As any cat owner knows, a pussycat springs to attention when it sees you holding a can opener—and, since it wants to eat as soon as possible, it might be willing to indulge you in a quick training session. Once it's had its fill, though, you can expect to be ignored until the next meal comes around.

Even if you do succeed in teaching your cat tricks, you'll have to be satisfied with a fairly limited repertory, like fetching and heeling—although some smart cats develop their own tricks, like learning how to open a refrigerator or cupboard where food is kept.

WHY is a cat's tongue rough?

Cats clean and comb themselves with their own tongues—a fascinating (and sometimes revolting) process. To help in its grooming regimen, a cat's tongue is coated with tiny, rough, backward-hooking barbs called papillae, made out of the same substance as its sharp claws.

WHY do cats get hairballs?

Cats are constantly shedding their fur, and they're also constantly cleaning themselves with their rough tongues. If you do the math, you can see that the average cat ingests a fair amount of loose fur, which it throws up occasionally in the form of a gross, wet, lumpy (but usually completely harmless) hairball.

WHY do cats have whiskers?

A cat's whiskers are kind of like a bug's antennae: they help it navigate through and around obstacles and maintain its balance (which is why cats can scoot so easily down inch-wide railings). These whiskers are longer and deeper than normal hairs, and their roots are unusually rich in blood vessels and nerve endings.

HOW does a cat see in the dark?

Like any creature, a cat cannot see in absolute, total darkness. But thanks to a special layer of cells in the back of its eyes—which collects dim light like a mirror—a cat can see in near-total darkness much better than a person can. These special cells are also why you can see a cat's eyes "glowing" if you look at them from a certain angle as the light reflects from its retinas.

HOW do cats sharpen their claws?

As any cat owner knows, it's usually by tearing apart the most expensive piece of furniture in the house. Cats keep their claws sharp by honing them on any available rough surface. In the wild that might be a tree trunk, but domestic cats use anything ranging from a specially designed "scratching post" to your best upholstery. Strangely, even when a cat has been de-clawed, it will still go through the motions of sharpening its non-existent nails.

HOW do cats purr?

Cats have been kept as purring pets for thousands of years, but scientists still don't agree on the purring mechanism. The best guess is that purring is generated by vibrating blood vessels in the cat's chest, though some experts believe purrs emanate from the cat's diaphragm, like a hiccup. Scientists have even advanced the idea that a soft, soothing purr helps to heal damaged bones and tissues in the cat's body.

Despite what you may have heard, cats don't only purr when they're happy. They will also make this mysterious sound when they are sick, anxious, or simply hungry.

HOW sharp is a dog's sense of smell?

Dogs have over 200 million scent cells in their noses, compared to about 5 million for people—so in a way, dogs can smell roughly 40 times better than people can. Trained dogs also have a good "memory" for scents, which is why they're used to track missing people or search for disaster survivors who might be hidden under rubble.

WHAT is the biggest breed?

Some individual Great Danes or golden retrievers can grow to enormous size, but the consistently biggest dogs are mastiffs and St. Bernards, which can reach well over 200 pounds. These two breeds are used in very different ways, though. Mastiffs make good guard dogs, while St. Bernards are more companionable (and helpful) "people dogs."

WHY do dogs sniff each others' butts?

For the same reason people shake hands—as a way to say hello! For dogs, it's even better than shaking hands, because with their good sense of smell, sniffing another dog can give them information about its gender, diet, and social status (that is, whether the pooch is aggressive or submissive).

WHY do dogs wag their tails when they're happy?

Thousands of years ago, before they became domesticated, wild pack dogs used to communicate with one another by wagging their tails (in addition to other behavior like barks, howls, growls, and body posture).

Pet dogs today—who have had most of their "wild" behavior bred out of them—mostly wag their tails when they're happy. But you should be careful: dogs also wag their tails (with a slightly stiffer motion) when they're angry, and in yet another way when they're frightened. Yet another kind of tail wag can indicate confusion, as when a pooch is uncertain whether to approach you or run away.

WHY do dogs fetch?

Dogs have been kept as pets for thousands of years, but in ancient times they did more than romp in the park and sleep on the sofa. Some dogs were trained to be "retrievers"—when its owner shot a bird with an arrow, the pooch ran over and brought it back. As more and more dogs were bred for the hunt, this behavior became ingrained, meaning that today pretty much any dog can be taught to fetch.

HOW many commands can a dog understand?

With proper training, an eager dog can be taught to follow a few dozen commands: sit, heel, talk, roll over, play dead, come, shake hands, and others. But it's important to realize that a dog doesn't understand words the way a human does; it pays equal attention to its owner's tone of voice and body language when it's figuring out what it's supposed to do.

WHAT is the smallest dog?

The tiny, bug-eyed Chihuahua weighs less than a big rat—anywhere from one to five pounds. Although there are heavier breeds of Chihuahua, they are not allowed to compete in dog shows.

WHY do dogs bury bones?

Dogs are separated by only a few thousand years from their nearest relatives, the wolves, so they haven't quite lost all their wolfish habits. In the wild, wolves are known to bury leftover food, then return to it later for another meal. Even though a dry bone doesn't really count as a "meal," dogs still indulge in this wolflike behavior.

HOW did dogs become pets?

Dogs are descended from wolves, and wolves are pack animals—meaning the members of the pack follow the lead of the "alpha," or dominant, wolf. Thanks to this pack behavior, thousands of years ago, a stray wolf puppy that happened to wander into a human village was likely to obey the commands of the person who raised it. As more and more wolves learned to live alongside people, the process of "domestication" took hold, and the animals were taught helpful behaviors like hunting, fetching, and companionship.

As ancient people learned to live with dogs (and vice-versa), they slowly learned the art of selective breeding: mating two dogs to produce a litter of puppies with characteristics (such as size and temperament) best adapted to life among humans. That's why there's such a large diversity of dog types today, ranging from huge Great Danes to tiny Chihuahuas.

WHAT is the difference between a horse and a pony?

About what you'd expect: ponies are much smaller. Horses and ponies belong to the same species (meaning they can mate and produce offspring), but adult horses reach a height of about five feet at their shoulder, while ponies are a couple of feet shorter.

HOW was the horse domesticated?

The domestication (that is, taming and purposeful breeding) of the wild horse was one of the most important developments of human history. Cavalry (soldiers atop horses) won some of the ancient world's crucial battles, and before the invention of the car, a horse was the only way to reach one's destination quickly.

It's unclear which civilization was first to domesticate the horse, but the process was well under way by 2000 B.C., when horses were already being used for transport (pictures of horses have been found in cave paintings from thousands of years earlier, probably because they were hunted for food). Like dogs, horses were domesticated when young foals were separated from their mothers, raised by people, and trained for specific tasks.

By the way, the horses of thousands of years ago were much smaller than today's thoroughbreds, so they were probably only used to pull wagons and carts.

HOW fast is a racehorse?

A thoroughbred racehorse can sustain a top speed of 45 miles per hour for about one mile. It helps if the horse has a light rider (since carrying extra weight slows it down), which is why professional jockeys tend to be small in stature. By the way, the name "thoroughbred" means the horse has been specifically bred for racing.

WHAT is a wild ass?

Okay, you can stop laughing now. One of the rarest mammals on the planet, the African wild ass is the direct descendant of the common donkey. Today, there are only a few thousand of these creatures in the grasslands of Africa near the Red Sea.

WHAT is the difference between a donkey and a mule?

Technically, a donkey is simply a smaller, funnier-looking variant of the horse. We know these two creatures belong to the same species, because a male donkey can impregnate a female horse, who will then give birth to a mule. A male horse can also impregnate a female donkey, resulting in an animal called a "hinny." However, because a hinny or mule has a different number of chromosomes (units of genetic material) than a donkey or a horse, it is sterile, meaning it is unable to reproduce.

Another kind of donkey, the wild burro of the American southwest, is descended from the pack animals used by Spanish explorers in the 16th century. These creatures are a lot tougher than ordinary donkeys, capable of losing up to 30% of their body weight in water (a valuable skill in a hot desert climate).

By the way, the word "donkey" is fairly new, adopted over the last couple of centuries to replace this creature's original name, the "ass." (And yes, the change was largely made to avoid confusion with you-know-what.)

WHAT is a lipizzaner?

In the late 16th century, the emperor of Austria imported a large, sturdy breed of horse from Spain, with the intention of creating a "royal" mount suitable for state occasions. Thanks to careful breeding, these lipizzaners are easily trained (you may see them "dancing" in circuses or TV commercials), but they're very rare—there are only a few thousand stallions, mares, and foals in the world today.

WHY do horses need shoes?

A horse's hoof is basically a gigantic toenail—and like any nail, it can chip or split if it's not cared for properly. Shoeing a horse protects its hooves from damage, and also makes it easier and safer for the horse to walk on irregular surfaces (since horses evolved to live on grass, they're not really designed for roads and pavements). In medieval times, making horseshoes was one of the many tasks of the village blacksmith.

WHY do rats have bare tails?

A large part of what makes people afraid of rats is their ugly, furless, skeletal-looking tails.

The reason the rat has a bare tail is to regulate its temperature: in hot weather, the rat can dissipate excess heat via its tail, which would be much more difficult if it had a thick (or even a thin) coat of fur.

WHAT is the biggest rodent?

If you're afraid of mice (or mouse-like creatures), stop reading now. The capybara, a rodent native to south and central America, weighs anywhere from 60 to 100 pounds, about the size of a large dog! Amazingly, scientists have identified the prehistoric remains of an even bigger rodent, weighing about 10 times as much as the capybara, which has been nicknamed the "guinea-zilla."

WHY do beavers build dams?

Real beaver dams aren't quite as spectacular as the ones in cartoons, but they're impressive nonetheless. The reason beavers stop up a creek with grass, dirt and leaves is because the resulting "lake" is a good place to hide from predators. By the way, scientists think beavers know their dam is "finished" when they can no longer hear the sound of rushing water.

HOW many nuts can a squirrel hold in its cheeks?

A squirrel's cheeks are almost as elastic as balloons, allowing it to store a total of four times its own weight in nuts. It's not a good idea to do this for extended periods of time, though: when its cheeks are stuffed to capacity, a squirrel can't even close its own eyes because the skin on its face is stretched so tight.

When it's not storing them in its cheeks, a squirrel hides nuts the way people hide gold, burying its stash in a few different locations (so in case one is found by a rival squirrel others will sustain it through the winter). Scientists aren't sure yet how these furry critters locate these hiding places after weeks or months, but it's most likely that they use their advanced sense of smell (which can detect a pile of nuts even through several feet of snow).

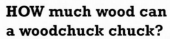

WHAT is the difference between a gerbil and a hamster?

Most people use these two names interchangeably, and to be fair, all hamsters and gerbils look pretty much alike. But there are some subtle ways to tell the difference.

There are about a hundred different kinds of gerbils, and many are related to central Asian critters called jirds ("jird" is Mongolian for "large desert rodent"). Hamsters are a bit less exotic and diverse than their gerbil cousins, but both species share the same common ancestor—the rat.

As to which makes the better pet, that's a matter of personal preference. Hamsters are slightly bigger and tougher than gerbils (meaning they're more likely to survive rough handling), and are most active at night. Gerbils are smaller, with fluffier tails, and they're slightly more active. They occasionally venture out during the day, so kids can get to see more activity, instead of just having to listen to their hamster squeaking away in its wheel at night.

WHY do moles have bad eyesight?

Since they spend so much of their time burrowing below the ground, moles don't have much need for 20-20 vision. A mole compensates for its tiny, beady eyes by having sensitive hairs around its nose, which lets it "feel" its way through its burrow. The mole's fur is also extremely soft, so it doesn't catch on obstacles and create friction as it moves back and forth.

HOW much wood can a woodchuck chuck?

Woodchucks don't really chuck (throw) pieces of wood, but that hasn't kept some enterprising people from trying to answer this question. As it digs its burrow, a woodchuck throws out about 35 cubic feet of dirt. If this dirt were occupied by the same volume of wood, it would total about 700 pounds!

HOW do flying squirrels fly?

Like many other "flying" creatures—fish, for example—flying squirrels don't fly the way birds do. Instead, these furry critters launch themselves and glide through the air on wide flaps of skin that connect their front and back paws. The Giant Flying Squirrel, which lives in the Far East, can glide almost 1,500 feet at a time.

WHY do deer have antlers?

A male deer has antlers to ward off predators (lions really hate getting a mouthful of antler) and to spar with other males during the mating season. Interestingly, reindeer are the only species of deer in which the females also have antlers, probably so they can dig through packed snow to reach the tasty grass underneath.

By the way, antlers (which deer, moose, and caribou have) are very different from the horns of goats, sheep, and cattle. First, unlike horns, growing antlers are covered by a soft, fuzzy layer of skin called "velvet," which drops off during mating season. Second, the horns of goats and bulls are permanent, while antlers are shed every winter and a new pair grown all over again. And third, antlers are made out of bone, while horns are made out of keratin (the same protein that makes up your hair and toenails).

HOW do llamas survive at high altitudes?

As befits a beast that lives at extreme altitudes (in the Andes mountain range of South America), the llama is uniquely adapted to its habitat. First, its blood carries more oxygen than other mammals, since the air is thinner at 10,000 feet. And second, the llama has unusually long, thick fur, which—in addition to its ability to carry baggage—makes it a valuable resource for mountain dwellers.

WHY do goats eat tin cans?

They don't, as you may already have guessed—in fact, if any animal could successfully digest a tin can it would probably be a top story on the evening news. This myth may have started because goats like to nuzzle strange and unfamiliar objects, and (like any animal) will sometimes try to lick out the leftover contents of an empty tin can.

HOW do camels store water?

For a long time, people believed that camels stored water in their humps. However, it's since been discovered that a camel's hump actually contains food reserves (in the form of fat), and will become flabby if the beast goes too long without eating. As for water, that's stored in the camel's stomach—about one or two gallons at a time.

WHAT is the difference between a buffalo and a bison?

Don't tell Buffalo Bill, but there were never any buffalo in North America. The two species look very much alike, but buffalo are native to Europe and Asia, while the shaggy beasts hunted by American natives and western settlers were actually bison. The confusion arose when Europeans first settled in North America, saw vast herds of familiar-looking animals, and promptly called them "buffalos."

There used to be many, many more bison than people in the American Midwest only 150 years ago—anywhere from 30 to 70 million before they were driven nearly to extinction. These herd animals were hunted for food and pelts, then vast numbers were slaughtered to make way for the laying of the new railways, so only a few hundred remained by the late 1800's. Thanks to conservation measures, the population is now protected and has rebounded on reclaimed prairie land to about a quarter of a million today.

WHAT is hay?

Ruminants like deer and cows survive on a steady diet of grass. If fresh grass isn't available, these creatures find hay—a mixture of dried grass and pasture flowers—to be an acceptable substitute. Like other dried foods, the good thing about hay is that it lasts much longer than fresh grass, and is readily available during the winter.

WHAT is a ruminant?

The word "ruminant" derives from "rumen," a special stomach that allows animals like sheep, goats, and cows to digest grass. You can recognize a ruminant by its constant chewing, as it grinds down its "cud" of semidigested grass.

WHAT country has the most sheep?

Based on sheer numbers, China has more sheep than any other country in the world: almost 150 million out of the world's total population of 1 billion. But if you consider the sheep-to-people ratio, New Zealand is the clear winner: this small nation has almost 50 million sheep, meaning there are about a dozen sheep for every human being.

WHY are polar bears white?

Look at it this way: if you were a seal, would you notice a polar bear sneaking up on you during a blinding snowstorm? The main reason polar bears are white is to blend in with their surroundings, either to pounce on unsuspecting prey or to elude human hunters (since people are the polar bear's only natural enemy).

WHY do bears hibernate?

In the winter the foods that bears eat—nuts, berries, the occasional camper—become very scarce. Rather than spend its days hunting for scraps, the bear curls up in a cave and hibernates (that is, goes into a very deep sleep) until spring. To survive its long snooze, the bear makes sure to fatten up in October and November, since it can lose up to 30 percent of its body weight by the time it awakens.

Unlike other hibernating animals such as chipmunks and squirrels—which have to wake up every few days to maintain their body temperatures and go to the bathroom—a black bear can sleep for months at a stretch. During this time, it maintains a body temperature of about 88 degrees Fahrenheit (compared to its normal temperature of 100 degrees), largely thanks to its thick coat of fur. Smaller hibernating animals can lower their body temperatures to as little as 40 degrees!

WHAT is the most dangerous bear?

As dangerous as a grizzly can be, it's a pussycat compared to its more vicious cousin from the north, the polar bear. This huge beast subsists on a diet of seals, walruses, reindeer, and the occasional whale, and it's powerful enough to pound through thick ice with its front paws. If you don't think that's intimidating enough, a full-grown male can rear up to a height of 10 feet!

HOW long is an anteater's tongue?

The tongue of the giant anteater (which lives in South and Central America) is a whopping two feet long. When you subsist on a diet of ants, you have to have a way to catch a whole bunch at the same time—and by flicking its long, sticky tongue into an ant mound (up to 160 times a minute) the anteater can feast on tens of thousands of tiny bugs at a single sitting.

HOW does a bat fly in the dark?

These little flying mammals aren't nearly as blind as people think, but they have evolved a unique way to navigate in the dark: sonar! As it flies, a bat emits tiny squeaks and buzzes, and it "hears" its surroundings by the way these sounds echo off walls or objects in its path.

HOW do sloths hang upside-down all day?

If ever an animal was adapted to an upside-down life, it's the sloth. This animal's toes are long, sharp, and curved, so they can hook easily over tree branches, and it has unusually strong muscles in its arms, legs, and shoulders. When it's in its natural habitat, the sloth is indistinguishable from a big lump of moss, which protects it from predators and allows it to (pretty much) sleep the entire day.

WHY do warthogs have warts?

Not the handsomest creatures on the face of the earth, warthogs earned their name because of the prominent "warts" on their muzzles (which are larger on males than females). These aren't real warts—a human skin condition caused by viruses—but pads of skin that help protect the warthog's faces, especially when the males fight with each other over available females.

HOW did vampire bats get their name?

Vampire bats feed on the blood of pigs, horses, cattle, and even large birds. Like a vampire, this small creature emerges only at night, then cuts through its victim's tough hide with razor-sharp teeth and laps up—but doesn't actively suck—the blood that oozes out. Vampire bats need to feed at least once every few days; hungry bats have been known to get mouth-to-mouth "transfusions" from well-fed companions!

As creepy as they are, vampire bats (which usually keep their distance from humans) have been a valuable resource for scientists. In fact, the chemical these creatures use to keep their victims' blood from clotting (called "draculin") has inspired a genetically engineered drug that helps stroke victims.

It's tempting to think that vampire bats inspired stories of human vampires, but this isn't the case: these creatures are native to Central and South America, whereas the first tales of vampires arose in central Europe.

HOW do dolphins breathe?

Because it's a mammal, a dolphin needs air just like the rest of us. It gets its fill by surfacing every now and then to quickly breathe in and out through the blowhole on top of its head (which is a kind of specialized nostril). Usually, dolphins breathe every two or three minutes, though in a pinch they can hold their breath under water for up to 10 minutes (which is a lot longer than a person can!)

While we're on the subject, a lot of kids (and even adults) don't know the difference between dolphins and porpoises. Well, porpoises are much smaller than dolphins, growing to about 7 feet (or less) in length compared to a full-grown dolphin's 10-plus feet. Also, porpoises have much shorter life spans, only living for about 20 years, while healthy dolphins can live for 50 years or more.

WHAT is a manatee?

Long believed to have inspired the mythical mermaid, the manatee is a roughly human-sized sea mammal with an expressive face and no hind limbs (just a thick flipper). Like its cousin, the dugong, the manatee has long been hunted for its meat, hide, and body part,s which are sometimes ground up and used in traditional medicines.

WHY do people hunt whales?

"Whaling," as it's called, is much less common than it used to be. Up until the end of the 19th century, whales were hunted primarily for their blubber (which was rendered down to oil to be burned in lamps), and for whalebone, which was used to make corsets. Sperm whales were also prized for a special substance stored in their heads (called "spermaceti") that was turned into a precious perfume. When people hunt whales today, it's usually as a source of food, or to protect commercial fisheries.

WHAT is whale blubber?

Whales live in the some of the world's coldest waters, so they need a reliable way to keep warm. Blubber is a thick layer of fat just beneath the whale's skin, which serves as both insulation from the cold and a convenient place to store food. Some arctic tribes like to eat whale blubber, but it's definitely an acquired taste!

WHY do walruses have tusks?

Although a male walrus's huge tusks occasionally come in handy for chopping through the ice (these huge beasts live in the Arctic Circle, which is frozen all year long), their main function is to attract female walruses. The bigger the tusks, the healthier and more dominant the male appears, making him a good prospective mate.

WHY do whales sing?

The haunting, musical, booming sounds made by whales are their means of communicating with other whales. The reason a whale song sounds so "alien" is that it's meant to project through water, not through air, the medium by which humans and other land animals communicate. In fact, whales and dolphins "talk" this way all the time, because their vision is so limited in the murky depths of the ocean.

HOW high can a whale spout water?

A whale spouts water as it surfaces to breathe, so it can clear its blowhole to take in plenty of fresh air. Most whales spout seawater only a dozen or so feet in the air, but the giant blue whale has been known to create a fountain nearly 40 feet high—about the height of an office building.

WHAT is the biggest animal?

You probably guessed it was some kind of whale, and you're absolutely right: the blue whale is the biggest animal on earth, measuring up to 100 feet from head to tail and weighing as much as 150 tons. Not only is the blue whale the biggest animal living today, it's also the biggest that ever existed, outweighing even the most massive dinosaurs by about 50 tons (or 100,000 pounds).

Ironically, this most titanic of all the earth's creatures subsists on a steady diet of some of the smallest: tiny, one-celled animals called plankton, which it harvests from ocean water using a special filter in its jaw. But don't let the blue whale's diet fool you into thinking that all whales are harmless filter-feeders. Sperm whales have been known to feast on the occasional seal, and the aptly named killer whale hunts for large prey in packs, like wolves!

WHY are there so few giant pandas?

A number of factors have combined to make the giant panda of China one of the rarest large animals in the world. First, pandas breed very slowly (a female typically produces only one surviving cub every few years); second, these creatures depend on a steady diet of bamboo, which is often destroyed to create human settlements; and third, pandas are sometimes hunted for their "magical" body parts. Thanks to intensive efforts, the panda population has stabilized, but the species still hovers on the brink of extinction.

WHY do people hunt rhinos?

It has long been believed in the countries of the Far and Middle East that ground-up rhinoceros horn has medicinal properties. Although these horns are mostly made of keratin (the same stuff as our fingernails and toenails!), the trade in rhinoceros horn has been so profitable that the population of the Black Rhinoceros of Africa has been reduced by 97 percent, to about 2,000 individuals.

WHAT is an ecosystem?

No animal—not even humans—can survive completely apart from other living things. An ecosystem consists of the complicated web of relationships between various species (ranging all the way from bacteria to large mammals) and the physical environment in which they live. The reason many animals are endangered is that a seemingly harmless change to one aspect of their ecosystem sets off a chain reaction that causes a rapid fall in population.

HOW is it decided that a species is endangered?

As used by the International Union for the Conservation of Nature, the organization that tracks vanishing species, the word "endangered" has a very specific meaning. It applies to creatures with a total world population of 500 to 2,500 individuals (such as the giant panda), or to a species living in a total area of under 5,000 square kilometers, or about 1,900 square miles, whose population is declining (such as the spotted owl or the Bengal tiger).

The classification "Endangered" actually falls somewhere in the middle of the IUCN's scale. Some species are judged to be at "low risk," which means they may possibly be declining in numbers but don't yet merit intervention, while other species are classified as "vulnerable," meaning they have experienced a definite fall in population. A species may also progress past the "endangered" stage to become "critically endangered" (less than 250 individuals remaining), or "extinct in the wild," meaning the only survivors are found in zoos. Finally, of course, there is the sad classification: Completely Extinct.

WHY are so many big cats endangered?

If any animal was equipped to fight its own extinction, you'd think it would be the leopard, tiger, or panther—after all, these creatures can actually defend themselves, unlike other vanishing or extinct animals like giant turtles and dodo birds.

The trouble is that a tiger rarely has the opportunity to defend itself in hand-to-claw combat. Big cats are hunted from a safe distance by people with powerful rifles. Usually they are shot by herdsmen or ranchers to protect their cattle or other domestic animals, but they are also stalked for their beautiful pelts, or to provide primitive remedies, or even just for the thrill of the hunt.

Despite what you may think, though, most big cats aren't killed by guns. These predatory beasts need large areas in which to hunt and enough wild game to sustain themselves and their families. A single panther, for example, requires a territory of about 50 square miles. As cities and towns expand into previously wide-open spaces, and the amount of wild prey diminishes, the cats' territory shrinks and their population gradually dies out.

WHAT is poaching?

Poachers are people who hunt (or capture) animals illegally. Some poachers disobey regulations (say, by hunting out of season or killing more deer than the legal limit), while others are brazen enough to sneak onto wildlife preserves and kill endangered animals. In most countries, poaching is a crime, though this law can be hard to enforce if the authorities don't pay attention—or if they accept bribes from the poachers.

WHAT is the main reason animals become endangered?

That's easy to answer: people! Although human beings don't deliberately set out to destroy species, the rapid growth of the world population—and the pressure this puts on natural resources—leads to (for example) the cutting down of forests and the conversion of open savannah into farmland. As humans impinge on the natural habitats of animals, many species are in increasing danger of becoming extinct.

WHAT microbe has the most DNA?

Scientists have long known that most of an organism's DNA is "junk"—that is, it doesn't carry any genetic information (even human DNA, as far as we know, is 99 percent nonfunctional). Even so, you may be surprised to learn that the DNA of one species of amoeba is about 200 times the size of the human genome! As gigantic as it is, though, this amoeba's DNA only comprises a few thousand genes, while a much smaller strand of human DNA contains about 30,000 genes.

WHY do bacteria become resistant to antibiotics?

When it comes to survival, bacteria have two major advantages: the speed with which they multiply (a single bacterium can produce millions of ancestors in just a few days), and the ease with which their DNA mutates.

Antibiotics (drugs that kill disease-causing bacteria) usually succeed in wiping out most of their targets, but one or two bacteria may develop a mutation that makes them more "resistant" (that is, harder to kill). So, even if a drug wipes out 10 million bacteria in a single dose, the one or two left alive can continue to multiply and make the patient even sicker.

For most bacterial diseases, drug resistance isn't a problem—if one antibiotic doesn't do the trick, another, more powerful one will kill the stragglers. Doctors are concerned, though, that the indiscriminate and frequent use of antibiotics for mild illnesses that don't really need them may be breeding a population of "superbugs" that are almost impossible to destroy with our current medicines.

WHAT are cyanobacteria?

Much different from the "ordinary" bacteria found in humans, cyanobacteria are a kind of "missing link" between the bacterial and plant kingdoms. Like plants, these organisms derive their energy from photosynthesis, but they lack other components found in plant cells. Cyanobacteria can easily grow to a visible size, which is why they're sometimes called blue-green algae.

HOW do bacteria swim?

Most bacteria have at least one flagellum, a small, whip-like cord that propels the organism through the water. The reason you see bacteria "tumbling" in a microscope is that their flagellae abruptly start rotating in a clockwise rather than a counterclockwise fashion (or vice-versa), creating a brief moment of confusion until the cell heads off in a new direction.

WHAT are diatoms?

Among nature's most beautiful creatures, diatoms are microscopic, one-celled organisms that live in tiny shells of silica (the same substance that makes up sand). What makes these shells so distinctive is that they're perfectly symmetric, and come in an array of intricately etched shapes (wheels, diamonds, etc.) and colors. As diatoms die, their discarded shells accumulate into rocks and mineral formations called "diatomaceous earth."

WHY is E. coli so important?

Trillions of rod-shaped E. coli bacteria live in our intestinal tracts, helping us digest food. However, this common bacterium is also important for another reason—because it's easily cultivated, scientists have studied it in exhaustive detail. In fact, E. coli was one of the first organisms to have its genetic code (that is, the information contained in its DNA) described in full.

WHAT are the sturdiest bacteria?

For years, scientists believed organisms could only survive in relatively moderate conditions—which (in biological terms) encompasses everything from the frigid cold of Antarctica to the baking heat of the Sahara Desert. That view changed, though, when a primitive form of bacteria was discovered on the ocean floor, thriving in the superheated water above a "thermal vent" (that is, a crack venting hot gases from beneath the earth's crust).

These "archaebacteria," as they're called, thrive in conditions that would be instantly fatal to most other organisms. Besides the intense heat (up to a few hundred degrees Celsius, although water doesn't boil at these depths because of the intense pressure), these primitive microbes tolerate extreme acidity, and they "breathe" corrosive gases that float up from the vent.

So many different archaebacteria have been discovered, in so many extreme conditions, that some biologists believe these were the first organisms from which all life evolved.

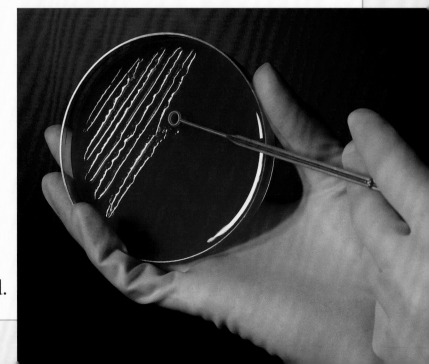

HOW powerful is the shock of an electric eel?

A full-grown electric eel can generate a shock of about 500 volts, enough to stun (if not kill) most small animals. The eel creates this current using thousands of ultrathin, stacked "plates" around its vertebrae, similar to what you'd find inside a battery. It can modulate its output to deliver either a small zap (to capture and eat a small fish) or a big one (to knock a hungry crocodile silly).

An electric eel doesn't only use its shocking talent to eat or avoid being eaten. Its electric plates are also useful for navigation (since they allow the eel to orient itself according to weak electric currents in the surrounding water) and for communication with other eels.

By the way, although electric eels get all the attention, you may be surprised to learn that some other ocean creatures are electric as well, including a species of freshwater catfish and a type of manta ray!

HOW sharp are a porcupine's quills?

A porcupine has about 30,000 quills, and they aren't just for show—each one is as sharp as a needle. When it's threatened, the porcupine doesn't shoot its quills like arrows, but bumps into the pursuing beast and gives it a faceful of needles. Needless to say, very few animals will attack a porcupine twice!

WHY do fish have scales?

For the same reason people have skin—to protect their internal organs! A fish's scales are flexible enough to wriggle back and forth as it swims, and hydrodynamic enough to glide through the water without creating too much resistance. By the way, not all fish have scales—some shield their bodies with a thick layer of mucus instead.

HOW do oysters make pearls?

An oyster produces a pearl when a piece of sand (or some other foreign substance) slips into its shell and irritates the soft tissues inside. In response, the tissues secrete a protective substance called "nacre," which coats the irritant and renders it harmless. Over the course of a few years, the tiny nacre nub grows into a pearl.

WHY does a puffer fish puff?

Puffer fish puff themselves up like water balloons when they're threatened, so they're too big to be swallowed by predators. They accomplish this feat by 1) having unusually elastic, stretchy skin, and 2) not having any ribs. Puffer fish are also extremely poisonous, which doesn't keep them from being a popular restaurant dish in Japan (chefs are careful to trim away the poisonous parts before the fish are cooked and served!).

HOW do insects protect themselves?

Bugs are way down at the bottom of the food chain, so they'd be a quick afternoon snack for a bird or lizard if they didn't have a reliable way to protect themselves. One strategy is camouflage. An insect that has evolved to look like a plain, ordinary stick, or a leaf, has a better chance of being passed over by an unsuspecting bird searching for food.

A ladybug's spots serve another purpose entirely—to warn away predators. Many brightly colored insects, frogs, and snakes are poisonous, so predators avoid them. Ladybugs are not at all poisonous, but they trick predators into thinking they are. (By the way, most ladybugs have red or gold shells with black spots, but some species have black shells with red or gold spots.)

Other cases of deceptive markings can be found on certain butterflies. When you see two big round spots on a butterfly's wings, the reason they're there to trick an insect-eating bird into thinking it is looking down on a frog or some other creature with big, round eyes that is not on its menu.

WHAT makes a skunk smell?

Skunks have two special glands in their behinds that secrete a substance called "musk," a powerful, stinky, and (in large doses) dangerous chemical that it uses to ward off enemies or people. When it's threatened, a skunk can spray its musk as far as 15 feet.

HOW does a chameleon change its color?

Despite what you see in cartoons, a chameleon can't blend in with just any pattern, like polka dots and stripes. But thanks to special pigment cells in its skin, this small lizard can change gradually between shades of green, brown, and gray, perfect for hiding against leaves and tree trunks or absorbing more heat from the sun.

HOW big was a dinosaur's brain?

Dinosaurs—especially the big, lumbering ones—were notorious for having tiny brains. The stegosaurus, which was almost 30 feet long and weighed over a ton, had a brain the size of a walnut! However, scientists now believe that smaller dinosaurs had brains comparable in size to modern mammals like dogs, which must have made it easy to outwit a T. Rex.

HOW big were a saber-toothed tiger's teeth?

Technically, a saber-toothed tiger should be called a saber-toothed cat, since these prehistoric beasts weren't related to tigers. Whatever the case, they were best avoided, since an adult's fangs were at least six inches long. Oddly, saber-toothed tigers are also known as "smilodons," which just might give a person the wrong idea!

WHAT caused the Ice Age?

The earth has gone through plenty of cold snaps in its history, but the Ice Age stands out because it was the first to be endured by humans, about 25,000 years ago. No one knows for sure, but this "modern" ice age was probably caused by a slight change in the earth's axis of rotation (which altered the amount of sunlight reaching the ground), or possibly by a change in the amount of carbon dioxide in the atmosphere.

With its wintry temperatures and ice sheets that extended inland for thousands of miles, the Ice Age certainly made life difficult for prehistoric people. But it did have one unexpected benefit: by opening up a frozen "land bridge" between Siberia and Alaska, it allowed primitive tribes to cross into the North American continent and spread from there to Central and South America.

HOW woolly were woolly mammoths?

Very woolly, but it's unlikely any cavemen were brave enough to shear these 10-foot tall, five-ton beasts and make sweaters (though they did use the wool from already-dead mammoths they happened to find laying on the ground). The now-extinct mammoth's hair ranged from a few inches to a couple of feet long, and if you managed to peel one whole, its pelt would cover about 20 square meters—enough to carpet your living room!

HOW big was the biggest dinosaur?

This is a hard question to answer, since archeologists are constantly digging up the remains of bigger and bigger dinosaurs. For now, the largest dinosaur that's known to have existed is the argentinosaurus, which was 100 feet long and weighed about 100 tons. Like other huge dinos, the argentinosaurus was a slow, gentle, none-too-bright plant-eater that went extinct long ago.

HOW small was the smallest dinosaur?

As with all dinosaur-related questions, it's hard to answer this one conclusively until more evidence is found. For now, scientists believe the smallest dinosaur was the compsognathus, which was about the size of a chicken. Footprints have been found of dinosaurs that may have been even smaller, but it's hard to tell if these were full-grown dinos, or just the babies of bigger species.

WHY did the dinosaurs become extinct?

For a long time this was a mystery, until a scientist proposed a strange idea: what if a giant meteor hit the earth millions of years ago? Besides leaving a huge crater, the impact would raise enough dust and ash to blot out the sun, killing the plants dinosaurs depended on for food and causing the dinosaurs themselves to die out over the next few centuries.

Well, not only have most scientists accepted this theory, but they think they've found the crater of the meteor responsible. The Chicxulub crater in the Yucatan (a large peninsula in southern Mexico) is about 125 miles wide, and was created millions of years ago, around the time of the dinosaurs's extinction, by one of the largest meteors ever to strike the earth.

WHY did T. Rex have such tiny arms?

The tyrannosaurus was a strange dinosaur: it had enormous teeth, powerful hind legs, and arms so tiny they didn't even reach its mouth. Most scientists think that T. Rex's arms were vestigial—a useless holdover from the creature T. Rex evolved from. In fact, if T. Rex had continued to evolve for a few million years, it might have wound up with no arms at all!

WHY don't spiders get stuck in their own webs?

Not all strands of a spider web are sticky. A spider cleverly keeps track of where it places the sticky and nonsticky strands (which are made of two different kinds of silk), so it doesn't tangle itself up accidentally like an unwary fly. Even with this simple precaution, though, some clumsy spiders do get trapped in their own webs.

Spider silk, by the way, is an amazing substance: the silk of some species is stronger, and more flexible, than an equal quantity of steel wire. Since spiders are so adept at spinning high-quality silk, you may

wonder: Why do we get silk from silkworms rather than spiders? The reason is that scientists haven't found an efficient way to "harvest" spider silk, and in any case, spiders don't produce nearly as much silk as silkworms (and they're certainly not as easy to manage!).

HOW big is the biggest spider?

So big that you can practically put it on a leash and walk it down the street. The Goliath Birdeater, a species of tarantula native to South America, measures a foot from end to end, and is big and strong enough to catch, kill, and eat a full-grown mouse at a single sitting. Even scarier, the females of the species can live up to 15 years, which is longer than many house pets!

WHAT is a daddy longlegs?

Technically, what most people call a daddy longlegs isn't really a spider, but a close relative called the "Harvestman." It's also possible they're referring to another long-limbed (true) spider called the Daddy Longlegs Spider. In any case, both of these species are relatively harmless; the Harvestman only eats already decayed food, and the bite of the Daddy Longlegs isn't especially serious.

WHY are spiders technically not insects?

Scientists classify species (or families of species) according to the characteristics shared by all its members. Spiders differ from insects in one major respect: an insect's body has three main parts (the head, the thorax, and the abdomen), while a spider's head and thorax are fused into one piece, called the cephalothorax.

HOW does a spider kill its prey?

If you're a fly, death by spider is a particularly unpleasant way to go. After the fly becomes trapped in the spider's web, the spider cocoons the bug into a ball of silk, injects it with a substance that dissolves its internal organs, then sticks in its fangs and slurps the gooey guts out.

WHAT is arachnophobia?

"Arachnid" is the latin word for "spider," and "phobia" means "fear of." So if you suffer from a bad case of arachnophobia, you probably skipped this part of the book!

WHAT is the most dangerous spider?

Perhaps because it has such a catchy name, the black widow has garnered an unearned reputation as the world's most dangerous spider. But the black widow is about as deadly as a newborn puppy compared to the Australian funnel web spider and the brown recluse (which is found all over the world).

Just a tiny bite from the tree-dwelling funnel web spider is enough to kill a full-grown man. Oddly enough, though, this spider's venom barely affects smaller animals like dogs and rabbits.

The bite of a brown recluse spider, on the other hand, is usually not fatal. But it is extremely painful, and potentially disfiguring, because the spider's venom eats away at surrounding tissues, causing a deep, open, spreading wound that takes months to heal.

By comparison, a black widow bite is a walk in the park. Although this spider's venom is extremely toxic, it is delivered in such small doses that death (or even injury) is unlikely to result. The usual symptoms are swelling, pain, and nausea, which usually all go away after a couple of days.

HOW many eyes does a spider have?

Unlike people—the vast majority of whom have two eyes—the number of eyes a spider has varies by species, ranging from zero to as many as 12, with most varieties having an even eight. Usually, the two central eyes are the ones that do most of the work, while the surrounding eyes improve the spider's sensitivity to light (which help it to hunt prey and avoid predators).

Section 2

Civilization

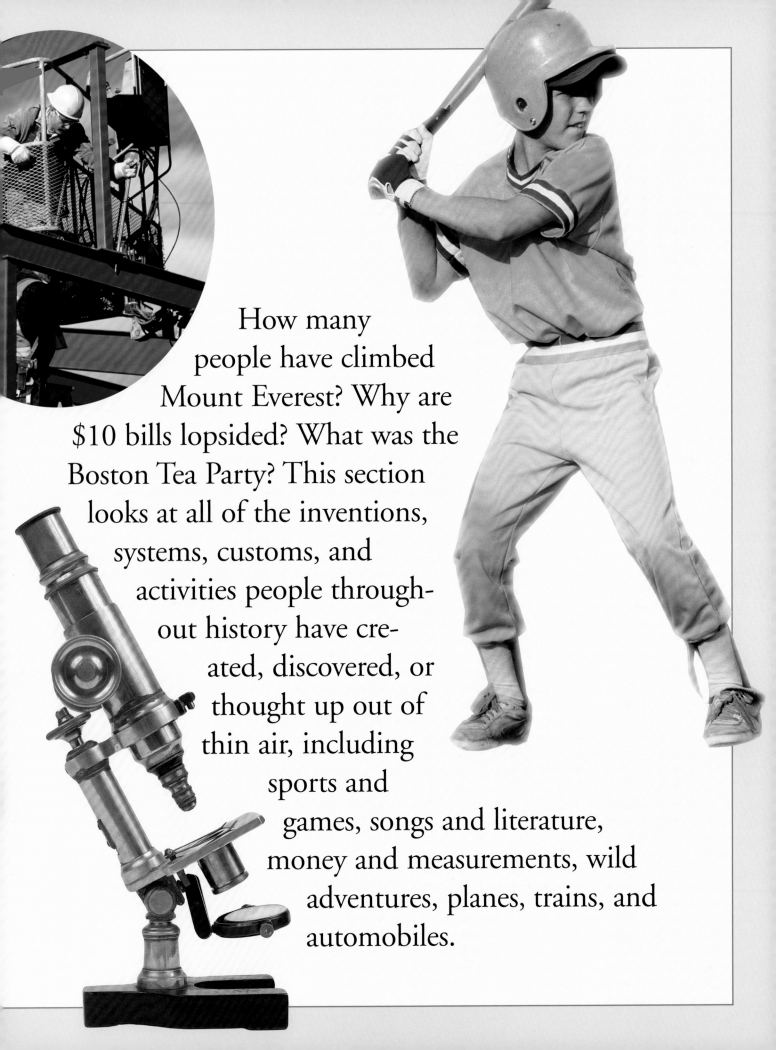

How many people have climbed Mount Everest? Why are $10 bills lopsided? What was the Boston Tea Party? This section looks at all of the inventions, systems, customs, and activities people throughout history have created, discovered, or thought up out of thin air, including sports and games, songs and literature, money and measurements, wild adventures, planes, trains, and automobiles.

WHAT are crayons made of?

The typical crayon has two main ingredients: colored pigment and paraffin (the same kind of wax used to make candles). Since wax melts at a relatively low temperature (about 120 to 140 degrees Fahrenheit), it's easy to melt the paraffin, mix in the pigments, and pour the mixture into a crayon-shaped mold. When the crayon solidifies, it's wrapped in paper and put in the box.

HOW do art dealers authenticate paintings?

With works by Renaissance artists commanding tens of millions of dollars, authenticating paintings (that is, confirming that they were in fact done by the artist in question) is of crucial importance in the art world. The problem is that many of these "old masters," as they're called, had devoted students who painted in a style nearly indistinguishable from their teachers.

Unlike detecting modern counterfeits of ancient works—which can usually be accomplished, say, by analyzing paint with high-tech equipment—authentication is a much trickier affair. It helps to have an unbroken chain of "provenance" (that is, ownership by various people), dating back to when the painting was made, and experts are often called in to analyze brushstrokes for unmistakable signs of the master's touch. Still, the process of authentication is far from foolproof: at least some famous paintings hanging in museums were probably done by someone else!

WHY does something rattle around inside a spray can?

What causes that rattling sound is usually one or two small metal or glass marbles that help mix the paint together. They move around inside and blend the paint's chemicals together more quickly than if there was nothing to stir them.

WHY doesn't glue dry up in the tube?

Most ordinary, household glues are water-based—that is, they become sticky as the water mixed up inside them slowly evaporates. If you're careful to leave the cap on the tube, the glue inside won't dry up, since there's nowhere for its water to evaporate to.

WHAT is paint made of?

There are all different kinds of paints—acrylic, oil, etc.—but they all share three basic ingredients: pigments, binders, and solvents. The "pigments" are the chemicals that give paint its characteristic color, while the binders make sure the color sticks to the wall after the paint has dried. Solvents are the chemicals (often poisonous!) in which the pigments and binders are dissolved.

WHY is it called "modern art?"

In a broad sense, modern art is whatever art happens to be popular when you're alive. In a more specific sense, though, what historians call "modern art" refers to a movement starting in the 1880's, in which artists felt free to move away from realistic subjects (like portraits and landscapes) toward more abstract modes of expression. The first modern artists of the late 19th century were hugely controversial, but today what we call "modern art" is pretty much the norm.

WHAT is papier-mâché?

Although it has a French name (which can be translated as "chewed paper"), papier-mâché dates all the way back to ancient China, when warriors mixed paper pulp with glue to make helmets (which presumably weren't very effective against iron swords!). Today, papier-mâché is popular in elementary school art classes, though some adult artists and stage designers use it too.

WHAT is the world's oldest painting?

As long as you're not too attached to modern concepts like canvases and frames, the first true paintings date all the way back to prehistoric times. In 1940, in France, two boys stumbled across an ancient cave, the walls of which were covered with animal drawings. Scientists later determined that these drawings were made about 15,000 years ago by primitive cavemen.

Up until the 15th and 16th centuries, the vast majority of paintings and drawings in the western world had a religious theme, and were found almost exclusively in churches or chapels. The concept of private individuals collecting framed art didn't really take root until the Renaissance, when royalty and the wealthy nobility commissioned portraits of themselves to hang on their walls or bestow as gifts (remember, this was long before the invention of photography).

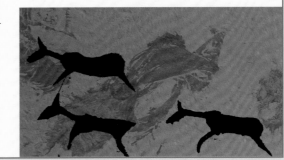

WHY was the printing press an important invention?

Until the mid-15th century, when the German Johann Gutenberg invented the printing press in order to print the Bible, manuscripts had to be copied out by hand, meaning even the most popular books only had very limited distribution (and could be afforded only by the nobility). By enabling the printing of hundreds or thousands of books in a short amount of time, the printing press began the spread of literacy (and knowledge) among the "lower" classes.

WHAT was the first novel?

This is a hard question to answer, because there was really no "first" novel in the sense that there was a first car. If you're willing to accept that an unwritten (that is, orally transmitted) verse epic qualifies as a novel, then the form dates all the way back to Homer's *Odyssey* and beyond. However, many experts cite Daniel Defoe's *Robinson Crusoe* and Henry Fielding's *Tom Jones*—both written in the 18th century—as classic early examples of the modern novel.

WHAT was the Library of Alexandria?

Until its destruction in the first century B.C., the Library of Alexandria (in a port city by that name on the north coast of Egypt) was the largest and most famous in the world. Historians estimate that it contained anywhere from 400,000 to 700,000 scrolls (the modern book, with its front and back covers, is a relatively recent invention), encompassing all the scientific and philosophical knowledge of antiquity.

To this day, historians and archeologists disagree about how the Library of Alexandria was destroyed. Some believe the culprit was the Roman general Julius Caesar, who set the harbor of Alexandria (and, unintentionally, the library) on fire during his invasion of Egypt in 47 B.C. Others say the library (or at least a part of it) actually survived until the third century A.D., when it was destroyed in the course of an Egyptian civil war. Whatever the case, the loss to knowledge has been incalculable, because many of the scrolls the library contained were the only copies, and they have been lost forever.

WHAT was the first comic book?

Although newspaper comics have been around since the late 19th century, the first comic book didn't appear until 1933, when a publisher collected various strips and reprinted them in an eight-page pamphlet called "Funnies on Parade." By the way, the world's most expensive comic book is "Action Comics #1", published in 1938—the very first appearance of Superman!

Most kids own anywhere from a few dozen to a few hundred comic books, but that's small change compared with professional collectors, who own tens of thousands (at about $2 per comic book, that's an expensive collection!). The reason most people collect comic books is that, occasionally, a title will become very rare and very expensive, and can be sold for thousands of dollars.

WHAT was the first children's book?

As long as there have been kids, there have been kid's books—or at least (before the age of printing) specially bound folk tales meant for children. The oldest known collection of these tales that has been found in book form is the 2,000-year-old Panchatantra from India. Since ancient books were rare and expensive, it's a good bet that the child who read the Panchatantra was a prince or princess!

WHAT is Dracula based on?

The character Dracula was invented by author Bram Stoker in 1897, but the legend dates back much farther. Some historians believe the myth of a blood-sucking count originated in 15th-century Transylvania (a territory in Eastern Europe), thanks to a ruler named Vlad Tepes. According to legend, Vlad killed his enemies by impaling them on giant stakes, and thus earned the nickname "dracul" (meaning "dragon" or "devil.")

WHY do we read from left to right?

There's no one "right" way to read a piece of text. Like all languages originating in Europe, English is read from left to right, but other languages around the world have different rules: Hebrew, for example, is read from right to left, and Chinese (which is spoken by a billion people) is read up to down, in adjoining columns!

HOW did language start?

We'll never know the details of the first language spoken by humans. However, linguists (scholars who study language) believe that many of the world's major languages—including English, Russian, and Hindi—trace their roots back to Proto-Indo-European, spoken by the people of Southeastern Europe and Asia thousands of years ago. Languages like Chinese and Japanese, as well as other languages in Africa and Australia, presumably also shared a common ancestor in ancient times.

You can get a sense of how Proto-Indo-European is related to modern tongues by considering its word for mother, "mat." This simple syllable gave rise to "mother" (in English), "madre" (in Spanish), and "matar" (in Sanskrit, the ancient language that preceded Hindi, the language of modern India). The same applies to Indo-European number names like "dvi" and "tri," the source of the English "two" and "three."

WHAT is the world's most widely spoken language?

That's an easy one: although English is the language most commonly used for international commerce and diplomacy, the most populous language by far is Mandarin Chinese—it's the native tongue of over one billion people, compared with a little over half a billion English speakers.

WHAT is the strangest language?

!Kung, spoken in Africa by natives of the Kalahari Desert, uses sounds that don't even exist in other languages. That exclamation point in front of the name isn't a typo; it represents a strange popping sound that !Kung tribespeople employ in their language, along with numerous explosive-sounding "clicks."

WHAT language has the smallest alphabet?

Among languages spoken by more than a few thousand people, Hawaiian has, by far, the fewest letters: only 12, less than half as many as English. That's why Hawaiian words have so many K's, N's, M's and L's, since these account for the majority of the language's consonants.

WHAT is the hardest language to learn?

It all depends on the individual, of course. But for many English-language speakers, the hardest language to learn is Chinese, since its pronunciation is very different from English and it uses an entirely different kind of writing, based not on letters, but on symbols called "ideograms." To keep things in perspective, though, many Chinese speakers think that English is the world's most difficult language!

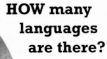

HOW many languages are there?

The world is home to thousands of languages, but most are spoken by only a very small number of people, ranging from a few dozen to a few thousand (and once these people are gone, the language disappears forever). Today, the world's major languages (English, Chinese, Hindi, etc.) account for the vast majority of speakers.

WHAT country has the most languages?

You probably thought it was a big country like the U.S. or China, but the nation with the most languages is tiny Papua New Guinea in the South Pacific. Although most of the five million natives of New Guinea speak English or a language called Moto, there are a multitude of small, mostly primitive tribes that speak over 700 distinct languages, ranging from "Abasakur" to "Yakaikeke."

This proliferation of tongues makes New Guinea a favorite destination of linguists, who study how languages originate and evolve. However, this task is complicated by the fact that the vast majority of small, tribal languages—including those of New Guinea—have never been written down, and lack even a basic alphabet. Because of this oral-only tradition, a tribal language usually dies with its last speaker.

WHAT is a dialect?

A dialect is a version of a particular language spoken with such different pronunciations and different meanings of words that it is very hard for people to understand. Dialects are most often found in areas that are cut off from contact with other communities, such as a mountainous region populated by an isolated tribe.

What is semaphore?

A low-tech communication system using flags, semaphore used to be a cheap, efficient way for ships at sea to communicate with one another over long distances (it came into its own in the early 17th century, after the invention of the telescope increased the range of its signals). However, semaphore was rendered obsolete in the mid-19th century by the invention of the telegraph.

WHY does Morse Code use dots and dashes?

Back when Morse Code was invented—in the first half of the 19th century—telegraph wires were just starting to come into use. Because there were so few cables and so many customers, messages had to be transmitted in code, and the shorter the code, the better. Morse Code was the most economical and easiest to learn, so its dots and dashes became the standard.

WHY was the transatlantic cable built?

Before the invention of wireless radio—that is, antennas that transmitted radio waves through the air to receivers—telegraph signals had to be sent by wire. This was easy enough to do on land, but in the early 19th century, governments grappled with the problem of hooking up North America with Western Europe, which involved laying a cable over almost 2,000 miles of the Atlantic sea bottom.

The first transatlantic cable—which, oddly enough, went into operation only a few years before the first transcontinental railroad—was laid in 1858 by two ships (carrying some very large spools of wire!) that met in the middle of the Atlantic Ocean. Unfortunately, this cable lasted only a few weeks before failing permanently, and it was only in 1866 that a more durable link was established between the two continents.

WHAT are hieroglyphs?

Letters—that is, written symbols that stand for sounds, from which words are assembled—are a relatively recent innovation. Ancient cultures like the Egyptians and Mayans used hieroglyphs, complex symbols that denote entire words and concepts; for example, a picture of a throne might mean "king," or an open mouth might mean "speak."

HOW does a CD player work?

A compact disc stores music in digital format—that is, as billions of digital bits, or "1"s and "0"s. A CD player uses a laser beam to read the surface of the disc, then converts this stream of bits into sound. A DVD player works exactly the same way, except that DVDs can store much more digital information than can regular audio CDs.

HOW did people get news before newspapers?

Way back in the Middle Ages—when there weren't any newspapers, and most people didn't know how to read anyway—ordinary folks kept up with current events via gossip, sermons at church, and occasional proclamations by the town crier.

The fact is, the average villager usually had no idea what was going on in the outside world, and often didn't even know what his own king or queen was up to.

Traveling minstrels, peddlers, and tinkers (who mended broken metal things such as pots) provided another means to disseminate news. These people would travel from town to village to city, selling their wares and services to anyone that would have them. They became walking newspapers, picking up news ranging from the goings-on at court, the movement of armies or the sacking of towns, to whose pig got stolen or who was marrying whom.

WHY do we drive on parkways and park on driveways?

The word "park" doesn't apply only to cars: it also means a public place set aside for a specific purpose, which is where the term "parkway" comes from (as in, the way through a state park). As for driveways, they earned that name because they allow a person to drive right up to the front of a house and park the car (the word "parkway" was already in widespread use, so calling a "driveway" a "parkway" would have been too confusing).

WHAT is a palindrome?

A palindrome is a word, name, number, or phrase that reads exactly the same forward and backward. "Anna" and "Otto" are palindromic names, "1001" and "232" are palindromic numbers, and one of the most famous palindromic phrases is "A man, a plan, a canal: Panama!" (Try spelling this backwards to see how it works.)

Palindromes are only one of a variety of popular word games. Many people also enjoy playing with "anagrams"—that is, words whose letters can be rearranged to form other words (or a series of words). For example, the word "punishment" can be written as "nine thumps," and the phrase "the morse code" can be turned into "here come dots."

HOW many words are in an average person's vocabulary?

There are about a million words in the English language, but the vast majority of people don't use nearly that many. According to linguists, the average English speaker knows about 20,000 words, and uses about 2,000 in conversation in any given week. People who are especially well educated—or who are very good at Scrabble—may have an active vocabulary of 100,000 words or more.

WHAT is the longest word in the English language?

This is a tough one to answer, since chemists and biologists use all kinds of enormous, specialized words that (technically) aren't even English at all! That said, the longest English word is a real mouthful: "antidisestablishmentarianism," meaning a belief system that opposes removing the tie between church and state. Try dropping that into your next conversation!

HOW did the teddy bear get its name?

Teddy bears are named after Theodore "Teddy" Roosevelt, the 26th president of the United States. One day in 1902—or so the story goes—Roosevelt and his friends went out hunting for bears, but when they couldn't find an adult grizzly, his pals captured a wounded bear cub and tied it to a tree for the president to shoot.

A believer in fair play, Roosevelt refused to go along, since the bear cub couldn't defend itself or run away. A journalist who accompanied the president on the trip mentioned this in his newspaper story, whereupon the public expressed its overwhelming support for Roosevelt's decision. The story became so popular, in fact, that an enterprising toy manufacturer decided to create a stuffed bear to commemorate the occasion. The rest is Teddy Bear history.

WHAT is the most common last name?

Taking a global perspective, "Chang" (or "Zhang") is by far the most popular last name, shared by 100 million Chinese. In the U.S., there are three million people whose last name is "Smith," followed closely by "Johnson," "Williams," "Jones," and "Brown."

HOW did the Dead Sea get its name?

Because nothing will grow in it! The Dead Sea, located in Israel, is so saturated with salt and minerals that nothing can live, or even sink, in it—if you jump in, you'll float straight to the surface. By the way, if Dead Sea sounds like an unappealing name, it's better than what geographers in the Middle Ages called it: the Stinking Sea, the Devil's Sea, or the Sea of Asphalt.

HOW did polka dots get their name?

Back in the nineteenth century, a polka-music craze swept across America (with its brass instruments and accordions, polka music is a lot different from rock or rap). People became so crazy about polka dancing that they started using the word to describe different things, including the colored-circle design that was often worn by polka dancers.

WHAT was the Gold Rush?

There have been a few gold rushes in American history, but the only one that deserves the capital letters is the California Gold Rush—which started in 1848 when a gold nugget was discovered in the town of Sutter's Mill near San Francisco. As word spread via newspapers, thousands of people flocked west from the cities of the East Coast—an arduous, months-long journey in the days before cars and transcontinental railroads.

Ironically, not many people struck it rich during the Gold Rush (except the shopkeepers who sold supplies to prospectors!), but the resulting "boom towns" helped put California on the map.

About 50 years later, in 1896, history repeated itself when gold was discovered in the Klondike (a Canadian territory near Alaska). Within a few years, nearly 100,000 Americans had ventured north in search of their fortunes—and most of them had about as much luck as the veterans of the California rush.

HOW much did the Louisiana Purchase cost?

By modern real estate standards, the Louisiana Purchase of 1803—in which the U.S. acquired over a half-billion acres of territory stretching from New Orleans to North Dakota—was an incredible bargain. The purchase price was $15 million, about $200 million in today's dollars (less than it costs to build most sports stadiums!).

WHY did settlers ride in covered wagons?

Covered wagons—or Prairie Schooners, as they were sometimes called—were the very first mobile homes.

Since settlers often traveled through dangerous territory, they needed a vehicle they could sleep, cook, and work in, especially if there was too much snow on the ground to pitch a tent or if they were afraid of hostile Indians.

HOW many Indians used to live in North America?

Historians believe that before Columbus arrived in 1492, there were anywhere between 2 and 18 million Native Americans in what is now the United States (it's hard to tell exactly, since the tribes were widely scattered and didn't keep records). It was much more crowded farther south, with as many as 30 million Indians living in what is now the country of Mexico.

WHAT was the Boston Tea Party?

One of the key issues leading to the Revolutionary War was "taxation without representation": citizens of the American colonies were required to pay taxes to England, but didn't get much say in how those taxes were raised or how the money was spent.

The Boston Tea Party was directly related to the issue of taxes. Because American colonists refused to buy tea sold by the (British) East India Company, the English government allowed this company to sell its tea without having to pay tax back home (American tea makers, on the other hand, still had to pay the tea tax, putting them at a competitive disadvantage).

For an international incident, the Boston Tea Party was quick and relatively nonviolent. One night in 1773, Samuel Adams and about 60 other colonists (all of them dressed as Mohawk Indians) stormed three British ships anchored in Boston harbor and heaved the crates of tea they contained overboard. In retaliation, the British government closed the harbor, the latest in a chain of events that eventually led to the rebellion of 1775 and the declaration of independence from British rule in 1776.

WHY are people taller now than they were 200 years ago?

Over the past 200 years, the average height of adults in industrialized nations (like the U.S. and the countries of Western Europe) has increased by about four inches. Scientists believe this is because kids today are better fed than they used to be, allowing them to grow to their full height.

WHY do cowboys wear spurs and big hats?

A cowboy's spurs—those circular, metallic objects on the heels of their boots—do exactly what their name implies: they "spur" a horse to giddyap by delivering a prickly kick to its flanks. The classic cowboy hat—called a "Stetson" or a "10-gallon hat"—also has an important function. Its wide brim protects cowboys from the burning sun of the midwest plains, as well as the occasional drenching rainstorm.

WHAT is Stonehenge?

Archeologists believe that Stonehenge—a circle of giant stones in southern England—was built by ancient Druids 4,000 years ago to make astronomical observations (by tracking the sun, moon and stars as they lined up with the rocks). There are other theories—including one claiming Stonehenge was used for human sacrifice—but these haven't been widely accepted.

WHAT is the oldest city on earth?

Lots of cities in the world are ancient, but have been long since abandoned—usually we don't even know about them unless an archeologist happens to dig one up! Historians believe the oldest continuously occupied city in the world is Damascus, now the capital of Syria, where people have lived for an unbroken span of at least 5,000 years.

HOW big is the Pyramid of Cheops?

Egypt's biggest pyramid is 449 feet tall and measures 745 feet on each side (it was the tallest man-made structure in the world from the time it was built, about 2600 BC, until the great European cathedrals of the 15th century). It's estimated that as many as two million slabs of stone were used to build this edifice, each weighing an average of 5,000 pounds.

HOW did the Egyptians build the pyramids?

The biggest pyramids weren't built in a day, or even a year. The Egyptians erected these huge structures over the course of decades, using hundreds of thousands of laborers (many of them slaves). Archeologists believe thousands of workers at a time transported huge slabs of stone from nearby quarries to the building site, where they were pushed up enormous ramps and cemented in place.

All of this work is doubly remarkable because—unlike another enormous structure, the Great Wall of China, which was built to keep out invading armies—the pyramids had just one purpose: to preserve the remains of departed Pharaohs, as well as their servants and possessions. The Egyptians believed strongly in the afterlife, and so the Pharaohs were expected to build gigantic tombs befitting their stature.

This isolated island in the south Pacific is one of the world's great mysteries. When Europeans first landed here hundreds of years ago, they discovered strange-looking sculptures of enormous heads scattered all over the island. The civilization that built these statues, the Rapa Nui, has long since disappeared, so we may never know what they were were meant to portray.

WHAT is a mummy?

A mummy is a body whose soft tissues (skin, muscles, and internal organs) have been preserved for an unusually long time. The ancient Egyptians created mummies by pumping preservatives into newly deceased bodies. By the way, mummies aren't only found in Egypt: ancient corpses have been found (accidentally) preserved in swamps and glaciers around the world.

WHAT is Macchu Pichu?

One of the most spectacular sights in South America, Macchu Pichu (which means "Old Peak" and is also known as "The Lost City of the Incas") is the remains of an ancient Incan settlement in Peru, nestled by a mountain ridge over a mile above sea level.

Historians believe Macchu Pichu—in which can be found the remnants of a large temple and several smaller palaces—wasn't really a city at all, but a kind of vacation retreat for the Incan nobility and priesthood (probably less than a thousand people lived there at any given time).

Macchu Pichu had a very short time in the sun. Archeologists believe the city was built in the mid 15th-century, then abandoned after the Spanish conquest of Peru in 1532. The site was rediscovered in 1911, and excavations there shed valuable light on Incan civilization. Today, Macchu Pichu is a major tourist destination, visited by nearly half a million people a year.

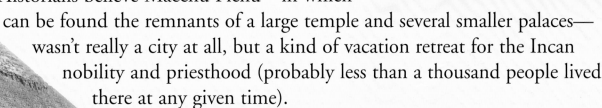

WHY was the Magna Carta so important?

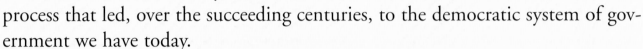

The Magna Carta—a document drawn up in England in the early 13th century—may seem like a distant curiosity, but it started a process that led, over the succeeding centuries, to the democratic system of government we have today.

The Magna Carta was forced on King John of England in 1215 by a group of dissatisfied English nobles. Up until this time, the English king—like the vast majority of monarchs elsewhere in Europe—enjoyed "absolute" rule, meaning he could confiscate property, raise taxes, or have people put to death simply by his command. The Magna Carta placed limits on the king's power, and even provided for a kind of "veto" by a committee of barons.

Succeeding kings ignored many of the Magna Carta's provisions, but they could never find a way around this famous clause: "No free man shall be arrested, or imprisoned, or deprived of his property, or outlawed, or exiled, or in any way destroyed…unless by legal judgment of his peers, or by the law of the land."

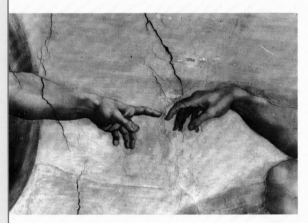

WHAT was the Renaissance?

The Renaissance—French for "rebirth"—wasn't a single event in European history, but a centuries-long transition between the Middle Ages (which were characterized by ignorance and superstition) and the modern age (marked by rationality and creativity). Most people associate the Renaissance with 16th-century painters like Michelangelo, but William Shakespeare was also part of the Renaissance, as were Italian musicians like Monteverdi.

HOW did the Black Death start?

The Black Death or Black Plague is a deadly viral disease that causes lymph glands to swell into "buboes" (large black lumps in the underarm). Historians think it originated in China, then was carried west by fleas and rats. When it reached Europe in 1348, the Black Death killed one-third to one-half the population, literally tens of millions of people, in the space of a few years.

WHY did Columbus sail to the New World?

When he set out on his historic journey in 1492, Christopher Columbus had no intention of discovering a new continent—he was seeking a sea route to India, which was already known to Europeans from overland trade. So, he actually discovered North America by accident!

WHAT was the Russian Revolution?

Of all the countries in 19th-century Europe, Russia was by far the most oppressive, since the Tsar (its ruler) had unlimited power. After World War I, in which Russia suffered heavy losses, this system of government became increasingly unpopular and unstable, allowing the "Bolsheviks" led by Lenin and Trotsky to seize power and declare a "worker's republic" in 1917.

WHY was the guillotine used during the French Revolution?

Compared with the other methods of execution in 18th-century France, the guillotine, a long, weighted blade that sliced off a person's head, could actually be considered humane, since it was very quick and sure. Considering the thousands of people who were put to death during the French Revolution, this was an important consideration. It was also a machine, not a person, so it could never get tired!

WHAT are the Balkans?

The Balkans are a collection of small countries in southeastern Europe, including Bulgaria, Yugoslavia, and Greece. This area of Europe has historically been very unstable—stretching back for centuries—mostly because the nations are constantly battling each other over territory. Some of the wars are internal and some involve neighboring countries from the north and east, like Turkey and Russia.

WHY was the Hundred Years' War so long?

This protracted conflict between England and France (which started in 1337 and ended in 1453, so it was really 116 years long!) wasn't a war in the modern sense of the word. In medieval times, even the most powerful nations could only sustain armies of limited size, and couldn't overpower their enemies with sheer force. Also, since England and France are separated by the English channel, neither country could successfully invade the other and bring the war to a conclusion.

The cause of the Hundred Years' War was the claim of the English king to a sizeable portion of French territory (at that time, monarchy was a fluid concept, so it was normal for a ruler in, say, Germany to also hold sway over territories in Spain). The war proceeded in fits and starts, with long periods of uneasy truce and only a few major battles. Technically, France "won" the war by holding on to its territory, but the fact is that the people of both countries were sick and tired of this conflict by the third or fourth decade!

WHY do judges in England wear wigs?

English judges started wearing heavy, powdered wigs in the mid-17th century, when England was just recovering from a bitter civil war that pitted "roundheads" (named for their bowl-shaped haircuts) against normal-haired "loyalists." By wearing a wig to conceal his own haircut, a judge showed his impartiality, a practice that's persisted to the present day.

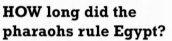

HOW long did the pharaohs rule Egypt?

The Egyptians had a thriving kingdom for thousands of years before later civilizations (like the Romans and Greeks) emerged on the historical scene. There's evidence for a continuing line of pharaohs dating from about 3000 B.C. to 800 B.C., when Egypt was conquered by its neighbors. Even after that, the institution of pharaoh persisted until the fourth century A.D.

WHY do kings have "I" or "V" after their names?

Those symbols after the names of kings are actually roman numerals, and denote the "number" of that king's name in the history of his country. For example, Richard III, pronounced "Richard the Third," was the third king named Richard in medieval England. Some ordinary folk do this as well: if you ever meet anyone named Howard Ellis IV, that means he's the fourth person named Howard Ellis in the history of his family.

Here's another interesting fact about what people have called their rulers. Back in ancient Rome, the emperor bore the title "princeps," meaning "first citizen" (this is the same root word as is used in the word "principal"). Later, European nations adopted this word to mean not the king, but the king's son, because they deemed their kings to be rulers, not citizens. So a "prince," being next in line to the king, was the first citizen. (The word "king", by the way, derives from ancient German.)

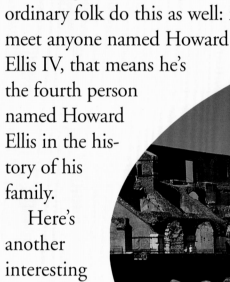

WHY do kings wear crowns?

Fancy hats and robes have been an emblem of power since the beginning of recorded history. In ancient times, kings (who were also religious leaders) wore tall, conical hats to set them apart from commoners. The "solar," or circular, crown worn by European kings had its origins in Asia Minor in the 4th century B.C., and was first adopted in the west by the conquering Romans.

As another symbol of their power and wealth, emperors, kings, and other high government officials wore robes dyed with purple, a fashion statement out of the reach of the common people. In ancient times, dyes were rare and expensive—especially purple dye, which cost even more than gold.

HOW big was the Roman Empire?

At its greatest extent—in about A.D. 200 —the Roman Empire stretched from Britain and Spain in the west to Egypt and Palestine in the east, south to Northern Africa, and north to all of France and pieces of Germany. The only reason the Romans didn't expand further east into India and China was because of the Persian Empire, which they never quite managed to conquer.

HOW old was Alexander the Great when he conquered the world?

People grew up fast in ancient times: Alexander of Macedon (a country north of Greece) started conquering the world in 330 B.C., when he was 20 years old, and accomplished this feat in the space of about ten years. But there's a catch here: In Alexander's time, the known world consisted mostly of the countries of the eastern Mediterranean (Greece, Egypt, and northern Africa), the Middle East, and parts of India.

WHAT was a gladiator?

In ancient Rome, convicted criminals and prisoners of war were trained in combat and made to fight each other to the death as entertainment for emperors and cheering crowds. If a gladiator put together a string of victories, he might win back his freedom, but the odds against him were high—most gladiators only lasted a few weeks or months.

WHY do soldiers wear uniforms?

For two reasons: first, soldiers need to cooperate with one another, and it builds cohesion (and helps maintain discipline) to have everyone dressed the same way. And second, just like a football game, battles on the ground are much easier to follow when your side is wearing a different uniform than the other side.

HOW does a catapult work?

Think of a medieval catapult as a very large, weirdly shaped bow. As it's pulled back, the ropes holding the catapult's payload gradually take on more and more tension, so that when they're finally released, the entire machine springs forward with enormous force. The biggest catapults could launch heavy objects the distance of a football field!

HOW do night-vision goggles work?

There are two different kinds of goggles that soldiers wear to see better at night. One kind (called "passive") amplifies the available light, kind of like turning up the contrast on your TV set. These goggles won't work in total darkness, since they need at least a little dim light to do their work.

The other kind of goggles (called "active") send out a near-infrared beam of light to illuminate the surroundings, then amplify the signal so the wearer can see what's going on. Unlike the first kind, these infrared goggles can be used in total darkness.

Like much technology originally developed for military purposes, today's night-vision goggles have become cheap enough (and declassified enough!) to be purchased by civilians to play around with.

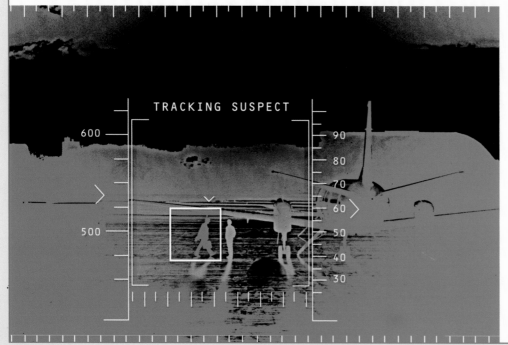

TRACKING SUSPECT

WHY did knights wear armor?

A knight without armor wouldn't have been much good on a battlefield, and he certainly wouldn't have been successful in a joust. Though incredibly heavy (up to 100 pounds), a full suit of medieval armor was effective against most of the weapons of the day—spears, arrows, and swords—though of course a knight could still be killed by a well-struck blow.

WHY do military people say "sixteen hundred" instead of 4 o'clock?

In the army, precision is vitally important. Rather than setting an invasion, say, for 4 o'clock, and confusing soldiers about whether that means 4 in the morning or 4 in the afternoon, the military uses a 24-hour clock starting at midnight: 4 in the morning is "0400 hours," noon is "1200 hours," and 4 o'clock in the afternoon is "1600 hours."

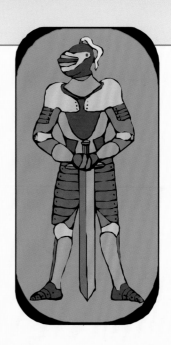

HOW big were cannonballs?

Cannonballs—whether they were used by pirates or armies—came in all different sizes, but most were about the size of a grapefruit and weighed between 12 to 24 pounds (during the Civil War, a "24-pounder" referred to the size of the cannon that was required to shoot 24-pound cannonballs). By the way, cannonballs didn't actually explode; the idea was to mow down advancing armies by shooting the balls waist-high at high speeds.

WHAT was the first tank?

Although the concept had been floating around for a while before then, the very first tank—an armored vehicle designed to be impervious to light enemy shellfire and roll over and through obstacles—was used by the British army in 1916, during World War I. (According to some histories, the young Winston Churchill—who was later to lead England during World War II—suggested the tank as a way of overwhelming enemy troops dug into trenches.)

The tank really came into its own during World War II, in which Germany's fast-moving Panzer tank was a key element of its "Blitzkrieg" (lightning-fast combat) strategy. Although tanks figured in all the key battles of the Second World War, they were the main stars of the battle of El Alamein in 1942, in which 500 German tanks (and about 100,000 soldiers) squared off against 1,000 Allied tanks (and 200,000 soldiers). The Allies won, though not quite as easily as you'd think considering their two-to-one advantage!

WHY did Copernicus keep his discovery a secret?

In the early 16th century, the Polish astronomer Nikolaus Copernicus wrote a book explaining his "heliocentric" system—that is, his discovery (based on astronomical observations) that the earth revolves around the sun, and not the other way around. The reason "On the Revolution of the Heavenly Spheres" was published only after his death is that Copernicus feared the reaction of church authorities, who believed the heliocentric theory contradicted the word of the Bible.

WHAT is the oldest science?

Since we can be pretty sure that the civilizations of thousands of years ago weren't tinkering with atomic reactors or revving up internal-combustion engines, the earliest "science" probably involved simple observations of the sun, moon, and stars. This ancient version of astronomy had some practical uses (keeping track of time, for instance), and many more speculative ones (like, say, predicting a ruler's fortune).

HOW did Newton discover the law of gravitation?

A popular story has it that the English mathematician Isaac Newton had an inspired moment one day in the mid-17th century as he was resting under a tree, an apple dropped suddenly and bonked him on the head, shaking loose the equation describing how an object falls in a gravitational field. This makes for a funny image, but it's almost certainly not true: what's more likely is that Newton was already working out his equation when he happened to see a falling apple (or, even more likely, that apples had nothing to do with it at all!).

While we're on the subject, there's not much evidence for another "aha!" moment in the history of science: the day in 1752 when Benjamin Franklin proved the existence of electricity by flying a kite in a thunderstorm. Franklin himself never wrote about this experiment; rather, the story appeared fifteen years after the fact in a book published by the British chemist Joseph Priestley, who claimed the details were communicated to him straight from the founding father. (Franklin never disputed the account, so the story may be true after all.)

Most measuring units in physics are named after the scientists who first investigated or discovered them. So, the "volt" (which measures the electric potential of a current) is named after Alessandro Volta, who invented the first battery in 1800; the "ampere" (which measures a current's rate of flow) is named after Andre-Marie Ampere; and the "ohm" (which measures a current's resistance) is named after George Ohm. (The inverse of the ohm, the "mho," is also used by electricians.)

HOW were modern numbers invented?

Since the earliest times, humans have always known how to count—either temporarily (using their fingers) or more permanently (by notching marks into sticks). As ancient city-states grew larger and more difficult to administrate, various counting systems were devised, many of them resembling the "four lines and a slash" prisoners use to keep track of their sentences. One of the most advanced systems of antiquity was that used by the Romans, in which (for example) XVII meant "17."

However, since Roman number symbols are virtually impossible to multiply and divide, modern mathematics had to wait until a later development: the invention of a standardized set of numerals (1, 2, 3….9), as well as the all-important zero. These innovations were first used by Indian mathematicians in the first millennium A.D., and were later exported to the countries of the Middle East (which is why they're known as "Arabic" numerals). Unlike earlier counting systems, Arabic numerals are easy to manipulate, and led to an explosion of mathematical knowledge.

HOW powerful was the first microscope?

The use of a single crystal or glass lens to magnify objects two or three times dates all the way back to antiquity. The first "compound" microscope (that is, a microscope using two or more lenses for added magnification) was invented in the late 16th century, and further developed by the scientist Anton Leeuwenhoek. Leeuwenhoek's microscopes could attain a magnification of nearly 300, which allowed scientists to examine tiny objects (like bacteria and red blood cells) in great detail for the very first time.

What was the biggest battle of World War II?

You wouldn't know it from watching the movies, but the biggest battle in the biggest war in history didn't involve Americans at all. In the Battle of Stalingrad, in 1942, desperate Russian troops tried to dislodge occupying Germans from a strategic city on the Volga River. In a few days of desperate hand-to-hand fighting, about a half-million soldiers were killed on each side, and an equal number wounded. The Russians won, a key turning point in the war that eventually resulted in the defeat of the Nazis.

After that story, you may not be surprised to learn that the Soviet Union suffered the most casualties of any country involved in World War II: over 20 million soldiers and civilians. By contrast, the United States got off fairly lightly, with about 300,000 combat fatalities and virtually no civilian deaths (since the war was never fought on American soil).

HOW did the War of 1812 start?

This conflict between the U.S. and Great Britain isn't very well-known today, but it was crucial in confirming America's independence (which had only been won a couple of decades before). The main cause of the war (besides the lingering bad feelings, of course!) was the British navy, which Americans felt impeded free commerce on the high seas. The War of 1812 marked the last time enemy forces landed on American soil, when British troops burned down most of Washington, D.C.

WHAT is the Mason-Dixon line?

This famous boundary between the northern and southern states of the eastern U.S.—which runs along the straight bottom of Pennsylvania and down past Delaware—is named after Charles Mason and Jeremiah Dixon, two surveyors hired from England in 1763 to settle a property dispute. The Mason-Dixon line became famous during the Civil War, when it served as a boundary between the Union and the Confederacy.

WHAT was the Cold War?

After its creation in 1917, the Soviet Union was a natural adversary of the U.S.: Russia's leaders disagreed violently with the political and economic system of the United States, and vice-versa. However, the two countries put aside their differences during World War II, when they joined forces against a common enemy, Hitler's Germany.

After World War II, these old differences reappeared with a vengeance. The Soviet Union emerged as a powerful, industrialized nation, the only one in the world in a position to challenge the still more powerful U.S. Although the two countries never engaged in an actual shooting war, they struggled against each other in more subtle ways, trying to align the countries of Europe, Africa, and the Middle East to their own philosophies.

The Cold War, as it was called, effectively ended in 1991, when the Soviet Union broke apart into its constituent nations.

WHY hasn't there been a World War III?

At the very end of World War II, the United States introduced a powerful, terrifying new weapon—the atomic bomb. Since then, a number of other nations have acquired nuclear arsenals, which they keep ready to launch against their enemies at a moment's notice. A big reason there hasn't been a Third World War is that government leaders realize a world war involving nuclear weapons could destroy all life on Earth.

WHAT was the Vietnam War about?

During the Cold War, the U.S. was vigilant about stopping the spread of Communism—the political system of America's two biggest adversaries, China and the Soviet Union. When a Communist uprising in northern Vietnam (a country in southeast Asia) threatened to engulf that entire nation, the U.S. committed troops to keep this from happening. The Vietnam War is notable for being one of the few conflicts the U.S. has lost—the last American troops evacuated South Vietnam in 1975, leaving the entire country under Communist rule.

WHAT was the War to End All Wars?

Since people didn't know at the time that there would be a Second World War, what we call World War I was originally called either the "Great War" or "The War to End All Wars." The causes were complex, but it basically boiled down to an arms race among various European countries, chief among them England and Germany. The spark that set it off was the assasination of Archduke Franz Ferdinand, heir to the Austro-Hungarian throne.

HOW do skywriters work?

Sometimes at the beach you can see a small plane "writing" a message in the sky. This is done with a special smoke canister attached to the back of the plane that the pilot turns on and off as he spells out his message. The reason beaches are popular locations for skywriters is that the air over the ocean on sunny days is especially calm, so a message will last longer before it drifts away.

WHY are runways so long?

The runways at most international airports are about two miles long—which is a good thing, since a landing plane needs plenty of room to decelerate and brake from a speed of a few hundred miles per hour. Runways are also about three feet thick, so they can handle a plane's massive weight (almost a million pounds for a fully loaded 777). Most major airports have at least four or five runways, though smaller ones can make do with one or two.

With such long runways, it's no wonder that airports need a lot of space. The largest in the world is King Khalid International Airport in Saudi Arabia, which takes up 81 square miles. As big as it is, though, Khalid is far from the busiest airport; that honor is shared by the international airports in Atlanta and Chicago, which between them handle over 100 million passengers a year.

WHY do helicopters have two propellers?

We can all see the top propeller of a helicopter, which sweeps out in a wide circle above the cabin. But a 'copter couldn't get off the ground (and, if it's already in the air, probably couldn't land) without its smaller tail rotor. This propeller, mounted in back, stabilizes the cabin and prevents the top propeller from spinning the entire helicopter around in circles.

WHY are airplane trips longer when you're going west?

When an airplane flies west (say, from New York to California), it's moving against the "jet stream," a steady current of air high up in the atmosphere caused by the earth's rotation. On the return trip, from L.A. to N.Y., the plane moves with the jet stream, and reaches its destination much faster—shaving about an hour off the trip.

HOW high can a plane fly?

Most commercial jets cruise at an altitude of 5 or 6 miles, but military aircraft regularly soar to about 10 miles. Any higher than that, and a plane runs into problems with cabin pressure, because the outside air is extremely thin at higher altitudes. Despite this, some experimental airplanes have climbed (briefly) to as high as 15 miles.

Because most planes capable of flying higher than 10 miles are also very fast, they're often accompanied by a phenomenon known as a "sonic boom." Sonic booms (which sound like short claps of thunder) are caused by

planes that fly faster than the speed of sound, about 750 miles per hour. As a faster-than-sound plane approaches, you can't hear anything—but as it flies overhead, the tail end of its sound waves suddenly become audible all at once!

HOW does a blimp fly?

Think of a blimp as an enormous helium balloon. Because helium is lighter than air, it floats—and because the volume of a blimp is so big (about 100,000 cubic feet), there's enough helium "lift" to carry a cabin filled with people. By the way, blimps used to be filled with an even lighter gas—hydrogen—until it was discovered that hydrogen blimps had a tendency to catch fire and explode! The Hindenburg, a hydrogen-filled blimp, was destroyed by a spectacular explosion in 1937.

WHY do airplanes have two or three engines?

Two reasons: first, two or three engines provide more power than just one, and second, multiple engines are a good idea in case one stops working or simply falls off. Also, two or three small engines are less bulky than the one giant engine a big plane would need to get off the ground.

WHY can't you see a Stealth bomber?

Actually, if you're standing right next to it, you can see a Stealth bomber just fine! What makes it "stealthy" is that it's nearly invisible to radar—the radio waves that track moving objects. The outside of the bomber is made of a substance that either completely reflects or completely absorbs radio waves, so it's more difficult (although not impossible) for enemy radar to track it.

WHAT is a suspension bridge?

The main part of a suspension bridge (the deck, where the cars go) is suspended by cables. If that sounds a bit like lifting yourself up by your own shoelaces, bear in mind that these cables are attached to huge towers, which are planted firmly in the sediment under the river, and terminate in heavy "anchorages" on either shore. Essentially, the cables help support and stabilize the bridge's massive weight.

The most famous suspension bridge in the world is the Brooklyn Bridge in New York, which was completed in 1883 after 17 years of construction (and the deaths of a few dozen workers). The Brooklyn Bridge has four thick bundles of cable, each about two-thirds of a mile long and containing over 5,000 separate wires—for a total wire length of over 12,000 miles!

WHY do stop signs have eight sides?

Back in 1923, a committee met in Mississippi to standardize the shapes of road signs. It was decided that round signs would be used for railroad crossings, diamond-shaped signs for "slow" warnings, square signs to convey information (like "caution"), and octagonal signs to say "stop." The color of stop signs wasn't standardized until 1954, when the federal government mandated the color red, which grabs the attention of motorists.

WHAT is the world's longest bridge?

There are many different kinds of bridges—arch, suspension, concrete, etc.—and many different ways to measure them (end to end from the anchorages, the part spanning water, the longest span between supporting arches, etc.). That said, some experts say the longest bridge in the world is the Akashi Kaikyo bridge in Japan, with an archless span over water of 6,532 feet.

WHAT is a causeway?

Sort of a younger brother to a full-grown bridge, a causeway is an elevated, man-made road that connects two islands over shallow water or marshes. In the U.S., the best place to find these structures is in the Florida Keys, which are connected to each other and to the mainland by a network of causeways as long as several miles each.

WHY do highways have speed limits?

Studies show drivers are less likely to be involved in fatal accidents if they're traveling at 65 miles per hour rather than 100 or even 75 mph. Also, speed limits help conserve gasoline; a 65 mph trip may take a few minutes longer, but it consumes less fuel than a shorter, speedier jaunt at 75 mph.

WHY are traffic lights red, green, and yellow?

Before cars were invented, a signaling system already existed that used red for "stop,", green for "go,", and yellow for "caution"—the one employed by the nation's railroads. By the 1920's, most major cities had adopted standardized red, green, and yellow traffic lights, because drivers were already familiar with this color scheme.

WHAT is asphalt?

This common material used for roads and driveways is basically just crushed concrete mixed with tar. Asphault is better than pure concrete because it has more flexibility, and will keep its smoothness even after it's been driven over by hundreds of thousands of cars.

WHAT is the world's longest highway?

The 3,000-mile long Trans-Canada Highway runs all the way from the Atlantic to the Pacific oceans. But it may not be the champ for long: in Russia, there are plans to build a highway from Moscow in the west to

Vladivostock in the east, which would stretch a whopping 8,000 miles.

While we're on the subject, we inherited the word "highway" from medieval England, where it described a road extending a long distance from the safety of a city ("highwaymen" were bandits who would rob unwary travelers).

The words "freeway" and "thruway" are more modern terms, applied to large, multilaned highways that don't have traffic lights and stop signs to slow traffic down. A "thruway" does stop traffic occasionally at tollbooths to collect money from those who drive on it. A "freeway" has no toll booths, but it isn't really free; it's maintained by tax money from the state or states it runs through.

WHAT causes potholes?

Potholes usually start to appear in late winter, when snow and ice melt during the day, seep down into tiny cracks in the road, and freeze again at night. Since water expands when it freezes, this causes a bulge to form in a small portion of the road, and when cars drive over this bulge, the surface breaks off entirely—resulting in a big, gaping pothole.

HOW does a transmission work?

A car's transmission turns the energy created by its engine into movement via a complicated arrangement of gears that turn the axles (which in turn control the car's four wheels). The reason the transmission has more than one gear is because different speeds require different gear sizes, to allow the engine to work most efficiently.

There are two basic kinds of transmissions: manual and automatic. The newer, and now most common, automatic transmission adjusts its gear size to match the car's speed, without the need for any input from the driver other than to put the car in "drive."

A manual transmission, which is what all cars used to have, requires the driver to shift gears. For this, there are two extra pieces of equipment: a gear shift stick, located next to the driving wheel, and a "clutch" pedal on the floor beside the brake pedal. When the clutch is depressed it temporarily disengages the gears so the shift can be made. People who really enjoy driving prefer this method, as it requires more skill and gives drivers a better sense of control.

HOW fast can a car go?

Experimental drivers set speed records by strapping rockets to the back of their cars (not recommended for beginners!), but for an ordinary gas-combustion car, the speed record is about 240 miles per hour. At the world's fastest car race—the Indy 500—drivers regularly hit speeds of above 200 miles per hour, at least on the straightaways.

WHY do we drive on the right side of the road?

It's not more natural to drive on the right—that's just the way it happens to be done in the United States. In most of the world, including India, China, and Europe, motorists drive on the left-hand side of the road, for reasons that are still unclear—though it may have something to do with protecting the (then) numerous pedestrians back when cars first became popular.

WHY do windshields fog up in the cold?

During winter, the inside of a car is usually warmer and more humid than the outside, either because it's full of people or because the heater is on. As the warm air inside the car comes into contact with the cold windshield, the moisture condenses into a thin film that coats the inside of the glass.

WHY do cars have license plates?

Cars are big, heavy objects that can do a lot of damage if they're driven carelessly. The government requires them to bear identification so that if a car is stolen, involved in a hit-and-run accident, or just driven by someone who likes to go way over the speed limit, it can be tracked down more easily by the police.

HOW does a car engine work?

Basically, a car engine is a device for turning fuel into motion. The heart of the engine is its pistons, small tubes with chambers inside that expand and contract as the pistons pop up and down. On the upstroke, a drop of gasoline is mixed with air, and on the downstroke, this volatile mixture is detonated by a spark plug. The explosion drives the piston up, where its energy (along with the energy of the other pistons) is translated into motion via the car's transmission.

As you can guess, a car's horsepower is largely determined by the number of pistons (also called cylinders) in its engine. Most cars have four or six cylinders, but some powerful models have as many as twelve.

Although the engines of trucks and buses burn other kinds of fuel—usually kerosene or diesel—gasoline is best for cars because it combusts efficiently and (compared to diesel fuel) with a minimum of harmful emissions.

WHY is a car's engine in front?

The very first cars had engines in the rear. That changed in about 1900, when a French inventor put an engine in the front of his car, making the vehicle easier to balance and steer. Since then, the vast majority of cars have been designed with front-mounted engines, though the tiny Volkswagen Beetle was famous for having an engine in back.

WHY do cars have radiators?

When an engine burns gasoline, it converts most of the energy it creates into motion (which turns the car's wheels). But the rest of the energy is dissipated as heat, meaning the engine would become too hot (and might even melt) if it wasn't kept cool by circulating water from the radiator.

WHY are the letters on a keyboard out of order?

If you look at the keyboard of your computer, you'll see that the letters are arranged out of sequence. This is called the "QWERTY" keyboard (after the first few letters on the top row), and it was designed to reflect both the frequency of letters in the English language and the way people type. Inventors have since designed keyboards with different layouts, but QWERTY remains the standard.

HOW does a computer store information?

Computers "remember" things by storing them on hard drives—magnetic devices that hold information in binary form (that is, as strings of 1's and 0's rather than words or pictures). The information is retrieved by a tiny mechanical "head" that reads the drive, and the computer's processor converts the 1's and 0's into words or images on the screen.

HOW big was the first computer?

Most people consider ENIAC (the Electrical Numerical Integrator And Calculator), built in 1943, to be the world's first digital computer. Compared to

today's superfast, supercompact computers, ENIAC was a true monster: it weighed 30 tons, took up 1800 square feet of floor space, and used nearly 18,000 bulky vacuum tubes (transistors, which are much smaller, hadn't been invented yet).

The main reason computers have gotten smaller as they've gotten more powerful is a principle known as Moore's Law: manufacturers are constantly figuring out ways to fit more transistors (the basic logic elements of a computer) into the same volume of space. This trend can't continue forever, though: once transistors approach the size of individual molecules (which should happen in a few years), there's no way to make them any smaller.

Transistors—the main components of video-game consoles and computers—are basically tiny electronic switches that can either be in the "on" or "off" position. When a small amount of current is sent through a transistor, it can be made to store or pass on information in binary notation, that is, in the form of 1's and 0's. As small as it is, a home computer has hundreds of millions of transistors.

WHY do computers crash?

Unless you happen to trip over its power cord, the main reason your computer crashes is because of a glitch in its software—that is, one program tells it to do one thing at the exact same time as another program tells it to do another thing. This usually happens when, say, the game you're trying to play conflicts somehow with the computer's operating system. You can usually solve this problem by restarting the computer.

HOW did the computer mouse get its name?

When the first mouse appeared in 1964, its inventor described it as an "X-Y position indicator for a display system." Catchy, right? Soon, the little gadget was being called a "mouse" because 1) it was about the size of a small rodent, and 2) it had a "tail" where the cord connected it to the computer.

WHAT is the Internet?

It's hard to believe, but what we today call the Internet originated in the 1960's as a way for a handful of military computers to communicate with each other. Basically, the Internet isn't a "thing," but a system—a reliable way for computers large and small to send information (such as email, sound clips, and video) back and forth over phone or cable lines. Not only can't you pull the plug on the Internet, you couldn't even find the plug if you wanted to!

The decentralized nature of the Internet is its main strength—and its main weakness as well. Because it's so easy for computers all over the world to communicate with each other, computer viruses—small pieces of code that replicate themselves just like real viruses—can easily be transmitted, causing worldwide crashes and system outages in a matter of hours or days. That's why it's important to install anti-virus software on your computer, and never to open mail from people you don't know.

WHY was the Eiffel Tower built?

Of all the world's landmarks—the Empire State Building, the Great Wall of China, etc.—the Eiffel Tower in Paris is the only one that was built just for the heck of it. This purely decorative structure was erected to celebrate the Paris International Exposition of 1889, and has remained a tourist destination ever since.

HOW long is the Panama Canal?

The world's longest man-made canal is 51 miles long, spanning the country of Panama from the Pacific to the Atlantic oceans. Ships can't just zoom through, though—it takes 8 to 10 hours to navigate the canal, which includes a sophisticated system of "locks" that raise and lower the water level.

WHY does the Leaning Tower of Pisa lean?

The Leaning Tower of Pisa, in Italy, is one of the great architectural blunders of history. This stone edifice was erected in the 13th century in a completely unsuitable location: the sand and clay under one side of the base is spongier than on the other side, so over the years, the weight of the tower caused it to tilt increasingly in one direction.

Although most architectural landmarks are pretty much left alone (for reasons of historical preservation), that hasn't been an option with the Leaning Tower, since without some help it was liable to fall down completely. In 1990, scientists carefully excavated the tower's base and installed reinforcing steel cables, and ten years later, tourists were once again allowed to climb the structure (only 30 at a time, though, and only for 40 minutes).

WHAT is the world's biggest museum?

A museum under construction in Egypt may turn out to be the world's biggest, but for now, the honor belongs to the Louvre in Paris, which was once an enormous castle. The Smithsonian Institution in Washington, D.C., claims to be the world's largest museum, but technically it's a museum complex made up of sixteen separate buildings.

WHAT is the biggest U.S. national monument?

Mount Rushmore, in South Dakota, consists of 60-foot-tall busts of four U.S. presidents—George Washington, Thomas Jefferson, Abraham Lincoln, and Theodore Roosevelt. These likenesses were carved into the side of the mountain by 400 workers over the course of 14 years, and on a clear day, they can be seen from 60 miles away.

HOW long is the Great Wall of China?

That depends on who's doing the measuring. The Great Wall of China isn't one long, continuous structure, but a series of shorter walls with gaps in between, meant to keep out the hostile tribes of Mongolia to the north. The first of these walls was built in about 200 B.C., and additions were made over the next 1,500 years, some of which have since fallen into disrepair. Since experts disagree about exactly where the wall begins and ends, estimates of its length vary from 1,500 to 4,500 miles!

By the way, for a long time people believed that the Great Wall of China was the only man-made structure visible from outer space. However, this isn't true. From a low orbit of a few hundred miles, the Great Wall is in fact visible—and so are highways, railroads, and large buildings. But at an orbit beyond a few thousand miles, nothing on Earth can clearly be made out except oceans, clouds, and large continents.

HOW much does the Empire State Building weigh?

It's not as if you can find a scale big enough to plop it down on, but the Empire State Building—the tallest building in the world when it was completed in 1933—weighs about 365,000 tons (or 700 million pounds).

WHAT is the world's biggest castle?

There used to be a lot more castles than there are now, but the biggest to survive in one piece is Hradcany Castle in Prague, Czechoslovakia. Built in the eighth century, this enormous structure is over 500 yards long and a hundred yards wide. The biggest castle in England, Windsor Castle, is just a guest cottage by comparison!

WHAT is the fastest elevator?

If you live in an apartment house with a poky elevator, perhaps you'd like to move to the Taipei 101 Tower in Taiwan, which has an elevator that climbs and descends at close to 35 miles per hour. Even at this speed, the trip to the building's roof takes a full half a minute.

WHAT is leather?

Leather can be made from the hide of any large animal, but cows are most often used (since they have the thickest skin). Once the skin is removed, a tanner "cures" it by treating it with chemicals, that make it stronger and more weather-resistant. In the old days, tanners would collect peoples' urine, let it ferment for a week, and then use the resulting ammonia to cure the cowhide. Not surprisingly, tanners usually lived on the outskirts of town!

Because some people (many of them vegetarians) object to using the hides of animals for clothing, leather-like materials are often made from such substances as vinyl or canvas. A jacket made from "synthetic leather" is usually much cheaper than a real leather garment, and usually just as warm (though some people think fake leather isn't quite as stylish).

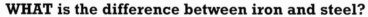

HOW does iron rust?

When a piece of iron reacts with the oxygen in the atmosphere—usually with the help of water or moisture in the air—a reddish film of iron oxide, or rust, forms on its surface. Because the iron oxide takes up more space than plain old iron, it rises up in bumps and flakes off, exposing new layers of iron that will also rust away—which is why rust should never be left untreated.

WHAT is the difference between iron and steel?

Because pure iron is susceptible to rust—and isn't quite strong enough to support tall buildings—most building in the world today is done with steel. Steel is iron that has been "alloyed" (mixed) with various other elements, such as carbon, manganese, or molybdenum, and is stronger and more durable than ordinary iron.

WHY are pipes made of copper?

Copper pipes have a long and illustrious history: they were used for plumbing way back in ancient Egypt! Copper is still used in pipes for two main reasons: first, it's fairly cheap, and second, it's relatively "ductile"—that is, it can be easily pulled and stretched into curved shapes.

HOW is paper made?

Most paper is made from trees. Huge logs are chipped into small pieces, and then "pulped" into a watery liquid that looks a lot like oatmeal. This pulp is fed into a machine that removes most of the water and flattens the soggy wood fibers into a papery shape. When these sheets are heated and dried, the result is paper. Fancy papers can be made using such ingredients as rice pulp or ground up-linen.

By the way, have you ever noticed that old newspapers turn yellow as they age? This happens for the same reason that fruit turns brown, or iron rusts: oxidation. Trees contain a tough, gluey substance called lignin, which is used in newspaper but not in other kinds of paper designed to last longer. As the lignin in newspaper is exposed to air, it slowly turns yellow.

WHAT is styrofoam?

Styrofoam is a mixture of 5 percent polystyrene (one of the world's most widely used plastics) and 95 percent air, which gives it its fluffy texture and appearance. Styrofoam is mostly used to cushion delicate items during shipping, but its heat-resistant qualities also make it a good insulator (which is why coffee is sometimes served in styrofoam cups).

WHAT are bicycle helmets made of?

Basically, bike helmets are made out of the same stuff as styrofoam—a puffy, air-filled plastic called polystyrene. And just like styrofoam protects a TV as it's being shipped, a bike helmet protects your skull in the event of an accident. According to one study, wearing a bike helmet can cut your risk of a serious head injury by 85 percent!

WHAT are disposable diapers made of?

Until a generation ago, most moms and dads swaddled their babies in cloth diapers, which—as you can imagine—had to be washed constantly. Today, many parents use disposable diapers, which are simply thrown away after they're soiled. Most disposable diapers contain artificial ingredients like plastics and treated wood fiber, as well as a chemical called sodium polyacrylate, which absorbs 100 times its weight in water.

HOW do heavy ships float in the water?

Any object will float if it weighs less than the water it pushes out of the way. Passenger liners and oil tankers are extremely heavy, but—because they take up so much space—they're not heavier, on average, than the amount of water they displace. A solid steel cube will sink right away, because of its high density and low volume.

WHY are ships christened with champagne bottles?

The tradition of christening, or naming, ships by smashing a bottle of wine on their bows has been around since the ancient Babylonian empire. Champagne is a bubbly wine used to celebrate joyful events like birthdays and anniversaries, so its use was carried over to the launching of new ships.

WHY is a pirate flag called a "Jolly Roger?"

The familiar skull-and-crossbones banner—first flown in the 17th century by pirates in the West Indies—looks anything but jolly, so its name has been an enduring source of mystery.

According to one theory, the Jolly Roger's predecessor was a flag dipped in red blood, which the French called joli rouge ("pretty red"). This was corrupted by English sailors into Jolly Roger. Another theory goes that because Asian pirates of the time hailed their captains as "Ali Raja," meaning "king of the sea," English sailors overheard them and translated the phrase as you-know-what.

However, the most plausible explanation is also the most boring. The word "roger" in British slang means "wandering vagabond," which applies pretty well to the life of a pirate. Since pirates could also be jolly (especially when they drank rum), this is most likely where the phrase "Jolly Roger" came from.

HOW many shipwrecks are on the ocean floor?

People have been sailing in ships for thousands of years, so it's not surprising that the ocean bottom is littered with sunken boats—as many as three million, by some estimates. Most of these wrecks are small and nearly impossible to locate, but salvagers occasionally dredge up a centuries-old pirate ship loaded with gold and jewels.

WHAT is keelhauling?

Until it was outlawed a couple of hundred years ago, keelhauling was the worst punishment a sailor could face. A rope would be tied around him, then he'd be thrown overboard on one side and dragged down under the "keel" (bottom) of the ship to the other side. The bigger the ship, the greater the odds the sailor would drown before he was hauled out of the water.

HOW long can a submarine stay underwater?

It used to be that submarines could only stay submerged for days or weeks at a time—because they needed to resurface for fuel. But modern subs can stay underwater for years without a break, if necessary, because a nuclear reactor provides all of the ship's energy needs.

WHAT was the first submarine?

As with many inventions, the idea of the submarine floated around for a long time before anyone could devise a working model. As far back as 1580, an English scientist theorized about an underwater craft, but it wasn't until 1776 that the first recognizable submarine—the "Turtle"—went into action. This small, one-man sub attacked a British ship in New York during the Revolutionary War, but didn't succeed in doing any damage. Submarines really came into their own during the Civil War, when both the Union and Confederacy experimented with this new mode of warfare. In New Orleans, Horace Hunley built a series of subs, the last of which was forty feet long and manned by nine sailors, including Hunley himself. Like many early subs, the C.S.S. Hunley (as it was dubbed afterward) came to a catastrophic end, sinking in Charleston Bay and killing everyone aboard.

HOW deep can a submarine dive?

Unlike scuba divers, who can't descend below a certain depth because of the high water pressure, a well-equipped submarine can theoretically dive as deep as the ocean floor. In fact, submarines have already visited the lowest place on earth, the Marianas Trench, which is about three miles below the surface of the Pacific Ocean.

HOW is wool made?

You can't just shear a sheep and have a sweater five minutes later. First the wool fibers need to be sorted (by waviness, thickness, color, etc.), washed with detergent to remove impurities, passed through a special roller, and bundled into balls of yarn.

Despite all this work, people have been making wool for thousands of years. Remains of woolen garments have been found in tombs in Egypt and in Peruvian settlements in the New World, while the ancient Romans developed rudimentary factories to speed along the wool-making process. Since fat, happy sheep are an essential component of the wool trade, an important historical development was the domestication and breeding of sheep to produce quicker, thicker, more easily shearable coats. Today, the prized wool-bearing sheep is the Merino, first bred in Spain and since exported to the rest of the world.

WHAT is dryer lint?

All clothes are woven from stringy materials, whether natural (like cotton or silk) or artificial (like dacron or rayon). Every time you put your shirts, socks or underwear in the dryer, small pieces of these textiles break off, accumulating on the bottom as a shapeless blob of lint.

WHY do dryers eat socks?

If you throw a really old, really holey sock into the dryer, it's possible that the spinning action will rip it to shreds and make it "disappear." Most of the time, though, those "missing" socks aren't really missing at all—they're hiding in the legs of your pants, say, or stuck to the top of the dryer's inside. If you take out and fold your laundry carefully, your dryer should never eat your socks again!

WHAT is velcro?

A combination of the French word for velvet, "velour," and hook, "crochet," Velcro is exactly what that word describes—soft fabric that's covered with tiny, intermeshing hooks, so two pieces stick together as if they'd been buttoned or zippered. By the way, the word "Velcro" is actually a corporate trademark, like "Xerox" or "Google."

WHY do cotton clothes shrink in the dryer?

When cotton becomes wet, its fibers swell up and become slightly thicker, and slightly shorter as well. If you dry a cotton shirt too quickly, the fibers become "frozen" in this shorter configuration. You can usually avoid shrinking cotton clothes by drying them on a clothesline, or on a very low heat setting.

WHY do black clothes get warmer than white clothes?

At night, white and black clothes have the same temperature. But on sunny days, a black shirt absorbs most of the sun's rays, while a white shirt reflects most of them back. That's why desert dwellers wrap themselves in white cloaks, because a stylish black cloak would make them really hot in a really short time!

WHY was the cotton gin so important?

A cotton plant doesn't produce pure, white, ready-to-sew fabric: the cotton fibers grow in small bulbs called "bolls," each of which contains about two dozen sticky cotton seeds. In the old days, these seeds had to be separated from the fibers by hand—meaning even the most industrious worker could turn out only a pound of cotton per day.

That's why the cotton gin was such an important development. This device, invented by Eli Whitney in 1793, mechanically separated the cotton seeds from the cotton fibers, so a single machine could turn out 50 pounds of pure cotton per day. Since cotton could now be a profitable crop, the effect was revolutionary: in the space of 20 years, the annual U.S. cotton harvest increased from 200,000 pounds to almost 100 million pounds.

WHY do engineers wear striped caps?

The blue-and-white striped engineer cap was invented a hundred years ago by a railroad engineer named George Kromer. Kromer's regular hat was always blowing off when his train hit top speed, so he decided to design a new hat that would stay put no matter what—and he just happened to give it a striped pattern. Other engineers liked the "Kromer cap" so much that it quickly became a railroad tradition.

WHY does a train whistle get lower as the train speeds away?

Sound is caused by the motion of waves in air. When a fast-moving source like a train emits sound, these waves have a higher frequency (and higher pitch) when they're approaching and a lower frequency (and lower pitch) when they're moving away. That's why the pitch of a whistle drops abruptly as soon as a train zooms past you on the tracks.

HOW long did it take to build the transcontinental railroad?

The first cross-country railroad in the U.S. wasn't conceived as a massive, east-coast to west-coast building project. When construction first began around 1862 (in the middle of the Civil War), two major rail lines already existed: the Central Pacific, which terminated in Sacramento, California, and the Union Pacific, which stretched from the east coast all the way to Omaha, Nebraska. In between lay 1,800 miles of nearly impassable desert and mountains.

To speed this project along, the U.S. government hit on a novel idea: the two companies would be paid according to how much track they laid. In the frenzied competition that resulted, the Central Pacific hired thousands of recent Chinese immigrants, and the Union Pacific thousands of Irish immigrants. Still, the project wasn't finished until May 10, 1869, when California governor Leland Stanford drove in the famous "Golden Spike" that joined the two rail lines in the town of Promontory Point, Utah.

WHY are subways underground?

Big cities have limited space, so it's better to devote aboveground building to housing or offices. Trams and elevated train lines ("els," as they're called in some places) take up valuable city real estate. Today, in New York City, all of the subways in Manhattan are underground, but trains in the more spacious outer boroughs still run aboveground.

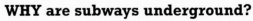

WHAT is a maglev train?

"Maglev" is a quick way to say "magnetic levitation," a mode of train transport that allows for faster, smoother rides.

Most trains get their power from an electrified third rail, with which the underside of the train must stay in constant contact, resulting in friction and loss of speed. A maglev train also depends on electricity, but in a different way. A power source electrifies coils on the maglev track, which produces a magnetic field. This field repels the magnets on the train's underside, so the train "floats" an inch or two above the tracks.

Because it experiences virtually no friction, a maglev train can go much faster than an ordinary train. In Japan, a new maglev line promises to hit speeds of about 300 miles per hour—about twice the average speed of the fastest electric train, and half the speed of a passenger plane!

WHAT is the world's longest railroad?

It's fitting that the world's longest continuous railroad line is in the world's longest continuous country. The Trans-Siberian express, in Russia, stretches all the way from Moscow in the west to Vladivostok (a city near Japan) in the east, a distance of over 8,000 miles.

WHY are there fewer trains today than there used to be?

Passenger jets have pretty much spelled the end of cross-country rail travel: today, you can fly from New York to Los Angeles in about six hours, compared to three or four days for the railroad trip. Although fewer people travel by rail, freight trains are still an essential means of transporting cargo (like coal and steel) over long distances.

HOW high can a hang glider go?

Theoretically, hang gliders can be launched from any altitude, but the extreme cold and thin air at jet-plane level makes such a dizzying trip impractical. That said, professional hang gliders can launch their craft from a height of over three miles, and coast for a distance of over 300 miles. Most ordinary folks are content with shorter trips of a few thousand feet up and a few dozen miles across.

WHAT was the first roller coaster?

It seems like it should be an American invention, but the very first roller coaster was built in St. Petersburg, Russia, in 1784 (it probably wouldn't have rattled a five-year-old, though, since it consisted of carriages rolling up and down gentle hills on grooved tracks). The first "scary" coasters, which plunged cars down from a steep incline, appeared in France a couple of decades later.

HOW many people have climbed Mount Everest?

Early in the 20th century, reaching the summit of Mount Everest was thought to be as unattainable a goal as landing on the moon. The main challenges that face climbers (besides the height) are the frigid climate and the thin air near the mountain's peak, which make breathing and physical exertion extremely difficult.

The first people to reach the top of Mount Everest were Sir Edmund Hillary and Tenzing Norgay, in 1953. (An expedition of decades earlier, by two English mountaineers, ended in disaster when they died before reaching the summit.) Since then, as climbers have learned the safest routes and best seasons to make the attempt, and as equipment has become more sophisticated, the number of people making the round trip successfully has multiplied.

To date, about 1500 climbers have climbed to the top of Mount Everest and back again. But just because this mountain has been successfully climbed doesn't mean that it has become any safer. In the year 1996 alone, 15 mountaineers died trying to reach the top, including a group of climbers who perished in a freak snowstorm just beneath the summit.

HOW did surfing become a sport?

Surfing originated about 500 years ago in Hawaii (long before this island, smack in the middle of the billowing waves of the Pacific Ocean, became a U.S. state). Called "he'e nalu" (wave-sliding), surfing was pioneered by the kings, queens and nobility of this island nation, whose surfboards, carved out of trees according to a ritual formula, were treated almost like religious items.

In the early 20th century, surfing became popular on the west coast of the U.S. and the beaches of Australia (both of which, like Hawaii, enjoy access to the Pacific Ocean). However, the sport really took off in the 1950's, when modern manufacturing techniques allowed relatively lightweight boards to be mass-produced out of synthetic material, such as fiberglass, rather than hand-made from wood. Not only were these new-style surfboards cheaper, but they allowed even beginning surfers to perform more intricate stunts.

HOW big is the Grand Canyon?

They don't call it "grand" for nothing. The Grand Canyon spans 277 miles of the Colorado River, ranges in width from 5 to 18 miles, and is about a mile deep. Oddly enough, most Americans didn't even know the Grand Canyon existed until after the Civil War, when a surveying expedition to the Colorado River happened to pass through it.

WHY shouldn't you go adventuring alone?

Just as there's a buddy system for swimming, it's always a good idea to honor this principle when you go on any adventure. This way, if you or your companion has an accident, one of you can help or go to get help. It's also very important to let people at home know where you and your friend are going. Millions of dollars are spent every year in rescue efforts for lost or hurt hikers, skiers, and whitewater rafters.

HOW dangerous is whitewater rafting?

Like any extreme sport, whitewater rafting (that is, steering an inflatable raft down a fast-flowing river) is perfectly safe, as long as you have adequate training and don't tackle a river beyond your experience level. Rivers in the U.S. are helpfully ranked on a scale of 1 to 6, with 1 being the easiest to navigate (kind of like the rafting equivalent of a bunny slope) and 6 being so dangerous that even professional rafters usually keep their distance.

WHY do clowns wear red noses?

The very first clowns appeared in the comedies of ancient Greece, where they kept audiences alert by throwing nuts into the seats. "Modern" clowns date back to the middle ages, when there were two main varieties: the quiet "white-face" clowns (who wore nothing but white makeup), and the zanier "red nose" clowns (who, as you probably guessed, wore big red noses).

Over the next few hundred years, these two clown types went their separate ways. The white-faced clowns can still be found in European circuses, but in the U.S. they evolved into silent mimes (street performers who mimic, say, climbing stairs). The funnier, and louder, red-nosed clowns became the American standard, a trend that was helped by the popularity of clowns like Bozo and Clarabelle on kids' TV shows from the 1950's and 1960's.

HOW big were the first TVs?

When black-and-white TV sets first began to be sold in the late 1940's, the most popular—and cheapest—models had screens that were only a few inches wide, so families had to sit up close to see anything. One company made a set with a 20-inch screen, which cost $2,500 in 1950 dollars—the equivalent of about $30,000 today!

WHAT was the first TV show?

Technically, the very first TV show was a drama called "The Queen's Messenger," an experimental broadcast in 1928—before anyone had TV sets to watch it! It's much harder to pin down the very first broadcast in the modern age of TV, starting in the 1930's and 1940's, but filmed radio shows (like those of the comedian Jack Benny) were a popular early choice.

WHAT is the longest-running comic strip?

The Katzenjammer Kids, a comic strip about a pair of mischievous boys, first appeared in a New York newspaper in 1897. Its creator (and his successor) has long since passed away, but the strip is still being drawn by younger artists. Because comic strips are "passed down" this way by the companies that distribute them to newspapers, there are plenty of incredibly ancient strips around, including Blondie (which dates from 1930) and Gasoline Alley (which first appeared in 1918).

WHAT was the first cartoon?

The very first cartoon, called "Fantasmagorie," was shown in Paris all the way back in 1908, but it didn't have any funny animals or pratfalls. Many people date the first kid-oriented cartoon to a few years later in 1914, when Winsor McCay (the creator of the popular comic strip Little Nemo) presented a short film called "Gertie the Dinosaur."

WHAT was the first musical?

Since musical theater evolved gradually from operas (which have been around for hundreds of years) and vaudeville (which dates from the last century), most historians say that *Show Boat*, from 1927, was the first musical in the modern sense of the word. It had original songs, spoken parts between the musical numbers, and a compelling plot line.

WHAT was the first movie?

There wasn't a first "eureka!" moment in motion-picture history—depending how you define the word "movie," you can even trace the first flick back to the oddly named "zoopraxiscope" in 1867. But most historians agree that the first movie in the modern sense of the word was presented by the Lumiere brothers in 1895. It didn't have a plot or special effects, but simply showed a couple of minutes of everyday life in Paris.

Silent movies (usually accompanied in theaters by a pianist) were the standard for the next few decades. That all changed in 1927, when *The Jazz Singer*—the first picture with sound—debuted to audience acclaim. Within a few years, all movies had sound—and then had to adjust to another big change barely a dozen years later, when the first big-budget color movie, *The Wizard of Oz*, had its premiere in 1939. Color took a longer time to catch on: black-and-white movies were still being made as late as the 1960's, but gradually faded away as color flicks took over.

WHAT is the oldest board game?

Checkers and backgammon may be thousands of years old, but they're Johnny-come-latelies compared to mancala, a game in which players move pieces around a double row of circular holes. Archeologists have found fossilized versions of this game in 7,000-year-old ruins in the Middle East, and it's also been dug up in Africa and Egypt.

Like tic-tac-toe, mancala can be played pretty much anywhere, and in any medium, which accounts for its popularity. Players can scoop holes into sand and use seashells, or scatter beans or pebbles into holes of mud. Genuine game boards, carved out of wood, are a later development, invented by the relatively advanced Middle Eastern civilizations of about 2000 B.C.

With such ancient roots, mancala has given rise to a bewildering array of related games. Virtually every tribe in Africa plays a version of Mancala, varying the rules and the number of holes used.

WHAT was the first video game?

"Pong"—a primitive tennis game consisting of two animated paddles on either side of a black screen and a single ball in the middle—first appeared in 1971. Despite (or because of) its simplicity, Pong became a huge hit, and it still occasionally pops up for other game systems in "greatest-hits" collections.

HOW many ways can you shuffle a deck of cards?

A standard deck has 52 different cards. This means the deck can be shuffled 52 times 51 times 50 times 49… etc. etc. ways, which produces a number that's about equal to 1 followed by 70 zeroes. By comparison, a billion is only 1 followed by nine zeroes!

HOW old is the game of checkers?

Games similar to checkers have been found in 3,000-year-old ruins in the Middle East, but it's impossible to know exactly how they were played. What we do know is that the first checkerboard was invented about a thousand years ago, and the first game that can be recognizably identified as checkers—called "draughts"—became popular in England in the 15th century.

HOW old is the game of chess?

They don't all agree, but most historians think chess originated in India around the 6th or 7th century A.D. (India is also the country that gave us modern numbers like 1, 2, 3, etc.). Back then, this game (called "chaturanga") was more of an exercise in military strategy than the familiar game of chess that we know today.

WHAT is the oldest card game?

"Tarocchi" appeared in Italy around the 14th century and probably originated in the far east much earlier than that. This card game has complicated rules (somewhat similar to bridge) and is played with a 78-card deck. In addition to the cards we're familiar with from modern decks (ace through 10, king, queen, and jack), the Tarocchi deck also includes a cavalier, a fool, and 21 numbered cards without suits, called "tarots".

If that last name sounds familiar, it's because those 21 numbered cards—with their illustrations of suns and moons, kings and queens, and jokers and magicians—were used by fortune-tellers in medieval times, and often pop up in fortune-telling scenes in movies or TV shows today. (By the way, the belief that you can predict someone's future with a Tarot deck is called "cartomancy.")

WHY do card decks have jokers?

Standard decks did just fine without jokers for hundreds of years, until a game called "euchre" became popular in the mid-19th century. In euchre, the standard 52 cards are supplemented with two cards called "bowers," which mutated into "jokers" (which is probably a corruption of "jacks.") In any event, practically nobody plays euchre anymore, but you can still find two jokers in most card decks.

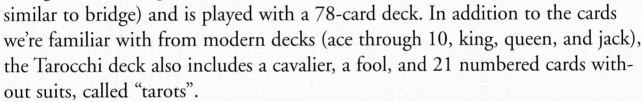

WHY is it so hard to win the lottery?

It sounds like a great deal: buy a ticket for a dollar (or ten tickets for ten dollars), and get a chance at a $100 million payoff. The trouble is, any time a lot of money is at stake, practically everybody in the country buys lottery tickets—putting your odds of winning at one in ten million or even one in a hundred million.

WHY do roses have thorns?

Because they are exceptionally succulent and tasty, roses need a way to protect themselves from hungry animals—and there's nothing like a mouthful of sharp thorns to convince a deer to seek its dinner elsewhere.

Despite their prickly nature, roses have been cultivated for thousands of years. The ancient Romans grew vast fields of roses, which they used for medicine, perfume, and confetti at parades (not to mention the rose petals that would sometimes be strewn in the emperor's path!). After the fall of the Roman empire, the rose ebbed somewhat in popularity, but by the time of the "War of the Roses" in 15th-century England the two opposing factions used emblems of red or white roses.

You should be aware that when you give roses as gifts, different colors have different meanings. Red symbolizes love and beauty, white symbolizes purity and innocence, yellow tells someone you are sorry, and pink is a perfect choice for friendship or to say "thank you."

HOW strong is a lily pad?

We know from cartoons that on top of every lily pad there's a big green frog, croaking happily. Well, frogs do occasionally perch on small lily pads, but it's also possible for a big lily pad (one that's two or three feet in diameter) to support a human being. You can't just jump onto it, though—you have to stand on a broad plank, which redistributes your weight across the pad's surface.

WHY do plants need fertilizer?

Plants get the oxygen, hydrogen, and carbon they need to survive from air and water, but other essential elements—such as nitrogen, phosphorus, and potassium—have to be obtained from the soil. Fertilizer (which is often made with animal dung) is rich in these elements, and helps plants grow.

HOW fast can a snail move?

Let's just say you wouldn't want one running to your rescue. A garden-variety snail can move about six inches a minute, but it usually goes much slower.

WHY do earthworms hide in the ground?

Earthworms thrive in dark, moist environments because direct sunlight dries out their skin, and since they don't have lungs, they need their skin moist to absorb oxygen from the earth. That's also the reason you see so many earthworms after a thunderstorm; with so many puddles around, they don't have to worry about staying wet.

WHAT is photosynthesis?

Put simply, photosynthesis is the method by which plants convert sunlight into food (usually in the form of sugar or starch). In most plants, the chemical that makes this possible is chlorophyll, though photosynthetic algae and seaweed often employ other compounds.

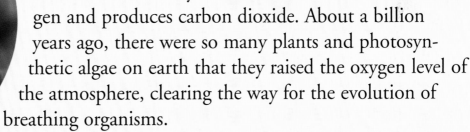

One interesting thing about photosynthesis is that it uses up carbon dioxide and produces oxygen—making it the opposite of the human respiratory system, which consumes oxygen and produces carbon dioxide. About a billion years ago, there were so many plants and photosynthetic algae on earth that they raised the oxygen level of the atmosphere, clearing the way for the evolution of breathing organisms.

All living organisms owe a debt to photosynthesis for another reason: by capturing and storing the energy of the sun as food, plants and photosynthetic organisms constitute the bottom layer of the food chain.

WHAT is organic gardening?

All gardening is "organic"—after all, people grow plants and flowers, not car fenders! "Organic gardening" is the term now given to the old-fashioned art of growing things without using synthetic or chemical fertilizers (to add nutrients to the soil) or pesticides (to kill plant-eating bugs). Synthetic and chemical compounds can sometimes have negative effects on people and the environment, so organic farmers use only natural substances and methods that can have no harmful side-effects.

WHAT is a gazebo?

Although the word sounds as silly as "whatchamacallit," a gazebo is actually a small, roofed building with open walls that is set in a pretty spot in a lawn or garden. These delightful structures were originally created for huge gardens as a means to provide shade or shelter from a sudden rain-shower. Now they are often used for outdoor weddings and dinner parties.

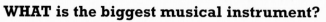

WHAT is the biggest musical instrument?

An old-fashioned pipe organ can be as big (and as complicated) as a jet plane, consisting of hundreds or even thousands of individual pipes, which produce notes when air blasts through them. Some of these organs have three or four keyboards stacked one on top of the other, as well as dozens of "stops" that alter the flow of air (and the sound of the notes).

HOW many people are in an orchestra?

Symphony orchestras don't come in one standard size; the number of musicians depends on the music being played. The first orchestras had only a dozen or so players, but as symphonies grew more popular (in the 19th century) orchestras employed 50 or 60 musicians, divided into winds, strings, brass, and percussion. Most modern symphony orchestras have about 100 members.

At this point you may be asking: what, exactly, is a symphony? When it first came into vogue—in the late 18th century—the symphony was an extended piece of music written for an orchestra of brass, string and various other instruments. "Classical" symphonies were usually divided into three or four "movements," three of them fast and brisk, one (in the middle) slow and leisurely. Today, however, a symphony is pretty much whatever the composer says it is!

WHAT was the first musical instrument?

We'll never know for sure, but it's likely that the first instrument played by prehistoric man was a hollow reed perforated with holes (that is, a primitive flute). As for stringed instruments, the lyre—a simpler version of the harp—first sprang up in the Middle East around the second and third millennia B.C.

WHAT is the smallest musical instrument?

In most orchestras, the smallest instrument is the piccolo—a thin, light flute that produces music an octave (that is, eight notes) higher than a flute. Outside an orchestra, the smallest instruments are harmonicas and kazoos, though you might have a hard time making the argument that the kazoo is really an instrument!

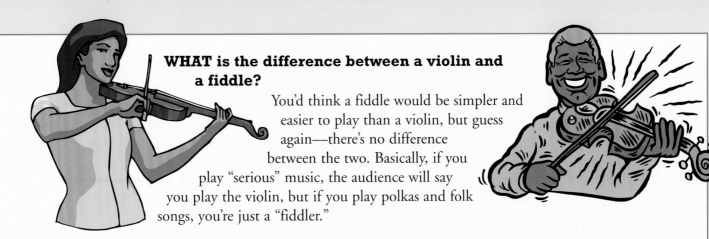

WHAT is the difference between a violin and a fiddle?

You'd think a fiddle would be simpler and easier to play than a violin, but guess again—there's no difference between the two. Basically, if you play "serious" music, the audience will say you play the violin, but if you play polkas and folk songs, you're just a "fiddler."

WHY do conductors use batons?

Despite what you see in cartoons, a conductor doesn't wave his baton and produce music out of thin air. The conductor's job is to rehearse the members of the orchestra and get them to play in unison, and in that regard, his work is pretty much done by the time you see a live performance. The reason he waves a baton during the show is to set the orchestra's tempo, that is, the pace at which it plays.

Early conductors didn't always use batons for this task. The first maestros simply waved their hands, and after that it became fashionable to thump a big wooden staff on the floor in a steady rhythm. This tradition ended—and the tradition of the baton began—when one famous conductor got angry at the way his orchestra was playing, accidentally thumped the staff on his own foot, and died of blood poisoning!

WHY does a piano have black and white keys?

The black keys on a piano have two functions. First, they mark the "sharp" and "flat" notes, which are a semitone different from the notes of the white keys (which are separated by whole tones and not semitones). Second, the arrangement of black keys helps players to memorize the layout of the keyboard.

HOW many keys does a piano have?

Surprisingly, pianos don't have a standard number of keys. A very few models have 85 keys, and one famous grand piano made in Germany has 97. However, most pianos you're likely to run into today have 88 keys, of which 52 are white and 36 are black.

WHY do footballs have an oval shape?

According to sports historians, the very first game of American football was played with a perfectly round ball. However, teams soon adopted the oval-shaped ball used in European rugby, because it was easier to hold onto while running and didn't squirt away from the action as easily as a round ball.

WHY are football players called "quarterbacks" and "halfbacks?"

The quarterback-halfback-fullback system was invented by Walter Camp, the "father of American football," in the late 19th century. Camp named players based on their positions behind the line of scrimmage: the fullback was all the way back, the halfback half as close as the fullback, and the quarterback half as close as the halfback. Today, you can find halfbacks, fullbacks, and quarterbacks all over the field, but the names have stuck.

HOW was football invented?

American football evolved from the English game of rugby—a sport that itself evolved from plain old football, which we call soccer here. While we're on the subject, the word "soccer" may have evolved from "association" (as in football associations, or teams), as a way of distinguishing this game from American football. Confused yet? (Oddly enough, American football doesn't have all that much to do with feet, except during punts, field goals and kickoffs.)

The American version of football became popular as a collegiate sport in the mid-18th century. By 1873, four universities—Rutgers and Princeton in New Jersey, Columbia in New York, and Yale in Connecticut—met to standardize the rules, setting team size at 11 players and field length at 100 yards. Other innovations followed—for example, the "down" system wasn't adopted until 1882, and there was no such thing as fourth down until 1912!

WHY can you hit balls harder with an aluminum bat?

There's a good reason the major leagues don't allow metal bats. As hard as it is, a wooden bat has a certain amount of "give," absorbing much of the energy of a pitched ball. An aluminum bat has very little "give," and allows the ball to keep more of its energy. Add the energy of the bat to the energy of the ball, and a line-drive hit with an aluminum bat could seriously injure (or even kill) an infielder.

WHAT is the world's most popular sport?

It's never really caught on in America—except among kids!—but soccer (which is called "football" everywhere but the U.S.) is far and away the most popular sport in the world. The World Cup championships, held every four years, attracts about two billion TV viewers from around the globe—or almost half the earth's population!

HOW fast is a baseball pitch?

In pro baseball, pitches range in speed from about 70 miles per hour (for a slow, lazy curve) to 100 mph (for a blistering fastball). The most powerful pitchers can throw at 103 or 104 mph, though they usually hit this velocity only a few times per inning.

HOW was baseball invented?

Most kids are taught that Abner Doubleday invented the game of baseball in 1839, but historians have since discovered the truth: baseball really owes its existence to Alexander Cartwright, who standardized certain features (number of innings, field size, etc.) that persist to this day.

Cartwright didn't just invent modern baseball out of thin air. Like football—which is based on the English game of rugby—Cartwright's game derived many of its rules from the English sport rounders, which involves balls, bats and other baseball-like features. In Cartwright's time, an early American version of rounders was called "townball."

By the way, Cartwright's team, the New York Knickerbockers, played the first modern game of baseball way back in 1845. As early as the 1860's, this new sport was already being described as America's "national pastime."

WHY do bowling balls have three holes?

A hundred years ago, bowlers used only two fingers—the thumb and middle finger—so balls only had two holes. Gradually, bowlers discovered they could better control the ball's velocity and spin by using three fingers (the two above, plus the ring finger), and that became the standard. By the way, you can occasionally find a bowling ball with five holes!

WHY is it called "pool?"

It's technically known as "billiards," but the cue-stick-and-balls game we call "pool" in America derived its name from "pool rooms"--illegal betting establishments where people "pooled" their money and wagered on sporting events. Since most pool rooms had a billiards table with which the visitors could kill time, the word attached itself to that popular game.

HOW fast can a bicycle go?

To answer this question, it's necessary to accept a loose definition of the word "bicycle" as a two-wheeled vehicle that runs on human power. Most speed bicycles look like the tiny, futuristic cars you see in science fiction movies, and can go 60 or 70 miles per hour over short distances (and even faster if they're going down a steep hill)—about the speed of your average car.

Even ordinary bikes are capable of attaining speeds of 20 or 25 miles per hour, and they hit this velocity plenty of times during the world's most famous bike race: The Tour de France. This annual three-week marathon in (you guessed it) France involves teams of cyclists from various countries, who make their way up and down hundreds of miles of hilly terrain in an excruciating test of endurance and speed.

HOW did Ping-Pong get its name?

It's catchy, for sure, but most people who take their Ping-Pong seriously prefer to call the sport by its formal name, "table tennis." The name Ping-Pong was created (and trade-marked) years ago by a toy manufacturer seeking to introduce the game, which is hugely popular in China, to the kids of America.

WHY is a marathon 26 miles long?

In 490 B.C., the Athenians of Greece fought a battle against the Persians at the nearby city of Marathon. Legend has it that a messenger ran the 26 miles from Marathon to Athens to tell the people of the Athenian victory (and then promptly dropped dead from exhaustion). That's why the distance of a modern marathon is 26 miles, though most people don't die after they cross the finish line!

WHY does tennis have such a strange scoring system?

15, 30, 40, love, deuce—sometimes it seems tennis comes from a different world. No one is sure where the numbers come from, although it's possible that in the country where tennis was invented, France, a clock on the court was read off at 15- or 20-minute intervals. As for "deuce," that derives from the French "deux," meaning two points, and "love" comes from "l'oeuf," which is French for "egg" (meaning a big fat zero).

WHAT is the most dangerous team sport?

Baseball and basketball both have their hazards, and various players have been seriously injured (and even paralyzed) while playing pro football. But on a day-to-day basis, the most dangerous sport is ice hockey, partly because players wield big, heavy sticks and sharp skates, but mostly because they "check" each other into the rink's walls with teeth-rattling force.

WHY do golf balls have dimples?

When golf was first invented (in Holland in the late 13th century), golf balls were perfectly round, like ping-pong balls. Dimples became popular when it was discovered that they create a thin layer of air turbulence around the ball, reducing drag by the surrounding air. That's why you can hit a dimpled golf ball much farther than an undimpled one!

While we're on the subject, for many years now, a legend has spread among kids that the inside of a golf ball contains some horrible poison (or even explosive). Well, not to burst your bubble, but a golf ball interior is pretty ordinary: it consists of a kind of rubber or tightly wound synthetic fiber that gives the ball a lot of "bounce" when it's struck by a club.

WHY doesn't the Chinese New Year start on January 1?

Not all cultures use the same calendar. We use the Gregorian calendar, a revised form of the Julian calendar invented by the ancient Romans. The Chinese calendar, which is even older, measures the year according to observations of the sun, moon, and stars, which is why the Chinese New Year is usually celebrated a few weeks after the first of January.

WHY does a week have seven days?

Unlike the twelve-month year, the seven-day week has nonscientific origins. In ancient times, the seven days corresponded to the seven known planets of the solar system. This system was then adopted by the Greeks and Romans, who named the days of the week after their gods. Today, the days of our week derive from Scandinavian mythology (for example, Wednesday is named after the Norse god Odin).

HOW long is a leap year?

A leap year, which occurs once every four years, is 366 days long, or one day longer than an ordinary year (the extra day is always added on February 29). Its purpose is to make the calendar more closely match the time it takes the earth to revolve around the sun.

WHAT is Sadie Hawkins Day?

Back in the 1950's, the popular comic strip Li'l Abner featured a character named Sadie Hawkins, who was so unattractive that no man would marry her--prompting her father, the mayor, to declare a holiday on which women could chase down men rather than the other way around. In many communities, Sadie Hawkins Day is celebrated on Leap Day (which occurs every four years, on February 29), usually with a school dance in which girls are encouraged to approach boys.

WHY does the year have twelve months?

Ancient civilizations arranged their calendars according to observations of either the stars or the moon. For the Egyptians, the year commenced when the bright star Sirius rose in the same place on the horizon as the sun, and was 365 days long. The Egyptians divided their year into twelve 30-day months, and added a five-day festival at the start to make up the difference.

Other cultures defined a year by the phases of the moon. Since a full moon occurs once every 29 and one-half days, the lunar year turned out to be a full day shorter than the solar year. It took centuries of tinkering, but finally the world has agreed on the standard 365-day, 12-month calendar, with a "leap day" every four years to keep things in sync.

February						
Sun	Mon	Tue	Wed	Thu	Fri	Sat
	1	2	3	4	5	6
7	8	9	10	11	12	13
14	15	16	17	18	19	20
21	22	23	24	25	26	27
28						

WHAT is Mardi Gras?

French for "Fat Tuesday," Mardi Gras is an annual holiday celebrated in New Orleans. It marks the end of "carnival," a weeks-long celebration just before Lent. The idea is to party and eat well on Fat Tuesday, because Ash Wednesday commences a time of fasting. This carnival tradition, which has its roots in medieval Christianity, is celebrated in other parts of the world as well, including Rio de Janeiro in Brazil.

WHY do we celebrate the Fourth of July with fireworks?

Ever since fireworks were invented, almost a thousand years ago, people have used them to celebrate important events, like coronations, holidays, and victories in battle. America marked its Declaration of Independence from England with a fireworks display, the first one of which occurred on July 4, 1777, and which has been an annual tradition ever since.

In France, Bastille Day (July 14) is similar to the 4th of July in the U.S. It marks the day in 1789 when a mob stormed the royal prison in Paris, the Bastille, and freed all the prisoners (they were surprised to find the Bastille was nearly empty that day). This was one of the major events of the French Revolution, in which the king, queen, and nobles were overthrown in favor of rule by the citizens.

WHY don't people work on weekends?

In the middle ages, life revolved around a six-day work week: the only day of rest was Sunday, when everyone was expected to go to church. Over the next few centuries, Saturday slowly became a day of rest as well, as productivity improved (meaning workers didn't have to put in as much time in the factory) and citizens clamored for a day they could spend as they pleased.

WHY do we paint eggs on Easter?

Easter is celebrated in early spring, so it's associated with the rabbit, a frolicsome, fertile creature. What do rabbits have to do with eggs? Well, hundreds of years ago, children believed rabbits laid eggs in the grass, which is how Easter egg hunts started. As for why these "rabbit" eggs are painted, that dates back thousands of years to an ancient Egyptian tradition. (Why did the Egyptians paint eggs? Nobody knows!)

WHAT country spans the most degrees of latitude?

You might think one of the countries of South America—say, Chile or Brazil—would span the most distance from north to south. But in fact, Canada takes the prize, spanning over 41 degrees of latitude between Middle Island, Ontario and Cape Columbia, Nunavut (near the North Pole). That's almost 3,000 miles from top to bottom! Brazil is a close second, spanning 40 degrees of latitude.

WHAT country spans the most time zones?

If you think it's annoying to keep track of the three-hour time difference between New York and Los Angeles, imagine what it's like to live in Russia. This enormous country spans eleven time zones, meaning that Vladivostok (on the coast of Siberia, near Japan) is almost half a world away from the capital in St. Petersburg.

WHAT is the Bermuda Triangle?

Many people are convinced that a triangular area of the Atlantic Ocean—with points touching the southernmost tip of Florida and the islands of Bermuda and Puerto Rico—is somehow hostile to air and sea traffic, with a mysterious number of "disappeared" planes and ships. This so-called Bermuda Triangle has inspired numerous books, movies and TV shows, all claiming that some supernatural force is at work.

Many scientists and statisticians have examined the Bermuda Triangle, though, and they've come up with a different explanation. It turns out that this relatively small sliver of sea has a disproportionately large amount of boat and air traffic, so it's not a surprising statistic that more planes and ships sink there—the unfortunate fact is, planes and ships do have accidents. Thanks to this scientific analysis, there's no need to involve ghosts or extra dimensions to explain the swallowed-up craft.

WHAT is the Continental Divide?

It's easier to visualize the Continental Divide if you picture the entire North American continent, and not just the United States. The divide (which marks the spot where falling rain or snow either drains east, toward the Atlantic Ocean, or west, toward the Pacific) runs from northwestern Canada, down through the Rockies, and on to Mexico. By the way, not only North America has a continental divide; so does every other continent in the world with the exception of Antarctica.

WHY is the earth divided into time zones?

Up until about 100 years ago, people determined the local time by following the position of the sun, which resulted in small differences from country to country (and even from town to town!). With

the advent of faster modes of communication—like the telegraph and the steam engine train—these time differences became unwieldy and potentially dangerous, creating the need for a uniform, reliable way to establish the local time anywhere in the world.

Some nations were quicker to adopt uniform time than others, but the problem was pretty much licked with the institution of Greenwich Mean Time in 1884. This system established a global clock "starting" in London at midnight (at the Royal Greenwich Observatory) and progressing through 24 imaginary time zones circling the earth.

Today, telling the global time no longer requires observation of the sun—instead, "Coordinated Universal Time" makes use of the precise measurements of atomic clocks.

WHAT is the Pacific Rim?

It sounds like something you can photograph from the air, but the Pacific Rim is more of an economic concept than a geological feature. It's used to describe the industrialized countries bordering the Pacific Ocean, which includes everything from the U.S. and Canada in the east to Japan and China in the west.

WHAT is the purpose of Daylight Saving Time?

First adopted in the U.S. in 1942 (after a brief, unpopular seven-month run in 1918 and 1919), Daylight Saving Time is the practice of setting clocks ahead one hour in the late spring (and going back to "standard" time in the late fall). The idea is to extend an extra hour of daylight into the early evening, rather than waste it in the early morning when most people are asleep!

STANDARD TIME DAYLIGHT SAVING

HOW deep is a fathom?

If you've ever seen an old submarine movie, you may recall objects being described as so many fathoms below the water. This ancient word, which means "outstretched arms" in Old English, corresponds to two yards, or six feet. Although the fathom has since been replaced by more modern measures of length (like the meter), it's still used by some sailors. (While we're on the subject of outdated measures, some ancient cultures determined length according to the "cubit," which was based on an outstretched human forearm.)

Another measure similar to the fathom is the knot, which is used to measure speed on the open sea. The knot is based on the nautical mile, which is 6,076 feet, compared to 5,280 feet for an ordinary land mile—so "50 knots" means "50 nautical miles per hour." (The nautical mile is longer than a land mile because it's derived from measurements of the earth's circumference.)

WHAT is a kilogram based on?

The basic unit of weight in the metric system, the kilogram is one of the few measures that is derived from an actual physical object: a small cylinder of platinum and iridium that was fabricated in the 1880's and has since been kept in a Paris vault. (In nonmetric terms, a kilogram corresponds to a little over two pounds.)

WHAT is a meter based on?

The meter (the metric unit of length, equivalent to a bit less than a yard) was originally calculated to be one ten-millionth of the earth's circumference. However, because the earth isn't a perfect sphere, the meter has since been defined as exactly 1,650,763 times the wavelength of light emitted by an atom of krypton in a vacuum. Since this quantity is the same anywhere in the universe, it eliminates the uncertainty caused by an Earth-based definition.

°C
50
40
30
20
10

°F
120
110
100
90
80

HOW does a thermometer work?

When liquid is heated, it expands in volume and takes up more space. The same is true for the mercury in an old-fashioned thermometer: when you hold the glass tube under your tongue, your body heat warms up the mercury, which expands to the level marked with a certain temperature. Newer, solid-state thermometers don't have mercury at all, but use electronic sensors to read your temperature directly.

By the way, there are three different ways to tell the temperature. The Fahrenheit scale—which is used in the U.S.—was introduced in 1724 by Daniel Fahrenheit. The Celsius scale—which is used in the rest of the world—is similar to the metric system; it divides the temperature scale into 100 degrees between the freezing and boiling points of water. And scientists tell temperature a third way, with something called the Kelvin scale.

HOW did people tell time before clocks?

The old-fashioned way: by looking at the sun's position in the sky. This gave them a rough idea whether it was morning, noon, or afternoon, and if more accuracy was required they could consult a sundial, a stick that casts shadows of different length depending on the time of day. On clear nights, time could be estimated by the position of the stars.

WHY are things counted in dozens?

In ancient times, some cultures counted by twelves because of the twelve phases of the moon. Also, the number 12 is divisible by many other numbers—2, 3, 4, and 6—compared to the number 10, which is divisible by only 2 and 5. For this reason, we persist in buying a dozen eggs or a gross (12 × 12 = 144) of handkerchiefs, even though most of the time we use the base 10 counting system.

HOW many dollar bills are there?

There are billions of dollar bills floating around the U.S. at any given time, and it's no wonder—the U.S. Treasury prints almost 20 million new dollar bills every day, most of them to replace old, worn-out bills, which are promptly shredded. A well-traveled dollar bill has a life span of about two years, though it can last much longer if you keep it safe at home in a cool, dry place.

While we're on the subject, you may wonder why the back of a dollar bill contains a pyramid with a single, glowing eye in the apex. Back when the U.S. currency was designed, at the end of the 18th century, many of the founding fathers belonged to a secret society called the Freemasons, which used the eye-in-the-pyramid to symbolize the "great architect of the universe." This symbol made its way onto the dollar bill, and tradition has kept it there ever since.

HOW many millionaires are there?

In the United States alone, there are over two million millionaires—the most of any country in the world. There are so many millionaires, in fact, that many people now aspire to be in the more exclusive club of billionaires (who are worth a thousand times as much). There are only a few hundred billionaires in the United States, and not many more than that in the rest of the world.

WHY are 10- and 20-dollar bills lopsided?

The government is always figuring out new ways to outsmart counterfeiters. A few years ago, large-denomination bills like 10's and 20's were redesigned so the portraits on front (of Andrew Jackson and Alexander Hamilton) were slightly off-center. This had two effects: first, it rendered older counterfeit bills obsolete, and second, it made the new bills that much harder to copy.

HOW does a credit card work?

A credit card allows you to spend money you don't have. The bank issues the card and extends you a "line of credit"—an amount of money you can charge (or borrow) on the card. You must pay the money back; a little at a time over a period of years, or in bigger amounts over a period of months. The bank charges you a fee, called interest, every month—so you wind up paying back more than you "borrowed" to buy what you wanted.

HOW much money is in an ATM?

An automatic teller machine can hold tens of thousands of dollars' worth of cash, mostly in $20 bills. Usually, though, a machine will allow a single person to withdraw only a few hundred dollars a day, even if you have a lot more than that in the bank. This is for your own protection: if you lose your ATM card, you don't want someone finding it and stealing your life savings!

WHY are pennies bigger than dimes?

It's not important that higher-denomination coins be physically bigger than lower-denomination coins (the way a quarter is bigger than a nickel). What is important is that when you reach into your pocket for change, the coins should be different enough from each other that you can tell them apart. Not only is a penny noticeably bigger than a dime, but it has a smooth edge, so you know what you're grabbing.

By the way, it's no longer the case that pennies are made exclusively of copper and nickels of, well, nickel. Modern pennies are made of zinc, with a thin copper coating, while nickels are mostly composed of copper (a 75 percent copper/25 percent nickel alloy, to be exact). If you're not confused enough yet, the dime—which decades ago was made out of silver—today consists of a 90 percent copper/10 percent zinc alloy, the same proportions that make up a quarter, which also was entirely silver before 1965.

WHY do they make $2 bills?

The two-dollar bill was introduced by the U.S. Mint in 1976 as a cost-saving measure (after all, it's cheaper to print one $2 bill than two $1 bills). Unfortunately, the denomination never really caught on with the U.S. public, and because it was printed in such small quantities many people wound up saving their $2 bills as good luck keepsakes rather than spending them.

WHY are black cats considered unlucky?

In medieval times, people believed witches kept cats as evil pets, or could even assume the form of cats (black cats, of course, since fluffy white Persians don't look particularly evil). A tradition developed among sailors that disaster awaited anyone whose path was crossed by a black cat, a superstition that persists to the present day.

WHY do people say "knock on wood"?

The phrase, "knock on wood"—usually uttered when you hear a remark like, "I hope it doesn't rain tomorrow"—has a few likely origins. In ancient times, people believed spirits lived in trees, and could be summoned for help with a quick knock. It's also possible the phrase derives from the game of tag, in which a kid can touch a tree (the "base") to avoid capture.

WHY does lightning never strike twice?

This is one of those sayings that's so completely wrong you wonder who made it up in the first place. Lightning strikes plenty of places twice, especially if that place is the tallest thing in the immediate vicinity (for example, the Empire State Building is struck by lightning dozens of times a year). If you're struck by lightning in an open field, and you're the tallest thing in that field, you're likely to be struck again unless you get away fast.

WHY is 13 an unlucky number?

No one knows for sure, but historians think the number 13 received its bad reputation from the Last Supper, the last meal Jesus Christ had before he was crucified (at which there were 13 guests). There's also an old story from Norse mythology in which the god of mischief, Loki, showed up uninvited at a party attended by the twelve other gods of Valhalla and precipitated a major disaster.

The superstition about the number 13 is so pervasive that some buildings don't have thirteenth floors. Although it's logically impossible for a tall building *not* to have a thirteenth floor, it's very likely that it won't be labeled as such—as you may have noticed if you've ever been in an elevator that goes straight from the twelfth to the fourteenth (which is really the thirteenth) floor.

WHY do witches fly on brooms?

There aren't really witches, of course, but that's not what people believed back in the middle ages. In the 15th century, a witch on trial "confessed" to flying on a magic broom (brooms were the main cleaning implements in medieval times, so pretty much every home had one), and pretty soon people believed that all witches got around this way.

HOW do magicians make things disappear?

It's impossible to make a child or an elephant actually, physically, vanish into nothing. Rather, a magician uses the art of misdirection, diverting your attention at the exact moment he pulls a lever or opens a box. Some magicians also use optical props (like carefully placed mirrors) to make the audience believe that his assistant has disappeared into thin air.

How did Halloween start?

The ancient Celts—who lived thousands of years ago in northwest Europe—celebrated a holiday at the start of November marking the end of the summer and fall and the beginning of the long, cold winter. On "Samhain," as it was called, the ghosts of the dead were believed to come back to mingle among the living.

After the Celts were converted to Christianity in the 8th century A.D., they renamed Samhain "All Hallow's Eve" (later "Halloween"), to honor the memory of departed saints. This was much more acceptable to the church authorities than a pagan holiday celebrating the dead.

So why do we dress up in costumes on Halloween? The Celts believed that, on Samhain, the spirits of the returning dead snatched up the souls of the living—who could avoid this fate by pretending to be someone else!

WHAT is a Jack o' lantern?

These grinning, hollowed-out pumpkins with flickering candles inside date back to eighteenth-century Ireland, when a blacksmith named Jack (so the story goes) outwitted the devil. To celebrate the event, Irish households kept Jack o' lanterns made of turnips—but switched to more abundant pumpkins when they emigrated to America.

WHY isn't there school in the summer?

Kids have it easy today, vacation-wise—a century ago, if anyone had suggested a three-month suspension of school from mid-June to mid-September, he'd have been laughed right out of the lunch room.

Back in the 19th century, schools in urban areas generally stayed open for the entire year. This was because parents could be more available to work in factories if they didn't have to make day-care arrangements for their kids. In some rural areas, by contrast, children received time off in the spring and fall, to help with planting and harvesting.

Today, the main reason for the long summer vacation isn't because it's too hot to learn, but because summer is (or used to be) the time when many parents have their vacation as well. But be forewarned: some adults think a three-month summer vacation is too generous, and have advocated new school calendars that give kids less free time.

WHY is there no "E" in letter grades?

This is a tough one. The most likely explanation is that, in some schools, the letter E is used to mean "excellent"—and if you got an E on a paper marked according to the A, B, C grading system, that would be very far from excellent! Most likely, the E was left out to avoid confusing parents, and to keep kids from passing off an "E" grade as good work.

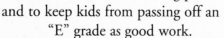

HOW did kindergarten get its name?

If the word "kindergarten" sounds foreign to you, there's good reason: it's German for "children's garden." The idea of sending five- and six-year-olds to school originated with a man named Friedrich Froebel, who established the first kindergarten in Germany in 1837. Unusually for the time, Froebel stressed the importance of play as well as instruction, which is why kindergartners spend so much time singing and finger-painting.

WHAT is chalk made of?

Believe it or not, when you draw on the sidewalk with a piece of chalk, you might be using the remains of millions of microscopic sea creatures! Real chalk is made out of limestone, which comes from the discarded shells of plankton and diatoms (which have accumulated over millions of years). However, much of the chalk sold in stores today is not found naturally in limestone deposits, but made from scratch in factories.

WHY are school buses yellow?

For decades, motorists have associated the color yellow with school buses. No one knows why yellow became the standard—bright red or green would have done just as well—but yellow buses became so common by the mid-20th century that a federal statute was passed in 1977 requiring all new school buses to be painted in "National School Bus Yellow." So it's not just a coincidence—it's the law!

WHY don't pens have erasers?

Actually, you can occasionally find a pen with an eraser, but its ink is specially formulated to come off when it's rubbed. Since most people want the ink in their pens to be more permanent (if they didn't, they'd use a pencil, right?), erasable pens have never really become popular.

WHAT did kids do before school was invented?

On the vast scale of human history, sending kids to school is a relatively recent innovation, only taking hold worldwide in the last couple of hundred years.

Up until the 18th century or so, going to school (or, more likely, having a private tutor to provide instruction in reading, writing, and philosophy) was a privilege that could only be enjoyed by the children of the very rich. Since most ordinary folks lived in rural areas, and survived on the crops they planted, they needed their kids close at hand to do farmwork and help with chores. As a result, not only didn't poor kids go to school, they usually never learned how to read and write!

While we're on the subject, until modern times, most kids didn't even have a "childhood" in the sense they do today. When a girl turned seven or eight, she was treated as a full-grown adult, and expected to pull her weight around the house.

WHY did prisoners wear striped clothes?

To distinguish them from prison guards (not to mention visitors) and make them immediately noticeable if they were to try to escape. Nowadays, not many inmates wear stripes—most jails now require prisoners to wear special, highly visible uniforms, like bright orange jumpsuits, for the same reason.

WHY do men wear ties?

The origin of the long, narrow necktie is lost in history, but we do know that the warriors of various ancient cultures wore neckpieces of one kind or another--for example, Roman soldiers and medieval knights used to wear pieces of cloth around their necks, probably to soak up the sweat caused by their armor. The modern tie is a direct descendant of the "cravat," a silk cloth worn by French nobility a few hundred years ago.

WHY do people get the "red carpet treatment?"

The phrase "roll out the red carpet" is used when guests are given a lavish welcome (sometimes there's even an actual red carpet on hand, as at the Academy Awards). This practice originated in India a few hundred years ago, when expensive red carpets would be unrolled in front of important visitors so their feet wouldn't have to touch the ground.

WHY do elevators beep?

For a simple reason: so blind people can know when they've reached their floor. In most modern buildings, elevators also have either raised numbers on their buttons, or numbers written in braille (a language using raised bumps) under the ordinary numbers, so blind people can find the appropriate floor.

WHY do barbershops have striped poles?

This one has an interesting answer, which may or may not be true. Barbers in the middle ages also doubled as surgeons and dentists, and, according to one historian, they'd hang white cloths with red blood stains outside their doors to alert potential customers. This accounts for the red stripes on a barber pole, but the blue stripes are more obscure—possibly they were meant to symbolize veins. Feel like getting a haircut now?

Though they're encountered far less often today, pawn shops (in which people can temporarily sell their possessions for cash, then buy them back later) often have three golden balls hanging over their front doors. This emblem was first used by the powerful Medici and Lombard banking families of renaissance Europe, which lent money to kings and nobility. (According to legend, a distant ancestor of the Medicis slew a giant with a sack of three rocks.)

WHY do soldiers salute?

Historians think the salute began when medieval knights politely raised their visors to greet guests at tournaments. The modern salute—a gesture of respect to officers by soldiers of more junior rank—originated in the British navy, and was soon copied by armies all over the world.

WHY do people shake hands when they meet?

As with many social customs, the origin of the handshake is clouded in history. Some people believe this tradition originated in the middle ages, when knights who encountered each other off the field of battle extended their bare hands to show they were unarmed. This may or may not be the case, but we do know that the Quakers of England—a peaceful religious sect—made a practice of greeting each other with handshakes in the 17th century.

Although handshaking is most common in the western hemisphere, it's also practiced in the far east, with one important qualification: it can be a deadly insult to shake with your left hand! This is because, in Arabic and Oriental societies, the left hand is traditionally used to wipe after you go to the bathroom.

In the west, some people (including Boy Scouts) shake with their left hands. This may also harken back to the days of yore: since a person usually held a shield in his left hand, deliberately shaking with that hand would be a clear demonstration of trust.

WHY are fire trucks red?

Actually, not all fire trucks are red—depending on where you live, you may see green, orange, or even multicolored fire trucks. What all these trucks have in common, though, is that they're bright and immediately noticeable, which prompts drivers and pedestrians to get out of the way.

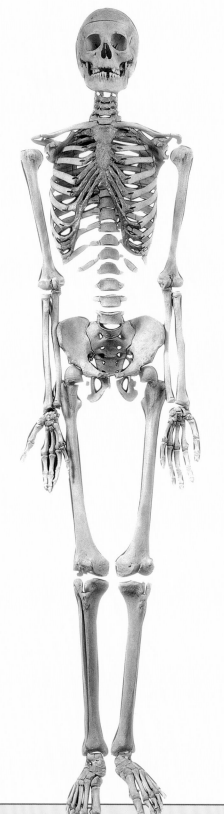

Section 3

Human Body

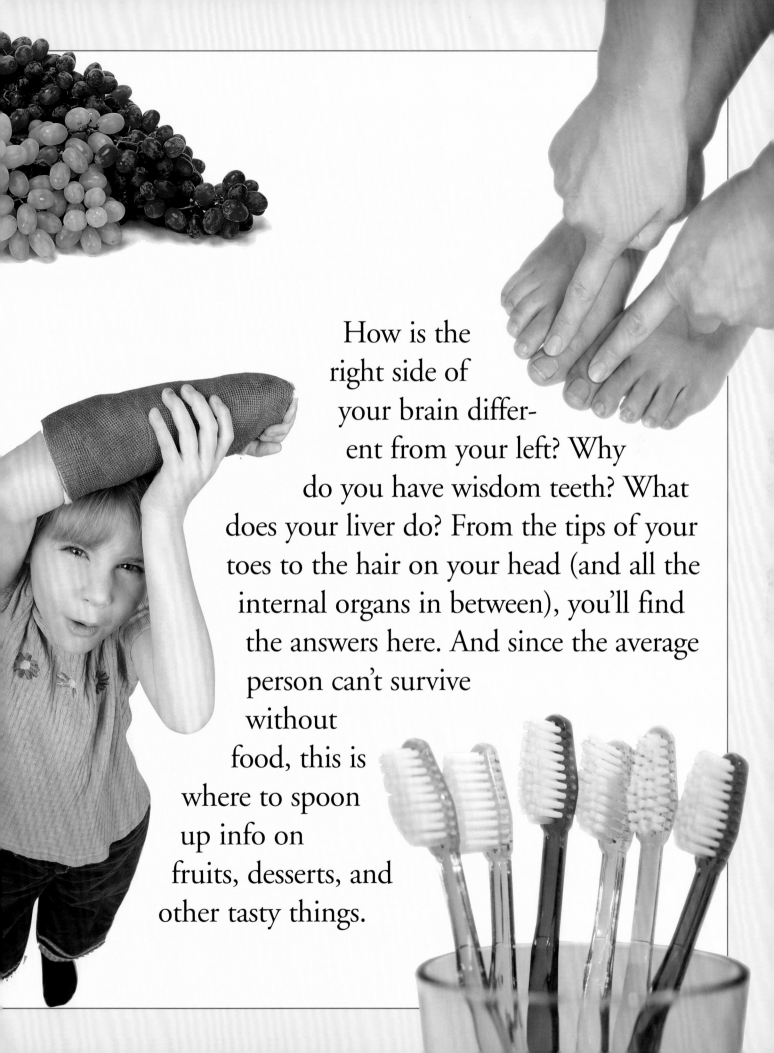

How is the right side of your brain different from your left? Why do you have wisdom teeth? What does your liver do? From the tips of your toes to the hair on your head (and all the internal organs in between), you'll find the answers here. And since the average person can't survive without food, this is where to spoon up info on fruits, desserts, and other tasty things.

WHY do doctors take blood samples?

When a doctor checks a patient's blood, he isn't just examining the condition of his red and white blood cells. A person's blood can contain clues to all sorts of non-blood-related diseases, such as diabetes (which causes a buildup of sugar) or certain types of cancer (which produce specific proteins that circulate in the bloodstream).

HOW much blood does a person have?

At any given time, there are about five quarts of blood coursing through an adult's body. Ninety percent of that is water, and of the rest, a little more than half is a clear liquid called plasma and the other half the red blood cells that carry oxygen.

WHY do people have different blood types?

All blood is essentially the same, except for one major difference: the blood "type," which is related to a kind of protein found on the surface of red blood cells. Most people have type A, B, AB, or O blood. Usually this isn't important, except when you receive (or donate) blood: if you don't get blood from a person of the same type, your body will "reject" the transfusion and you'll become seriously ill. This difference in blood types is the reason most hospitals have "blood banks"—that is, stocks of frozen or refrigerated blood that can be used for patients of a matching type. Most of the time, donated blood isn't used whole; it's separated mechanically into red blood cells (for transfusions), platelets (to control bleeding), plasma (the clear part of blood, also to control bleeding), white blood cells (to fight infection), and various components that regulate blood clotting.

WHY are bruises black-and-blue?

When you get a serious bump, the capillaries (tiny blood vessels) beneath the skin break and leak blood, which is why a bruise always looks red in its early stages. As the blood runs out of oxygen, it takes on a bluish-black color, and so does the bruise. Eventually, the dead blood cells are absorbed back into the body, and the bruise lightens in color and disappears.

WHAT is hemophilia?

About one in 5,000 people, most of them males, are born with a lack of "clotting factor" in their blood, meaning their cuts and bruises take a much longer time to heal. Depending on the severity of his disease, a hemophiliac can bleed to death from internal injuries that an ordinary person wouldn't even notice. Hemophilia is hereditary and can't be cured, but it can be controlled with regular injections of clotting agents.

WHAT is anemia?

More of a symptom of disease than a disease in itself, anemia is a shortage of healthy red blood cells in the bloodstream. It has various causes, including insufficient iron in the diet; lack of vitamin B_{12}; or a problem with the bone marrow (where red blood cells are manufactured). The most common symptoms of anemia are tiredness, short breath, and chest pains.

WHY is blood red?

The most important ingredient of red blood cells is hemoglobin, a large, complex molecule that carries oxygen into the blood and carries away carbon dioxide. Hemoglobin contains iron atoms, which give the molecule—and therefore your blood—a reddish color, for the same reason rusted iron has a reddish color. By the way, your blood is bright red when it's carrying oxygen, but a much darker red when it's not.

As a rule, all vertebrates (that is, animals with backbones, a category that includes everything from fish to birds to people) have red blood, but that doesn't apply to creatures lower down on the food chain. Because their oxygen-carrying molecules contain copper rather than iron, lobsters and crabs have blue blood, while (as you can easily see when you squash a bug) most insects have green or colorless blood.

HOW is blood made?

Blood cells are manufactured in the one place you probably wouldn't expect—in the marrow (soft insides) of your bones. There, specialized cells are responsible for creating three components of blood: red blood cells, which carry oxygen throughout your body; white blood cells, which fight invading germs; and platelets, which stop you from bleeding when you have a cut.

WHAT keeps your bones together?

Bones don't just fit neatly into each other like construction toys—they're connected at the ends by tough, stringy, but slightly elastic fibers called "ligaments," which are themselves connected to tendons and muscles.

Let's take the elbow as an example. The two main bones of your arm, the humerus and ulna, are joined by ligaments, which have a restricted range of movement (so you can't bend your arm backward) and hold the bones firmly in place in a juncture called a "joint." Tendons, which are slightly more elastic than ligaments, extend from this joint and other parts of the bone to the muscles in your arm.

By the way, not only do ligaments hold your bones together, but they also help support internal organs like your liver—which otherwise might slide all the way down to the neighborhood of your hips!

WHAT is the strongest muscle in your body?

You might guess one of the muscles in your arms or legs—or even your heart!—but the masseter (located on either side of the mouth) generates more pressure per square inch than any other muscle. The reason is that prehistoric humans had to bite and chew some very tough food, and needed big, strong jaws with equally strong jaw muscles.

WHAT is the smallest bone in the human body?

The body's three smallest bones are all close neighbors. When sound hits your eardrums, the vibration is passed on to the inner ear by a group of three bones: the hammer, the anvil, and the stirrup. The last bone in this chain, the U-shaped stirrup, is the smallest of the three, with a total length of only a few millimeters.

HOW many bones does a person have?

A full-grown adult has exactly 206 bones, more than half of them in the hands and feet (which makes sense, since hands and feet have the most moving parts). A newborn baby has over 300 separate bones, many of which fuse together as the child grows to create the adult total of 206.

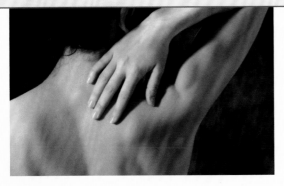

WHY do muscles cramp?

The sudden, sharp pain of a cramp is caused by an involuntary contraction of muscle fibers. Cramps don't have any one cause, but are most often brought on by overexertion (which can overstress muscles and put them temporarily out of whack). Leg cramps can be helped by getting more calcium in your diet.

WHAT makes muscles sore?

There are two different ways to strain your muscles. After a heavy workout, a substance called lactic acid builds up in muscle tissue, which causes the kind of acute soreness that goes away after about an hour. Doctors aren't quite sure, but they think long-term soreness is caused by microscopic tears in muscle, or a slow buildup of water and chemicals that throws the muscle fibers out of whack.

HOW long does it take a broken bone to heal?

As you know if you've ever fallen off a swing, a broken bone needs at least a few weeks to heal—and often longer than that if you're an adult (since adults heal less quickly than kids). A solid cast helps keeps the bone straight and in the proper position as surrounding cells secrete substances that close up the break.

WHAT are muscles?

The muscles of your body have two main components: long, tough, elongated muscle cells, and the proteins actin and myosin. When you flex a muscle, the actin and myosin molecules slide across each other, causing the muscle cells to contract, and the opposite happens when you relax. Because they have to be ready to respond at a moment's notice, muscles are well supplied with blood and nerve endings.

The body has two types of muscles. The "smooth" muscles lining your intestines, lungs, and blood vessels work autonomously (that is, on their own, without having to receive conscious commands). "Striped" muscles such as your biceps and triceps respond to conscious control, as when you flex your pecs. There are over 600 striped muscles attached to various parts of your skeleton.

Although the heart is technically a "smooth" muscle, its cells and proteins are so tough and durable that it qualifies as a unique muscle type of its own.

WHAT is the difference between the cerebrum and the cerebellum?

They sound alike, but these two main components of the human brain are very different. The cerebrum is the folded grey mass that takes up most of the inside of our skulls; it's responsible for reasoning, personality, and conscious perception.

Though they only add up to a fraction of the size of the cerebrum, the cerebellum and the attached brain stem (located at the rear base of the skull) are equally vital. These parts of the brain control "autonomic" nerve functions like breathing and digestion, keep the body balanced, and control complicated, largely unconscious muscle movements (such as are involved in walking or playing the piano).

The commands of the cerebrum and cerebellum are transmitted to the rest of the body via the spinal cord, which plugs into the back of the brain stem and extends all the way down the spine. Without a spinal cord, there would be no way for your brain to control the muscles of your body, and there would also be no way to transmit the sense of touch back to your brain.

WHY do brains have wrinkles?

If you crumple up a big sheet of paper, you can fit it into a small space. The same principle applies to brains: the reason they're wrinkled is to allow more grey matter to fit into our skulls. (Why don't we just have bigger skulls? Because if we did, it would be nearly impossible for babies to pass through the birth canal when they're born.)

HOW big is a human brain?

By weight, humans don't have bigger brains than some other animals—the average adult brain weighs about three pounds, compared to four pounds for a dolphin and twelve for an elephant. But our brains set themselves apart in three important ways: first, they're much bigger in proportion to the rest of our bodies; second, they have many more neurons, or nerve cells; and third, these billions of neurons are connected to each other in about 60 trillion different ways, allowing for more complexity in thought.

WHY are some people left-handed?

In a strict sense, a person is left-handed because the right side of his or her brain (which controls the left side of the body) is "dominant" over the left. In a larger sense, though, scientists don't know why 10 to 20 percent of the world's population is born left-handed. Some think it may be genetic (that is, programmed at birth), while some think it may have to do with chemical changes before a baby is born.

WHY can't you tickle yourself?

There are two ingredients to a successful tickle: a ticklish part of your body (your feet, your armpits, etc.) and the element of surprise. Even if your feet are ticklish, you can't tickle yourself because you can't surprise yourself—you always know what you're about to do, and your body prepares in advance so it doesn't have that "tickled" feeling.

WHAT is your funny bone?

The funny bone (that sensitive spot on the back of your elbow) isn't really a bone at all—it's the ulnar nerve, which reaches all the way down the forearm and into the fingers. A better question is why it's called a funny bone in the first place, since if you've ever knocked your elbow in the exact wrong way you know it's not a "funny" feeling at all!

HOW do we taste food?

Your tongue is coated with about 10,000 tiny bumps called papillae—or, as most people call them, taste buds. There are four different kinds, which respond to sweet, sour, bitter, and salty flavors (in any combination) and transmit this information to the brain. But they can't taste food all by themselves: the nerve signals from the buds have to be transmitted to special smell receptors in your nose. When your nose is stuffed, not only can't you smell outside odors, but you can't even smell the food you're eating—so it seems to have no taste at all.

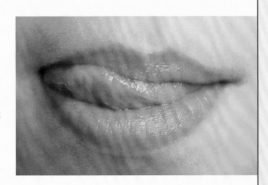

HOW is the right side of your brain different from the left?

Although they look exactly alike, the right and left sides of the brain are different in one important respect: the left side controls language and logical skills like math and science, while the right side is more involved with emotion and intuition. When you're an adult, damage to one side of the brain can affect the way you speak or process information. But if this damage occurs when you're young, the remaining half of the brain usually learns how to perform these tasks.

Strangely, the right side of your brain controls the muscles on the left side of your body, and vice-versa. Scientists aren't quite sure why this is the case—some think it's just an evolutionary accident (that is, the primates we descended from just happened to be wired this way), while a few suggest it may have something to do with balance or vision.

WHY does your voice sound different on tape?

"That's not me!" a person will say when he hears himself on tape for the first time. The reason your voice sounds weird on tape is because you're finally hearing it the way other people hear it—after it's traveled a few feet or yards. When you hear your voice during normal conversation, the sound travels only a few inches "inside-out," from your head to the inside of your ears!

HOW thin are your eardrums?

Because they need to be sensitive enough to detect very faint sounds, your eardrums are only about a tenth of a millimeter thick (with a total surface area of about 50 square millimeters). An eardrum can occasionally be punctured by loud sounds or sudden pressure changes, but will usually heal on its own within a month or two.

WHY does your voice get deeper as you grow older?

Your larynx—or "voice box"—is a tough, stringy organ in your throat that creates sound when air passes through it from your lungs. When you become a teenager, the larynx increases in size (much more for boys than for girls), creating a deeper sound when you talk.

If you're a boy, this process can result in an embarrassing (but mercifully short) interval when your voice "cracks," that is, shifts abruptly from a higher to a lower register. This happens because the part of the brain that controls your speech hasn't yet adjusted to the larger size of your vocal cords, and has to re-accustom itself to hearing the sounds they produce.

WHY does helium make your voice higher?

Helium is much lighter than the air we breathe (which is made of oxygen, nitrogen, and argon), and transmits sound at a higher speed. These two properties cause your larynx, the organ in your throat that produces sounds, to vibrate at a much higher frequency, giving you the voice of a cartoon character.

WHAT is sign language?

In a broad sense, sign language is any method of communication that uses the hands rather than spoken sounds. In a narrow sense, what most people mean by "sign language" is American Sign Language, which is taught to most deaf children. ASL has a signed "vocabulary" of thousands of words, making it a very effective communication tool.

WHY do ears have wax?

Ear wax isn't really a kind of wax at all—it's a sticky substance called "cerumen" that traps dust, small insects, and other contaminants that happen to find their way into the ear canal. Because cerumen is so sticky, it takes a long time for it to drain out of the ear, a process you normally don't even notice unless it builds up to bothersome levels.

WHY do loud noises make your ears ring?

Loud sounds can stun (or permanently damage) the sensitive cells in your inner ear that convert vibrations into sound, causing a steady hum or ringing sensation called "tinnitus." Tinnitus caused by sudden noise usually goes away after a few minutes, but constant exposure to ear-splitting music or jackhammers can cause the condition to become permanent.

WHY does spinning around make you dizzy?

Inside each of your ears is a tiny, delicate organ called the semicircular canal, which is filled with fluid and thousands of small, hairlike nerves. This is your body's balance system: when you tilt your head, the nerves inside the canal tilt as well and transmit their position to the brain, which adjusts your balance accordingly. Spinning around fast sends these hairs flying every which way, and the brain can't process the information quickly enough—which results in the sensation of dizziness.

As people age, not only does their hearing become less sharp, but the hairs in their semicircular canals begin to die off—which can result in dizziness and an increased susceptibility to falls. Damage to or infection of the inner ear can also cause a condition called vertigo, which makes you feel like your head is spinning even when you're standing perfectly still.

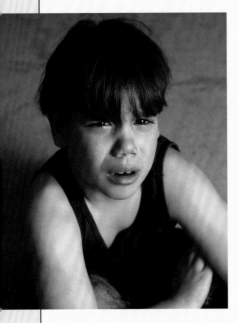

WHY are tears salty?

You don't only produce tears when you cry—the tear ducts in your eyes secrete them all the time to keep your eyeballs moist and wash them free from dust and other irritants. The salt dissolved in tears has a soothing effect on tissues, which is why eye drops sold in drugstores also contain salt.

WHY do your eyes get red when they're irritated?

The sclera—that is, the white portion of the eye around the iris—is covered with small, usually invisible blood vessels. When your eyes are irritated by dust, dry air, or direct sunlight, these blood vessels swell slightly and their color becomes more visible, giving you a bad case of "red eye."

WHY do we blink?

For the same reason cars have windshield wipers. Whenever we blink, a small tear (produced by the nearby tear duct) is spread over the cornea, the thin, transparent shield that covers the eye, keeping it free of dust.

HOW does laser eye surgery work?

A fascinating procedure, laser eye surgery is a way of shaping part of the cornea (the clear film covering the eyeball) so that it acts as a natural lens, correcting for nearsighted or farsighted vision. This eliminates the need for glasses or contact lenses, and is a reliable (although expensive) way to correct vision problems.

One of the most popular laser surgery procedures uses what is known as a "cold laser," which produces a tightly focused beam of ultraviolet light. Using this laser, an eye surgeon can "sculpt" a patient's corneas to within one-millionth of an inch, a delicate procedure requiring special equipment. The entire operation takes only a few minutes, and most patients start seeing better within days.

WHY do people have different color eyes?

The eye's iris (the band of muscle surrounding the pupil) has varying amounts of melanin, the chemical that gives skin its color. If the iris has little or no melanin, it's translucent, but looks blue because of the way it scatters light (this is the same reason the sky looks blue). If the iris has a little more melanin, it takes on a greenish color, and if it has lots of melanin, it appears brown or black.

WHAT is snow blindness?

When the sun shines on a large, unbroken field of snow and ice, it generates an incredible amount of glare, as well as eye-damaging ultraviolet radiation. This reflected light can burn the surface of your eyes, causing intense pain and difficulty seeing. It is possible to become snow blind even on an overcast day, which is why experienced mountaineers always wear sunglasses.

WHAT is color blindness?

The retinas of our eyes contain millions of light-gathering cells called "cones," which are sensitive to either red, green, or blue light (we see other hues, such as yellow, when the cones are stimulated by combinations of these three main colors).

In most instances, color blindness—an inability to distinguish between red and green—is caused by a lack of red and green cones in the retina. Although this may sound like a major problem, especially at traffic lights, it's often manageable because the affected person can learn to distinguish the two colors by shade, the same way you can tell apart two shades of grey in a black-and-white movie.

Because it's a genetic condition, the vast majority of people with color blindness are male. According to one estimate, millions of people in the U.S. suffer from color blindness to one degree or another.

HOW do contact lenses work?

Contact lenses float on the corneas of your eyes—the clear layer of tissue protecting your eyeball—in a thin pool of tears. They follow the same principle as glasses, but are much, much thinner and are flexible so they can fit comfortably in your eyes. The lenses bend and focus incoming light to correct for nearsightedness (not being able to see things far away) and farsightedness (not being able to see things close up).

WHAT makes hair curly?

The shape of a hair strand is determined by the shape of the protein, keratin, of which it's composed. Some peoples' keratin has an extra "kink" in its molecular structure that causes hair to grow out in natural curls. Hair can also temporarily curl (or straighten) because of high moisture levels in the surrounding air.

WHY do people have blonde, red, or brunette hair?

The easy answer to this question is: people have different-colored hair because they have different types of pigment cells in their hair follicles, which cause their hair to grow out yellow, orange, brown or black. What's more difficult to address is why people should have different hair colors at all: that is, what's the advantage of having blonde rather than black hair, since all hair does the same job (keeping the scalp warm) in any case?

Oddly enough, people with blonde hair have more hair per square inch of scalp than people with red, brown or black hair. The average person has anywhere from 100,000 to 150,000 hairs on his head, most of which are actively growing. Of these, about 100 hairs are shed every day, and usually wind up clogging the bathtub drain.

WHY does hair turn lighter in the sun?

Oddly enough, while prolonged exposure to the sun makes your skin darker, it makes your hair lighter! The reason is that the pigment molecules in a strand of hair are very fragile, and can be damaged by the sun's rays. The result is a loss of color, and what looks like a "lightening" of the hair.

WHY do people have eyebrows?

Think of eyebrows as nature's umbrellas—they prevent falling rain (or sweat from your forehead) from getting into your eyes. It's also possible that eyebrows evolved as a way for early humans to increase their range of facial expressions, back when spoken language had yet to be invented.

WHY do people go bald?

At any given time, about 85 percent of your hair follicles (the cells in your scalp that produce hair) are active, but the other 15% are dormant. In some people, these follicles shrink slightly every time they "reactivate" themselves, and in a few years they're so small they can't produce any hair at all—causing a bald patch to develop.

HOW long can hair grow?

It may seem like you always need a haircut, but hair doesn't actually grow all that fast: the average rate is a half-millimeter a day, or about half an inch every month.

A strand of hair doesn't grow forever—the hair-producing cells in the scalp are active for a few years, but switch off suddenly, causing the hair to fall out. Then they switch on again and produce a brand-new strand.

The growth rate varies among people, but the maximum length is about three feet, although there are some people who have been known to grow their hair almost to their own feet. By the way, some cultures believe in never cutting or shaving your hair, whether on the head or on the face.

WHY don't women have beards?

All people are born with the potential to grow facial hair, but in girls, female hormones suppress the growth of long hair everywhere but on the scalp. Beyond that, no one is sure why men grow beards and women don't.

WHY does hair turn grey when you get old?

As we age, the pigment cells in our hair follicles gradually die off, and the hair grows out grey or white (or even transparent!). By the way, young people can have grey hair, too, but this doesn't mean they're prematurely old—it's just a genetic trait they happened to inherit

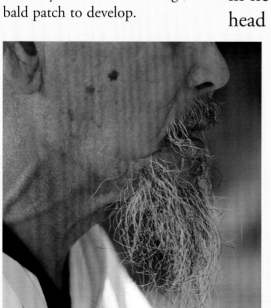

WHY do some people bite their nails?

Nail biting is what is known as a "nervous habit"—something little kids (and some adults) do to relieve stress, like hair-twisting or thumb-sucking. Most kids usually outgrow nail-biting by the time they reach elementary school, but the problem may require medical attention if they bite their nails so hard that they draw blood from their fingertips.

WHAT is a hangnail?

A hangnail isn't actually a piece of fingernail, but a small sliver of skin that separates from the cuticle (the edge of the fingernail where it meets the skin). A hangnail is usually harmless, but the pain it causes can be disproportionate to its size. It's best treated by having your mom carefully clip it off, then massage some lotion into the sore cuticle.

HOW fast do your fingernails grow?

All things considered, fingernails grow fairly slowly: a little less than an inch per year, compared to six inches per year for hair. The longer your finger, the more quickly the nail grows, so the nail on the middle finger of your hand grows the fastest and the nail on the pinky the slowest. Also—since you were about to ask—fingernails grow about four times as quickly as toenails.

Theoretically, your fingernails can grow to any size; one man in India has nails that are over five feet long! Practically, though, if you tried to grow giant fingernails, they'd break off accidentally before they even reached a couple of inches.

For this very reason, having long fingernails in ancient China was a sign of wealth and high standing, because it proved you didn't have to do any work and could pay servants to do everything for you. Chinese nobles used to have ornately carved and/or jeweled "nail sheaths" made to cover and protect their extremely long nails.

WHAT makes your knuckles crack?

It sounds like a bone popping, but that knuckle-cracking sound that drives your parents crazy is actually caused by gases that build up in the capsules of your finger joints. When you compress your finger in just the right way, these gases ooze out of the surrounding fluid and "pop" audibly into the empty joint.

WHY is it called a ring finger?

The tradition of putting an engagement or wedding ring on the third finger of the left hand (next to the pinky) dates back to antiquity. According to one theory, priests at Christian weddings would count off the Holy Trinity on a married couples' hands, landing on the ring finger. According to another theory, the ancient Egyptians believed the ring finger ran directly to a person's heart!

HOW do fingerprints work?

If you look closely at the tips of your fingers, you'll see a complex pattern of whirls and spirals, which make it easier for your hands to grip things (in the same way the treads of a tire give it a firm grip on the road). All human beings have fingerprints, but the patterns are so complex that no two are ever exactly alike. So, if you dip your finger in ink and press it on a piece of paper, you wind up with a unique "signature" by which you can be identified.

Using fingerprints for identification may seem like a modern idea, but Persia (modern Iran) was doing it way back in the 15th century. It took a while for this concept to take hold in the western world: it wasn't until 1900 or so that law-enforcement authorities in England and the United States began taking suspects' fingerprints. Today, the FBI has tens of millions of fingerprints on file, only a tiny percentage of which belong to criminals (most are collected as a simple way to identify law-abiding individuals).

WHY is it important to have an opposable thumb?

The opposable thumb—that is, a sturdy finger of the hand capable of moving inward to meet other fingers—has been essential to human evolution, since it allowed our primitive ancestors to grasp tools and weapons. Most apes and monkeys (and even some odd non-primates like koala bears and panda bears) have opposable thumbs, but only humans possess the fully flexible variety.

WHY do we have two of certain organs?

Having two copies of an organ in case one is injured or stops working is known as "redundancy," and it's an important concept in nature. That's mainly why we have two kidneys, two lungs, and two hands, feet, eyes, and ears, though there are other reasons for this duplication as well. We need two ears to pinpoint the location of a sound, for instance, as well as two feet to walk and two eyes to perceive depth.

WHAT do your kidneys do?

The main function of the kidneys is to remove harmful by-products of the digestive process from the blood, including urea (which is concentrated in urine) and ammonia—but they do other important work as well, including regulating blood pressure and maintaining the proper balance of salt in the bloodstream. Every day, your kidneys filter about 40 gallons of blood and make one or two quarts of urine, which is stored in the bladder and then excreted.

WHY is your heart on the left side of your chest?

Although people look symmetrical from the outside, they're lopsided on the inside. The heart is located on the left side of the body, along with the stomach and gall bladder, while the liver takes up more room on the right. The kidneys are arranged roughly symmetrically, but the lungs aren't: the right lung is slightly larger than the left, to make room for the heart.

Scientists have been puzzling over this jigsaw puzzle for a long time, and their best guess is that the body's internal asymmetry is required by nature, so that all of our vital organs can fit inside the smallest and most efficient space possible.

By the way, not everyone's heart is on the left side of his or her chest. Occasionally, people are born with the heart on the right side, and all the other organs flip-flopped as well. Scientists believe this "situs inversus" is caused by a specific mutation in the person's DNA.

WHAT does your liver do?

An amazingly versatile organ, the liver has three indispensable functions: to help digest food, to synthesize and store essential chemicals, and to remove harmful substances from the blood.

As part of its digestive work, the liver secretes a greenish, bitter substance called bile, which is necessary for digesting fat. This bile is stored in the nearby gall bladder, from which it's released as needed.

As the small intestine digests food, it sends the resulting chemical by-products—simple sugars, fatty acids, and amino acids (the building blocks of proteins)—to the liver, which turns them into proteins, complex sugars, and fats. The liver also harvests vitamins from the blood and stores them until they're needed by the rest of the body. Finally, the liver filters or breaks down various harmful substances from the blood, including dead or dying blood cells, alcohol, and various natural chemicals that can be poisonous in high concentrations.

HOW long is your small intestine?

Despite its name, your small intestine is much, much bigger than your large intestine: about 20 feet long if you uncoiled it from end to end, compared to only a few feet for its "large" companion. The inside of the small intestine is wrinkled in tiny folds, giving it an effective surface area of 250 square yards—enough to cover a tennis court!

WHY does your heart beat faster when you exercise?

When you run or work out, the cells of your body need more oxygen, which they use to create energy. Oxygen is carried by red blood cells, and red blood cells are pumped through the bloodstream by the heart. So when more oxygen is required by your cells, your heart pumps faster to meet the demand.

HOW many times will your heart beat in your lifetime?

The average person's heart beats about 75 times every minute—which scales out to 4,500 times an hour, 100,000 times a day, and 4 million times a year. Assuming you live to be at least 70 years old, your heart will beat a whopping three billion times!

WHAT is that beeping thing in a hospital room?

Lots of machines in hospitals make strange noises, but the device you're probably thinking of is the heart monitor, which "beeps" every time your heart beats. Unplugging the monitor won't make your heart stop, but it won't help the doctors and nurses do their jobs, either.

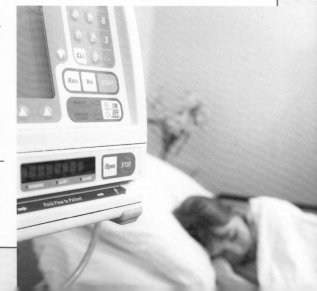

WHY do people have freckles?

Human skin contains melanin, a chemical that gives skin its characteristic color and offers protection from the sun. People with lighter-colored skin have less melanin, and so are more likely to develop freckles—tiny spots of melanin-rich cells—rather than an even tan when they're exposed to sunlight. Unlike sunburns, though, freckles are completely harmless—and lots of people think they're cute.

A close relative of the freckle is a mole—a collection of melanocytes, the cells in the skin that produce color (which is why moles are always brown). Most people have at least a few moles, usually on their arms or back. Moles are usually harmless, too, but a sudden change in a mole's size or color can be an indication of melanoma, a dangerous kind of cancer.

WHAT is a scab?

When you cut your skin, tiny cells in your blood called "platelets" rush to the site and stick together in a big, fibrous mass, plugging up the hole and preventing further bleeding. As the cut heals, this clump of platelets (and other assorted proteins) dries up and takes on a reddish-brown color, resulting in a scab. When the skin underneath is healed enough, the scab will fall off on its own. Picking a scab too early can make the scar bigger.

WHY do some injuries cause scars?

When you scratch the top layer of your skin, the cells quickly regenerate and cover it over like it was never there. However, if the scratch goes deeper to the tissue beneath, the skin manufactures collagen (a tough, stringy protein) to fill the gap. Collagen is a different color and texture from the surrounding skin, and results in a lasting scar.

WHAT causes sunburns?

Sunburns aren't caused by just any kind of sunlight—the culprit is high-energy ultraviolet light, which is just out of the visible range of the spectrum and especially prevalent in the summertime. A pigment called melanin (which gives skin its characteristic color) normally protects the skin from sunlight, but prolonged exposure to ultraviolet light is too much for the melanin to handle, and the result is a painful burn.

WHAT causes wrinkles?

As people get older, their skin cells divide more slowly, and the inner layer of their skin (called the dermis) becomes thinner and less elastic. This causes the proteins that normally hold the skin tight to loosen, and also reduces the skin's ability to retain moisture, resulting in wrinkles. By the way, prolonged exposure to the sun at an early age can dry out your skin and makes you more susceptible to wrinkles later in life.

WHAT is a rash?

A rash, which is technically known as "dermatitis," is a reddish irritation of the skin—sometimes rough, sometimes with many tiny bumps—that can be caused by anything from too-tight clothing to an allergic response to something you may have eaten or touched. Some people even get rashes from being nervous! Most rashes are harmless and easily treated with lotion, but rashes accompanied by a fever usually require a trip to the doctor.

What is the biggest organ in the human body?

When asked this question, most people would pick the lungs or the liver, or (if they thought they were really smart) the brain. But they'd be wrong: the skin is the out-and-out champion, weighing about 5 to 8 pounds in a fully grown adult, compared to only a few pounds apiece for the brain and liver.

At this point, you might be tempted to object, "but the skin isn't really an organ!" Well, that's partly true, insofar as one of the skin's non-organ-like functions is simply to protect the inside of your body. But human skin does much, much more than that: it regulates the body's temperature, conveys the sensation of touch, and excretes moisture via sweat glands, among other functions. In fact, some scientists think the skin is second in complexity only to the brain!

WHY do we have baby teeth?

When kids are small, their skulls and jawbones aren't strong enough to support a full set of adult teeth. Instead, they're born with a temporary set of 20 baby teeth, which fall out around the age of 6 or 7 and are replaced by permanent, adult teeth. This same process occurs in other mammals, but not in fish and reptiles, which lose and replace their teeth continuously throughout their lifetimes.

WHAT are fillings made of?

A few years ago, most fillings were made of amalgam (a blend of silver, tin, copper, mercury, or zinc) or just plain silver or gold. Because metal fillings can darken over time, and also because of possible long-term health issues, dentists today often use "composite" fillings, which are made of strong, durable plastic that more closely matches the color of teeth.

WHY do we have wisdom teeth?

Since millions of people need to have them removed, "wisdom teeth" sound like a pretty dumb idea. These strong, bulky teeth grow way in the back of the mouth between the ages of 15 and 25, when most people already have a pretty full set. If there's not enough room for these four extra teeth, they have to be removed by a dentist before they cause permanent damage.

If they cause so much trouble, why do folks have wisdom teeth at all? The answer is, long before dentists, prehistoric humans chewed a diet of very tough vegetables and uncooked gristle, and needed an extra set of large, flat teeth to grind down their meals. Adults lost their teeth at an early age to decay or injury, so the extra pressure caused by growing wisdom teeth pushing these new teeth forward was not a problem, as it filled in gaps where earlier teeth had fallen out.

WHY do kids need braces?

Some kids' teeth don't grow in perfectly straight all by themselves—the teeth in the upper jaw jut out over the teeth in the lower jaw, or vice-versa. By fitting you with braces, an orthodontist can make sure that all your teeth grow in evenly. This not only gives you a more attractive smile, but prevents serious dental problems later on, when you're an adult.

HOW do teeth get cavities?

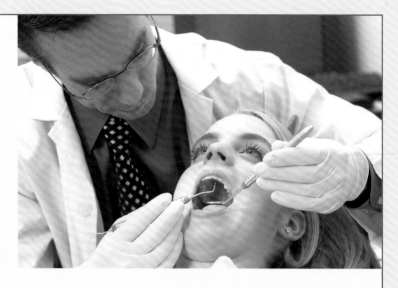

Despite what you may think, sugar by itself doesn't cause cavities—it's the bacteria inside your mouth that eat the sugar. These bacteria convert sugar and other kinds of food into a sticky substance called plaque, and this plaque contains a mild acid that slowly, over the course of months or years, eats away at the tooth's hard enamel surface, resulting in a cavity.

By itself, this wouldn't be so bad, except that teeth aren't hard enamel through and through—inside every tooth is a nerve, and surrounding this nerve is a relatively soft substance called "dentin." When a cavity reaches a certain size, the dentin is exposed to air, and the nerve of your tooth becomes susceptible to cold, heat, or pressure—resulting in a throbbing toothache. A filling solves the problem by plugging up the hole and protecting the nerve.

WHAT is toothpaste made from?

Depending on the brand, a tube of toothpaste contains all kinds of ingredients, including fluoride (which helps prevent cavities), antibacterial agents (which combat bacteria-causing plaque), baking soda, and various sweeteners and desensitizers. Some toothpastes also contain mild abrasives, which scour the enamel of your teeth and (supposedly) makes them whiter.

WHAT are teeth made of?

We need our teeth to do lots of heavy-duty chewing, so it makes sense that they're the hardest things in our bodies (and that includes our bones and fingernails!). The outer portions of teeth are made of enamel, a tough mineral the main ingredient of which is "hydroxyapatite." Inside the tooth is a slightly less rigid substance, dentin, which surrounds the sensitive nerve.

WHY don't people have tails?

Actually, people do have tails for a brief period of time—before they're born! In its first few months, a human embryo has a "tail" about one-tenth the length of its body, which is gradually absorbed into the body as the backbone takes shape (you have a remnant of this primitive tail in your "tailbone", which is the last vertebra of the spine that curves down under your backside).

A closely related question is: why don't people have fur? The reason lower mammals have thick coats of fur is to stay warm, first and foremost, but also to discourage predators and protect themselves from injury. Millions of years ago, our first human ancestors had thick pelts as well, but as they started to wear the skins of other animals they slowly lost the need, and the ability, to grow fur.

WHY do people have gills?

You may be surprised by this question: after all, everyone knows people have lungs that breathe air, not gills that filter water! But the fact is, early in its development, a human embryo develops gill-like slits on its neck that disappear further on in its development. They aren't working gills, though. Some scientists speculate that they're an evolutionary throwback to the time when all life existed in the oceans, but it may just be a quirky stage in embryonic development.

WHY do we have an appendix?

The appendix—a small tube jutting out between the large and small intestines—is a classic case of a "vestigial" organ: millions of years ago, it served some biological purpose (probably having to do with digestion), but now it's just getting a free ride. Unless it becomes infected—a condition called "appendicitis"—you wouldn't even know it was there!

WHY do men have nipples?

No one is quite sure: unlike women, men don't give birth to babies, and they certainly don't breast-feed them. The best guess is that even though male nipples don't perform any useful function, they don't do any harm either, so nature hasn't gotten around to eliminating them yet.

WHY do people have toenails?

It's easy to figure out the purpose of fingernails—since we use our hands to manipulate objects, the sensitive tips of our fingers need to be protected. We only use our feet for walking, though, so that same argument doesn't seem to apply to toenails. The most likely explanation is that toenails are evolutionary hangovers from our simian ancestors, who used their feet like extra hands to groom themselves, or to hold firmly onto branches.

WHAT are vestigial organs?

In the long, slow process of evolution, an organ that performed a useful function in one species may be of little or no benefit to its descendants, millions of years further down the line. Most of the time, this organ gradually dwindles away and completely disappears, but every once in a while, the result is a vestigial organ (like the appendix), which takes up space in the body but doesn't make an essential contribution.

Although it may seem silly—after all, why should nature allow useless organs to take up valuable real estate in our bodies?—the existence of vestigial organs is actually of great interest to science. By comparing the vestigial organs in people today to what has been discovered of their functioning ancestors in the remains of ancient creatures (or to their counterparts in still-living creatures), scientists can figure out how the human "body plan" evolved over the course of millions of years.

WHY can't people move their ears?

Although some folks can wriggle their ears, no one can move his ears around at will like a dog or a cat. The reason is that dogs, cats and other animals hunt and eat much smaller prey—and it's easier to hear a tiny mouse when you can tilt your ears in its direction. This skill wasn't as valuable for prehistoric humans, which is why we haven't evolved moveable ears.

WHAT is the difference between corn and maize?

"Maize" and "corn" both refer to the same thing, a tall, seed-producing plant. (The word "corn" comes from the ancient word "grn," which is also the root of "grain," while "maize" is an old Indian word meaning "source of life.") As to why maize is speckled while corn is yellow, that's just a regional variation—they're still basically the same plant.

WHAT is the difference between an onion and a scallion?

What we call a scallion is the green, leafy portion of the onion plant, while the onion itself is the root. Generally, scallions are smaller and milder than onions. They're often used instead of chives, which is a very thin oniony-tasting grass.

WHAT is the difference between yams and sweet potatoes?

They may look and taste alike, but yams and sweet potatoes are entirely different vegetables. Yams grow in tropical climates (sometimes to giant sizes!) and are rarely cultivated in the U.S. The smaller sweet potato is grown on these shores, and is closely related to the morning-glory flower. Two things yams and sweet potatoes do have in common, though, is their high proportion of starch and their sweet taste.

WHAT is the difference between green and purple grapes?

There are all different colors of grapes, ranging from green to red to purple to black. In the U.S., one of the most popular varieties is the green California Thompson, a large, sweet, seedless grape that kids like to eat as a snack. These grapes probably wouldn't be considered "real" grapes in most other parts of the world, where the tart, seeded, purple variety is preferred.

Just as there are green and purple grapes, there are green and purple juices made from grapes. Although purple grape juice makes a nasty stain when you spill it on the carpet, doctors have discovered that it's an extremely healthy beverage (just as moderate amounts of red wine, which is basically fermented grape juice with alcohol, is healthy for adults). The reason is that purple grape juice contains substances called "flavonoids" that help fight certain types of disease.

WHAT is the difference between fruits and vegetables?

In the language of botanists (scientists who study plants), fruits are defined fairly narrowly: they are the ripened, seed-bearing ovaries of flowers. The purpose of a fruit is to drop onto the ground (or be carried away by people or another fruit-eating creature), so the seed can find fertile soil and grow a new fruit plant. Grains and most nuts are all kinds of fruits by this definition.

By contrast, what botanists call vegetables comprise a grab bag of seedless edibles, including leaves, stems, and flowers. Tubers, which include potatoes, carrots, beets, and radishes, are classified as root vegetables, but peas and beans are a branch of the fruit family called legumes.

If all this sounds confusing, you're not alone: many food experts differ about the exact dividing line between fruits and vegetables. The tomato is a classic source of argument: long considered a vegetable, it's technically a fruit (at least according to the scientific description), as are green peppers, avocados, and cucumbers.

WHAT is the difference between walnuts and pecans?

There's a good reason walnuts and pecans look alike: the trees these nuts grow on are closely related (although the pecan tree is more closely related to the tree that produces hickory nuts). Pecans are more delicate in both shape and taste, while walnuts are broader and bumpier and make for a healthier snack, since they have a much lower fat content than pecans.

WHAT is the difference between bananas and plantains?

Mainly this: you can't eat a raw plantain. Bananas ripen quickly and naturally from their "green" state, as the starch in the fruit turns into sugar. Plantains, on the other hand, ripen much more slowly, which is why they need to be cooked (usually in South American dishes) before they're eaten.

WHAT is the difference between waffles and pancakes?

It's all a matter of presentation. The ingredients in pancake and waffle batter are pretty much the same, consisting of flour, sugar, eggs, milk, and leavening. Pancakes, though, are fried flat in a pan, while waffles are cooked both sides at a time in a specially designed waffle iron, which gives them their bumpy texture.

WHAT makes lemons sour?

Like all members of the citrus family—including limes and oranges—lemons derive their sour taste from citric acid. By the way, citric acid isn't only produced by fruits; it's also manufactured by our cells as an essential component of human metabolism.

WHY are unripe fruits green?

When a fruit ripens, it gradually replaces its chlorophyll, the chemical that makes leaves (and unripe oranges and bananas) green, with other chemicals that turn the fruit orange, yellow, or red. These chemicals also convert starch (which makes unripe fruit taste bitter) into sugar (which makes it taste sweet). The point is to make the fruit edible, so animals will eat it and scatter it seeds.

WHY does bruised fruit turn brown?

The peel of an apple or banana protects the delicate pulp underneath. When the fruit's insides are exposed to air, the same chemical responsible for its tangy flavor—citric acid—becomes oxidized and turns brown. (Oxidation, by the way, is the same process that causes metal to rust.)

WHAT is the oldest fruit?

It's hard to know for sure what people ate or drank thousands of years ago, but based on references in the bible and other ancient sources, it's clear that two fruits vie for historical supremacy: dates and grapes.

Dates, which have been cultivated for at least five thousand years, are small, dark fruits that grow on a tree called the date palm, native to Africa and the Middle East. When fresh, the fruit of the date is very sweet, and becomes even sweeter when the date is dried (the way it's often eaten).

While dates were (and are) mostly eaten as food, the primary purpose of grapes has been to ferment wine, the beverage of choice of ancient civilizations (and some modern ones as well). Thousands of years ago, grapes were cultivated by the countries of the Mediterranean, but today they can be found all over the world.

WHY don't bananas have seeds?

Actually, bananas do have seeds—they're just so tiny that most people don't notice them. Banana seeds are embedded inside the tasty fruit, and look like tiny black dots. Unlike other seeds—like those inside an apple or watermelon—banana seeds are soft, harmless and easily digested.

If it seems like some pieces of fruit are all seeds, there's a good reason: fruits can harbor hundreds of seeds. This is nature's way of ensuring that some will drop onto the ground and produce new plants. By the way, despite their name, seedless watermelon and seedless grapes aren't entirely seedless: they're filled with immature (but edible) soft white seeds, and, occasionally, some hard seeds.

WHY do peaches have fuzz?

Peaches have fuzz for the same reason people have hair on their arms and legs—it helps keep away insects (and if you're a peach, it also helps keep away harmful fungi like mold and mildew). Granted, a thin layer of fuzz isn't as secure as the thick shell of a coconut, but that's usually all the protection a peach needs.

WHAT is a tangelo?

A tangelo is a cross between a tangerine and a buffalo. Just kidding! Actually, a tangelo is a cross between a tangerine (a close relative of an orange) and a grapefruit. (Some varieties of tangelo, grown in Florida, are hybrids of oranges and grapefruits). Tangelos are larger and contain less seeds than ordinary tangerines, but have the same delicious flavor.

WHAT is rhubarb?

Rhubarb isn't really a fruit at all, but a low-growing, leafy plant. The stems of rhubarb are thick and turn red when they are ripe, and it is this part of the plant that is sliced up and cooked. Rhubarb stems are very tart and tangy and are never eaten raw (in fact, its large, umbrella-like leaves are poisonous) but the stems are very good—and good for you—when cooked with lots of sugar. Rhubarb goes very well with strawberries, which is how it is most often eaten—cooked together in a delicious pie.

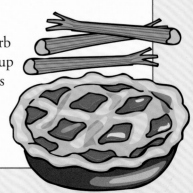

HOW does popcorn pop?

The inside of a popcorn kernel is filled with lots of starch and a little water. When the kernel is heated, the water and starch turn into vapor, which explodes out of the seed's hard shell as a fluffy mass. In case you're wondering why you can't pop, say, a walnut, a seed has to have exactly the right size and ingredients to accomplish this trick.

WHY do donuts have holes?

If you just plop a big ball of dough into a frying pan, odds are it won't cook evenly—the outside will be nice and crisp, but the center will be gooey and slightly underdone. Punching a hole in the middle of a donut (or bagel) allows you to cook it more quickly and evenly. By the way, the donut was invented 200 years ago by the Pennsylvania Dutch, who called it an olykoek, or "oily cake."

HOW are potato chips made?

Classic, everyday potato chips are made by frying, drying, and salting ultrathin slices of potato (some companies also make more healthful chips that are baked or use less oil and salt).

As with most junk foods, potato chips have an interesting history. This snack was invented by accident in 1853, when a chef in a New York restaurant had trouble making french fries (thick-sliced slivers of potato fried in oil). As the story goes, a particularly troublesome guest kept sending back his order of fries, saying they weren't done right. The chef retaliated by cutting the potatoes so thin, and frying them so crisp, that they couldn't be eaten with a fork—and to his astonishment, the guest liked them!

Potato chips became a national obsession in the 1920's, thanks to two important developments: first, the invention of the mechanical potato peeler eliminated the laborious process of thin-slicing potatoes by hand, and second, a traveling salesman named Herman Lay peddled his chips out of the trunk of his car, establishing a brand name that has survived to the present day.

POTATO CHIPS

HOW was the hot dog invented?

If you don't count the bun, the hot dog has a long and illustrious history. Sausages (ground pork and/or beef rolled up in a tube) date from the first millennium B.C., and are mentioned in Homer's *Odyssey*. This dish was especially popular in medieval Germany, where the town of Frankfurt-am-Main takes credit for the invention of the "frankfurter" in the late 15th century. However, the city of Vienna disputes this claim, saying it originated the "wiener" ("Wien" is what Vienna is called in German).

The bun was a relatively late innovation in hot-dog history. The classic frankfurter-in-a-bun with sauerkraut was first sold out of a single pushcart in New York City in the 1860's, and then from a store in Coney Island starting in 1871. This cheap gourmet item became a national fad thanks to Chicago Exposition 1893, when German immigrants with pushcarts sold thousands of hot dogs (complete with buns) to curious tourists.

WHY are pizzas round?

One of the earliest references to round pizza comes from the 3rd century B.C.! Although pizza has had many shapes throughout history—square, elliptical, etc.—round has become the standard, probably because (1) it's easy (and entertaining) to spin a big piece of dough into the shape of a circle, and (2) a round pizza can easily be sliced into equal quarters or eighths.

WHY does soda fizz when you shake it?

Soda is "bubbled" in the factory by injecting it with carbon dioxide (a harmless gas) at high pressure, then sealing it inside a can. Usually, the carbon dioxide remains dissolved in the soda, unless you happen to shake the can, which causes some of the gas to escape and rise to the top. When you pop the lid, the carbon dioxide spurts out, getting you (and anyone else in the vicinity) soaking wet.

WHY are raspberry-flavored fast foods blue?

Lots of fruits and berries are colored red—strawberries, cherries, and raspberries, to name just three. Food companies have been using strawberry and cherry flavors for years, so when they introduced raspberry drinks and ices, all the "red" colors were taken—which is why they came up with the idea of using bright blue.

WHY does milk go sour?

A gallon of milk, even when it's brand new, contains a certain amount of harmless microbes called lactobacilli. In the course of a week or so, these bacteria multiply, turning the milk's lactose (also known as "milk sugar") into lactic acid. When the lactic acid reaches a critical level, the milk goes sour and has to be thrown out.

WHY does eating ice cream give you a headache?

If you eat ice cream too quickly, it can cause your palate—the roof of your mouth—to signal your body to send less blood up to your brain. The blood vessels in the brain compensate for this by swelling slightly, which causes the sudden headache. But there's no need to worry—even a bad ice-cream headache will only last for a couple of minutes.

WHAT is pasteurization?

Pasteurization is named after the scientist Louis Pasteur, who discovered that the microbes that cause milk to turn sour can be killed by exposing them to heat.

Milk is pasteurized in two ways: by heating it in a big vat to a temperature of 145 degrees Fahrenheit for 30 minutes, or by heating it to 160 degrees for 30 seconds. Not surprisingly, the second technique is more popular, since it saves manufacturers time and gets the milk to grocery shelves faster.

Another word you often see on milk cartons is "homogenized." If you store a gallon of un-homogenized milk in the refrigerator, its fat will gradually separate out, resulting in a layer of cream floating atop a pool of skim milk. Homogenization is the process by which the fat globules are reduced to a smaller size, which lets them remain suspended in the milk for a much longer duration.

HOW was ice cream invented?

Ice cream has surprisingly ancient origins: there's evidence of a milk-and-ice concoction dating all the way back to 400 BC. Modern ice cream first appeared in the mid-nineteenth century, when the the hand-cranked freezer was invented. However, the dish didn't really take off until a century later, when mechanical refrigeration allowed stores to sell ice-cream year-round.

WHY do babies need milk?

A newborn baby can't eat solid food, so it has to get all its nutrition in liquid form. Mammals have evolved milk, a tasty mixture of fats, proteins, and carbohydrates, to fill this need. In prehistoric times, human babies would live on mother's milk for a few years, but nowadays most babies breast-feed for a year or less before moving on to solid food.

WHY is it hard to drink a milkshake through a straw?

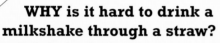

A milkshake has high viscosity—meaning it's very thick and doesn't flow easily (plain water, by contrast, has low viscosity). A drinking straw works via suction, and suction is more effective (and less painful!) with easy-flowing, low-viscosity liquids.

HOW is cheese made?

All cheese starts out as the most unappetizing substance on earth—sour milk. A special kind of bacteria and a substance called rennet (which comes from the stomachs of baby cows) are added to the milk, whereupon the mixture congeals into white, spongy bits called "curds."

In this early stage, cheese hardly smells at all. The stinky part starts when the bacteria get to work and "ferment" the curds by breaking down fats and proteins. This produces new chemicals, many of which are rather pungent (though that never scares away a true cheese lover).

In Swiss cheese, a special kind of bacteria produces big bubbles of carbon dioxide during the fermentation process. These bubbles are trapped in the cheese as it hardens, creating the familiar "holes."

WHAT is yogurt?

Originally eaten in the eastern European country of Bulgaria, yogurt is milk or cream that has been fermented by a special kind of bacteria, causing it to thicken and take on a tangy, slightly acidic flavor. Because plain yogurt can seem too sour (especially to kids), most yogurt sold in the U.S. is sweetened and either artificially flavored or mixed with fruit.

WHY is it called a "barbecue?"

No one knows for sure, but the most likely birthplace of the "barbecue" is the island of Hispaniola (home to Haiti and the Dominican Republic). Back in the 17th century, European settlers discovered natives cooking food on top of a frame of wooden sticks, which they called a "barbicoa." (The first reference to "barbecue" dates from 1733, in the journal of a citizen of Salem, Massachusetts.)

Most folks have accepted "barbicoa" as the most likely origin of "barbecue," but there are a couple of other theories (which you can judge for yourself!). Some trace the origin of this word to the French phrase "barbe a queue," meaning "from head to tail" (such as pig would appear on a spit). An even less likely story is that a pub advertised its "bar-beer-cue" pig in the late 18th century (meaning customers could drink beer, play pool, and eat a roasted pig at the same time!).

HOW did the sundae get its name?

So many towns claim to have invented the sundae that you could spend a month of Sundays trying to get the story straight. The most likely tale is that the sundae originated in Evanston, Illinois, where there was an ice-cream store that sold the sweet concoction on, you guessed it, Sundays. A local minister complained (saying kids should go to church on Sundays, not eat ice cream), so the store changed the spelling to "sundae."

WHY is a big sandwich called a hero?

The most likely source of the word "hero" is the popular Greek "gyro"—slices of roasted, spiced lamb wrapped in pita bread. Since Italy is very close to Greece, and heros were first served in Italian-American restaurants, this is one possible explanation. If you think about it, an Italian interpretation of a gyro could indeed turn out to be a meatball Parmigiana sub!

HOW did toll-house cookies get their name?

Toll-house cookies were invented in the 1930's by Ruth Wakefield, who ran a tourist lodge in Massachusetts called the Toll House Inn. One day, Wakefield was making a batch of cookies from an old colonial recipe, and decided to add a chopped-up chocolate bar to perk things up. The candy company later printed the recipe on its wrappers, and the rest is chocolate-chip history.

WHY don't egg creams have eggs or cream?

The egg cream, which originated in New York, is a tasty concoction of chocolate syrup, milk, and seltzer water. The original recipe called for a special syrup that was made with eggs, and cream was sometimes added to the milk for extra richness and flavor. This hasn't been the case for decades, but the name "egg cream" has stuck.

HOW did lollipops get their name?

According to one story, an American candy baron named his new treat after a popular racehorse, Lolly Pop. According to another story, the name lollipop originated in northern England, where "lolly" is another word for "tongue." Whatever the explanation, just be thankful: earlier this century, the lollipop was almost called "the born sucker."

WHY are French fries French?

They aren't. French fries got their name because cutting potatoes into small, narrow strips is called "frenching"—so what was originally called "frenched fries" soon turned into "French fries."

How was the hamburger invented?

As with all successful ideas, many people have claimed credit for inventing the hamburger. The likeliest story is that the first hamburger appeared sometime in the mid-1880's, when a cook in Ohio ran out of ground pork for his sandwiches and used ground beef instead. In the 1920's and 1930's, the hamburger became even more popular when the comic strip "Thimble Theatre" (home of Popeye the Sailor Man) introduced the hamburger-hungry scoundrel Wimpy.

The origin of another ground-beef concoction—the Sloppy Joe—is buried in history. Some people say this sandwich was invented in a Cuban bar called Sloppy Joe's (the American author Ernest Hemingway was a famous customer there). Others insist the name "Joe" is just a way of saying "anyone"—as in the expression "average Joe"—and it's no mystery how a dish this sloppy got its name.

WHY does food spoil?

As food ages, it becomes more susceptible to the microscopic organisms (mostly bacteria and fungi) that constantly lurk unnoticed in our homes. Even fresh food contains a small amount of microbes, but spoilage sets in when the bacteria or fungi multiply past a certain point and alter the food's chemical composition. You can see this process in action as a small spot of green mold grows, and spreads, on an old slice of bread.

In the old days, people preserved food by salting it, for two reasons: salt absorbs moisture, which bacteria and fungi need to grow, and salt itself has antibacterial properties. Nowadays, we preserve food mainly via freezing and refrigeration, but before electricity was discovered many heavily salted foods (especially meats and fish) could remain edible for weeks or months.

WHAT is freeze-drying?

Food can't spoil in the absence of water, since the bacteria and fungi that cause spoiling depend on a ready supply of H2O. Freeze-drying is a method of preserving food by removing all its water, converting it into a dry, powdery substance that can be stored safely for years (until you "just add water" and sit down for a meal). As an added bonus, freeze-dried food is about 90% lighter than its normal counterpart, so it's popular with astronauts and mountaineers who can afford to carry only a certain amount of weight.

WHY does meat need to be cooked?

Back in prehistoric times, cave-men cooked meat for two reasons: to warm up a frozen slab of woolly mammoth, or (more often) to make the meat tastier and easier to digest. Today, we cook meat because it tastes good, but also because the heating process kills germs. (By the way, raw meat is a popular delicacy at some fancy restaurants!)

WHY are some foods exposed to radiation?

Not all radiation is bad: although large doses can be dangerous to humans, small doses kill the bacteria that cause food to spoil. In the past few years, increasing numbers of foods (including fruit, beef, and chicken) has been irradiated in this way, though many people mistakenly believe that this makes the food "radioactive" and unsafe to eat.

WHAT is a pickle?

Pickles (cucumbers soaked for days in brine, or salty water, and then stored in vinegar) are a holdover from the days when food was regularly "pickled" as a means of preservation (since salt kills the germs that cause food to spoil). Although cucumbers are most popularly pickled today, you can also find such delicacies as pickled beets or pickled pig's feet.

WHAT is jerky?

Jerky is meat that has been smoked, salted, seasoned, and dried, resulting in a tough, chewy snack that lasts pretty much forever (which is why jerky was popular in the days before refrigeration). By the way, jerky doesn't have to be made from beef; some folks also enjoy elk, buffalo, or even turkey jerky.

WHY does bacon sizzle?

One reason bacon is so tasty is because it's salted and smoked to preserve it, but the other reason is because it contains a lot of fat. When you fry a slice of bacon, this fat melts and boils and spatters on the hot metal of the pan. The same thing happens with hamburgers, sausages, and many other fatty foods.

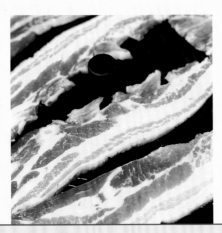

HOW does a refrigerator work?

Like an air conditioner, a refrigerator basically works by removing heat from its inside and discharging it to the air outside. This trick is accomplished by way of a mechanical device called a compressor, which squeezes a liquid refrigerant and pumps it into an evaporator. As the cold, compressed refrigerant evaporates, it becomes even colder, and thus absorbs heat from inside the refrigerator.

Until they were phased out in 1996, most refrigerators, freezers and air conditioners were cooled with chemicals called chlorofluorocarbons, or CFCs. Although CFCs are extremely efficient (and abundant) refrigerants, it was discovered that they had one very bad side effect: when discharged into the atmosphere, they destroy the ozone layer, which protects us from the sun's ultraviolet radiation. Older refrigerators still have CFCs, but newer models are designed to use less destructive refrigerants.

WHY were spices once more valuable than gold?

In medieval times, there were few spices native to Europe, so "exotic" seasonings like pepper and ginger had to be imported in long, slow caravans from India, China, and the Middle East. As a result, the price of spices skyrocketed—a serf could buy his freedom with a pound of peppercorns—and the demand for new supplies fueled the age of discovery. The reason Columbus set sail in 1492 was to find a sea route to India and its valuable spices.

Why was spice in such great demand? In medieval times, people often ate spoiled meat or vegetables, and needed strong spices to cover the unpleasant taste. Spices were also used in medications, wines, and perfumes, and as an emblem of wealth: the lord of a manor could vastly improve his social standing if he had pepper to spare for his guests!

WHAT is the most expensive spice?

In order to get a pound of saffron (a spice used mostly in Indian food), you have to process anywhere from 70,000 to 250,000 saffron flowers, making it the world's most expensive seasoning by far. Luckily, because saffron is so strong, only a teensy bit is needed to flavor a dish.

WHAT is cinnamon?

If you've ever dipped a hard stick of cinnamon into your hot chocolate, you know it's not quite like other spices. Cinnamon is actually the inner bark of a tropical tree, which is harvested during the rainy season, when it's more easy to strip off. Then, it's either curled into a stick and dried or ground up into the more familiar cinnamon powder.

WHY does pepper make you sneeze?

Pepper contains a chemical called piperine, which irritates the membranes inside your nose. When you breathe in ground pepper, the piperine stimulates the nerve cells in the mucous membranes, and the result is a big sneeze as your nose tries to clear out the offending substance as quickly as possible.

WHAT is the hottest pepper?

Believe it or not, there's actually a scientific measure of red-pepper spiciness—the "Scoville Scale." According to this system, the hottest red pepper in the world is the Red Savina habanero, which measures anywhere from 350,000 to 570,000—compared with "only" 5,000 or so for a plain jalapeño pepper.

WHAT is vanilla?

Few things in the world smell as good as a bottle of pure, natural vanilla extract—but it's a long journey from the vanilla bean to your dish of ice cream or container of yogurt.

Not really a bean at all, the vanilla bean is the fruit of a species of orchid (a type of colorful flower). This orchid blossoms once a year, for only a few hours, when its beans have to be harvested. For the next three to six months, the beans are heated in the sun by day and wrapped in damp blankets at night, which causes them to shrink and ferment, producing the familiar vanilla flavor.

As you might guess, not all companies are willing to invest the time and effort needed to produce natural vanilla—so they've developed a quicker, cheaper process for creating imitation vanilla, which doesn't taste nearly as good!

WHY is Asian and Mexican food so spicy?

As a general rule, the cuisines of nations in tropical climates—Thailand, India, Mexico—use hotter spices than the dishes of colder northern climates (like Europe and North America). There are two theories why this might be the case: first, eating hot foods makes you sweat, and sweating helps cool the body down. Second, since food spoils more rapidly in tropical climates, it's possible that extra-hot spices became popular for their antimicrobial (germ-killing) properties.

WHAT is garlic?

A first cousin of onions and leeks, garlic grows underground in small bulbs subdivided into smaller cloves (the same way the fruit of an orange is separated into sections). Garlic has been used for thousands of years, and not only to flavor food: it's widely believed (even by some scientists) that garlic can help prevent or cure certain diseases.

HOW is chocolate made?

The main ingredient of chocolate is the cacao bean, which grows in tropical climates. After they're harvested, the cacoa beans are crushed and processed to form cocoa butter, which is then mixed with sugar and milk-based products to create the familiar chocolate bar.

Because it doesn't have any cocoa in it, what we call "white chocolate" isn't technically chocolate at all. Real chocolate contains cocoa powder, which gives it its characteristic brown color. White chocolate, though, only uses cocoa butter, which is extracted from cocoa powder. The other main ingredients of white chocolate are milk and sugar, which give it its white (or very light tan) color.

By the way, the word "chocolate" comes from the Aztec word "xocoatl." The Aztecs used to drink a bitter, foaming beverage (very different from a milkshake!) brewed from cacao beans and flavored with vanilla.

WHAT is licorice?

Most kids know licorice from its use in candy, but ancient civilizations cultivated this plant for medicinal purposes (and some people still take licorice pills today). The licorice flavor comes from the root of the shrub, which contains the weirdly named chemical "glycyrrhizin" (a combination of the Greek words for "sweet" and "root").

HOW is root beer made?

There's no hard-and-fast recipe for root beer. In the old days, this concoction was made from a variety of spices—including juniper, wintergreen, and sarsaparilla—and sold as a medicine. Today, all root beers are based on sassafras root, but the other ingredients (the ones listed above, as well as birch bark, ginger, and even dandelion!) vary with the individual brand.

WHY is some lemonade pink?

Plain yellow lemonade is made from plain yellow lemons, so you might think plain pink lemonade is made from plain pink lemons. Well, you'd be wrong: what makes pink lemonade pink is a small amount of added cherry or pomegranate juice.

WHAT was the first candy bar?

Although bars of bittersweet chocolate were sold in the late 19th century, most people date the history of the modern candy bar from 1894, when Milton Hershey created the famous treat bearing his name. The Hershey Bar was made from milk chocolate (a sweeter, softer mixture of chocolate and evaporated milk), which was invented a few years before by another famous candy baron, Henry Nestle.

The Hershey Bar (and other candy bars that quickly followed) didn't really hit the big time until World War I. American soldiers stationed overseas got used to eating blocks of chocolate provided by the U.S. government, and when they returned home, they brought their taste for candy with them. The 1920's were the golden age of candy bars, with the introduction of Milky Way, Baby Ruth, and Mounds bars, as well as assorted non-bar treats like Chuckles and Milk Duds.

WHAT is rock candy?

The simplest kind of candy there is, rock candy is concentrated sugar syrup that has slowly been allowed to evaporate over the course of days or weeks, forming giant, clear, sharp-edged crystals of sugar. In other words, rock candy is as close as you can get to eating plain sugar right out of the jar!

WHAT is cotton candy?

Cotton candy is made by melting powdered sugar and spinning it in a special machine at high speeds, which forces the liquid sugar through tiny holes and into thousands of long "threads." These threads cling together naturally to create the cottony confection, and dissolve into a gooey mass of flavored sugar when they reach your mouth.

WHAT makes chewing gum chewy?

In the old days, the main ingredient of chewing gum—a rubbery substance called "chicle"—came from Sapodilla trees (there's evidence that the Mayans of central America chewed chicle a thousand years ago!). Today, though, the chewy part of most chewing gum is synthesized from less fun-sounding chemicals like styrene butadiene and polyethylene.

WHAT is broccoli?

Broccoli has a long and venerable history; it's been found on menus from ancient Rome. A dark green, leafy plant, broccoli is closely related to cabbage, cauliflower, and Brussels sprouts. Mostly its top, called the "flowerhead," is what is eaten, but the stems can be eaten too as long as they are well-peeled. Broccoli is good crunchy and raw, or steamed and buttery.

HOW do carrots help you see in the dark?

Carrots are rich in the chemical beta carotene, also known as vitamin A—and a lack of vitamin A impairs your ability to see in the dark. While it's unlikely that eating carrots will significantly improve your vision (since the human body derives its vitamin A from various foods), it may help to preserve your night vision well into old age.

WHY does celery have veins?

You've probably performed that classic school experiment: dipping celery into a beaker of red or blue dye and watching as the color travels to the top. The reason a stalk of celery (the stem of a celery plant) has such tough, stringy veins is because that's the way the plant transports water from the soil to its flowers.

WHY is it important to eat your vegetables?

Other than the fact that it's not healthy just to eat cheeseburgers and pizza all the time, vegetables are important because they provide essential vitamins and minerals. For example, green vegetables like broccoli are rich in vitamin A, and leafy veggies like spinach are a good source of vitamin E. Vegetables are also a handy source of calcium (which makes your bones strong) and iron (which helps your blood carry more oxygen).

Besides vitamins and minerals, vegetables (supplemented by fruits and grains) can provide sufficient protein, fats, and carbohydrates for a healthy diet. There are several different kinds of vegetarians—as they're called—who don't eat beef, pork, or chicken. Ovo-vegetarians eat eggs in addition to plant foods; lacto-ovo-vegetarians eat milk products and eggs; lacto-vegetarians eat milk products but no eggs; and "vegans" stick exclusively to a diet of fruits, grains, and vegetables.

WHY do potatoes need to be cooked?

Unlike other vegetables that grow underground—such as carrots and radishes—potatoes need to be cooked because they're loaded with starch, a stiff, crunchy substance that's extremely nutritious, but hard to digest. When you cook a potato—whether by boiling, baking, or frying—the starch is "gelatinized," meaning it absorbs enough water for it to be safely eaten.

Oddly enough for such a versatile vegetable, it took centuries before the potato was widely accepted in Europe (where it was introduced by Spanish conquistadors returning from the New World). Possibly because of its "pagan" origins, the potato was regarded as dirty and unwholesome, until the German ruler Frederick the Great persuaded his subjects to plant potato crops in the mid-18th century.

WHY can't people eat grass?

For the same reason cows can't eat hamburgers: we're simply not adapted to a grass diet. Grass is a tough and fibrous plant, which is why a cow needs four stomachs to digest it. Since humans only have one stomach, we have to settle for the occasional green vegetable, and leave the grass on the lawn where it belongs.

WHAT is an artichoke?

This bizarre vegetable—which looks like something from a science-fiction movie—is the flowerbud of a type of thistle plant. After it's cooked, you eat it by pulling away petals and scraping off the tasty meat at their base. The "choke" parts of an artichoke are the thistly stamens deep inside, which you must scrape off to get to the delicious bottom underneath.

WHY does slicing onions make you cry?

When you cut an onion in half, a complicated chemical reaction takes place: some of the proteins inside the onion's cells react with air to form a mild (but harmless) amount of sulfuric acid, which irritates your eyes and causes them to tear up. Putting onions in the refrigerator before you slice them will reduce the amount of escaping acid.

WHY do we eat cake on birthdays?

Birthday cakes have been around almost as long as people have. The ancient Romans used to celebrate birthdays with elaborate cakes of wheat and honey. In medieval Germany, kids ate small cakes shaped like the Baby Jesus, while in England birthday pastries were baked with small gifts (coins, buttons or rings) inside. The modern, circular birthday cake, complete with candles, first became popular about 200 years ago.

By the way, the song "Happy Birthday to You" was written in 1868 by two sisters, Mildred and Patty Hill, and is still under copyright—meaning the Hills' heirs have to be paid every time it's used for commercial purposes. That's why, when you see a movie or TV show with a birthday party, the guests usually sing a different song, since "Happy Birthday" costs the producers money!

WHY does skin form on chocolate pudding?

If you're like most kids, you peel off and throw away that yucky skin that forms on top of a bowl of chocolate pudding. This skin is mostly made of fat, which rises to the top of puddings and soups (the exact same thing happens with home-made chicken soup!) By the way, you can keep this skin from forming by covering the top of your freshly made pudding with plastic wrap.

HOW does jello jell?

Jello—or gelatin, to use the scientific term—is a form of the protein collagen, which holds cells together. When it's used in food, gelatin forms microscopic structures that trap water, which gives jello its bouncy shape and texture. What makes jello fun to eat is that the gelatin "melts" in your mouth, which produces more flavor than if you just drank an unjelled jello shake.

WHAT was the first breakfast cereal?

Believe it or not, until the middle of the 19th century, most adults in the U.S. would start their day with a nice slab of chicken or pork. That all changed in 1863, when a breakfast cereal called "Granula"—tough bran nuggets that had to be soaked in water overnight to be edible—was sold in stores. Like the popular cereal that followed a couple of years later—Grape-Nuts, which is still sold today—Granula was part of a "healthy breakfast" craze that swept the nation.

These first, sugarless cereals were aimed at health-conscious adults; it wasn't until the 1950's that food companies started to pay attention to kids, by adding lots of sugar and putting small prizes in cereal boxes to drive sales. All three of the very first breakfast cereals for kids—Rice Krispies, Frosted Flakes, and Sugar Smacks—are still sold in stores today.

WHAT is oatmeal?

This breakfast cereal is nothing more than cooked oat grains. Raw oats are rolled flat into flakes, to crack the hulls or outer skin of the grain. To cook the flakes, you boil them until they are soft. Nowadays most oatmeals are "pre-cooked" and flavored, so all you need to do is add hot water.

WHY does bread need yeast?

Besides giving bread some of its flavor, yeast—tiny, one-celled microbes—makes it fluffy as well. Yeast cells multiply in dough, creating carbon dioxide, which bubbles out and "lifts" the bread. Matzoh, which is eaten during the Jewish holiday of Passover, is flat and crisp because it's baked without any yeast.

WHY do pies have holes in the crust?

When you bake a fruit pie, the filling gets much hotter than the crust, because the moisture in the fruit evaporates into steam. Cutting "vent holes" into the crust allows the steam to escape, which keeps the pie from exploding in the oven. Putting the pie out onto the windowsill to cool is completely optional!

WHAT does "tutti-frutti" mean?

Tutti-frutti isn't a nonsense word—it's Italian for "all fruits," and was first used in the early 19th century to describe a pastry containing various kinds of chopped fruits. Today, the name "tutti-frutti" is used for ice cream, candy, or even toothpaste that contains a mix of different fruit flavors.

WHY are people allergic to cats or dogs?

Cats and dogs both shed "dander," small scales of dead skin that float in the air. (If that word sounds familiar, it's because it's related to "dandruff.") Some folks have an inborn sensitivity to dander, which is why they start sneezing and itching every time they come near your pet, and some are even allergic to their saliva.

WHY is carbon monoxide dangerous?

Carbon monoxide packs a one-two punch: first, it's odorless and colorless, so you can't see or smell it. And second, it prevents hemoglobin (the molecule in red blood cells that carries oxygen) from doing its job. In high concentrations, carbon monoxide molecules stick to the part of hemoglobin that normally carries oxygen, suffocating you slowly from the inside.

WHY are some kids allergic to peanuts?

Sometimes a specific food will cause the body to go into "anaphylactic shock"—which includes swelling of the vocal cords (so the victim can't breathe) and a sudden drop in blood pressure. It's not clear why some kids are allergic to peanuts while others aren't, but these allergies can be triggered by small amounts of peanuts—often in foods that aren't supposed to have them in the first place!

WHY are some pills bigger than others?

Some medicines (like aspirin) are only effective in large doses, while others (like anti-allergy medications) work in almost microscopic amounts. That's also why some pills need to be taken two at a time, because one pill would be far too big to swallow.

WHAT is dust made of ?

You may not want to know the answer to this one. Dust can be composed of lots of different things, but the most common are dead skin cells (either from people or pets), loose fibers from clothes, dead leaves, and tiny pieces of flies, roaches, spiders, and other creepy insects.

Of course, depending on where you live, these reliable components of dust may be supplemented by other substances. For example, homes located near factories often accumulate a fair amount of soot and ash, while folks who live in more rural areas may find themselves dusting away particles of pollen, topsoil (the dry surface of soil that tends to blow away in the wind), or dry particles from hay or wheat "chaff."

WHY does caffeine keep you awake?

Caffeine—which is found in many drinks, from coffee to cola—binds to the part of your brain that normally responds to adenosine, a chemical that slows down nerve activity and makes you drowsy. It also causes your body to secrete adrenaline, a hormone that keeps you alert. The combination of adrenaline and lack of adenosine is what makes you feel so jumpy and restless.

WHAT is the most toxic poison?

The word "poison" covers a lot of territory, including man-made chemicals, biological substances created by bacteria, and elements like plutonium and arsenic. Of all these, the most dangerous may be the botulism toxin created by a species of bacteria: a few billionths of an ounce is enough to kill a full-grown person!

WHY is iodine added to salt?

A lack of iodine (an essential element that's found in only a few foods, like seaweed and strawberries) causes a number of diseases, many of them involving the thyroid gland in the throat. In 1924, the U.S. government encouraged companies to add a small amount of iodine to table salt, a program that has virtually wiped out these diseases in this country. Just as iodine is added to salt, fluorine is added to water, because small doses of this element—which is poisonous in large amounts—can help prevent tooth decay in children. Since 1945, traces of fluorine have been added to public water supplies in the U.S., though not without controversy. Some people believe fluorine causes more health problems than it solves, but they haven't produced much evidence for their case.

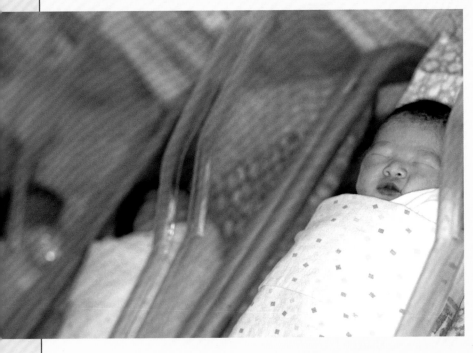

HOW many babies are born each day?

A whopping 400,000 babies are born every day, more than half of them in the world's fastest-growing countries, India and China. In case you were wondering, the number of people who die each day is less than half that, about 150,000. Do the math, and you can see that this means the world's population increases by one million people every four days, or close to one hundred million people a year.

WHY do people have belly buttons?

When a baby is in the womb, it is fed by an umbilical cord attached to its stomach that carries oxygen and nutrients from its mom's bloodstream. After the baby is born, the doctor ties off and cuts the umbilical cord, leaving a stump that dries up and falls off a short while after that. The result is a belly button, either an innie or an outie, depending on how close the tie-off was made.

HOW big is a human egg?

The eggs produced by a woman's ovaries are a tenth of a millimeter in size, so small you need a microscope to see them. The reason human eggs are so tiny compared to, say, chicken eggs is that a chicken egg needs to contain enough food to nourish the developing embryo, while a human embryo grows in the uterus and receives nutrition via its mom's bloodstream.

As small as a female's egg is, though, it's still thousands of times bigger than a male's sperm (the fertilization process begins when about a half-billion of these microscopic critters race toward the egg). Another key difference is that a female is born with a limited number of eggs, only a few thousand, while a male produces trillions of sperm over the course of his lifetime.

WHY do babies need to be burped?

Believe it or not, burping is a skill that has to be learned—and newborn babies can't burp any more than they can run or drive a car. By burping her baby after a feeding, a mom makes sure painful gas doesn't build up in the baby's stomach.

WHY do babies eat so often?

There's a reason the parents of newborns are so tired all the time. For the first few months of its life a baby needs to eat at least once every four hours, and sometimes every two or three hours. That doesn't sound bad, until you realize it applies to the nighttime, too—so mom (or dad) needs to get up at 2 or 3 in the morning. As a baby gets older, it usually learns to sleep most of the way through the night without demanding food.

HOW high can a baby count?

Scientists have proved (using clever experiments that are too involved to describe here) that a newborn baby can "count" to as high as four. It can't actually say the numbers, of course, but it can tell the difference between collections of two and three objects, and sometimes (if it's especially smart) between collections of three and four objects.

WHY do babies have such big heads?

The one thing that sets humans apart from other animals is the size of our brains, which are much bigger in proportion to the rest of our bodies than are the brains of cats, apes, or elephants. But having a big brain has one big drawback: babies have proportionately big heads, meaning the most difficult part of the birth process is getting the head through the birth canal.

As big as a baby's brain is at birth, it grows very quickly during early childhood (a 40 percent increase in size during the first two years). For this reason, a baby's skull is relatively soft and malleable, comprised of several patches of bone that grow and merge together as the brain expands.

Incidentally, this is the reason human children are so dependent on their parents. While a newborn horse can run and frolic within hours of being born, newborn babies have to wait for their brains to develop further before they can walk or feed themselves.

HOW much of a baby's body is made out of water?

About 60 to 65 percent of an adult male's weight is due to water, a figure that's slightly lower for adult women—about 50 to 60 percent. Newborn babies are almost 70 percent water, because their delicate bodies need extra cushioning.

HOW do you cure the hiccups?

There's no best way to cure a case of the hiccups, but all the successful tricks have one thing in common: they disrupt your breathing pattern, giving your diaphragm a "jolt" that gets it running smoothly again. These cures include: holding your breath, drinking a big glass of water, and eating a spoonful of sugar or peanut butter. If nothing works, don't worry—most hiccups go away by themselves after a few hours.

WHY do we need to sleep?

Scientists haven't quite figured this out yet. One theory is that sleep clears out residual chemicals from nerve pathways in the brain, literally allowing us to "think fresh" in the mornings, while another theory claims that sleep is simply an opportunity for the body to rest and recharge itself (during deep sleep, the body's heart rate, blood pressure, and temperature all drop). Some experts even think sleep has no purpose at all, but is simply an evolutionary adaptation to long, dark nights.

Dreaming is a mystery as well. Some scientists think dreams have a purely physical function, as a way to "exercise" the brain, while others believe dreams work out unsolved problems or bottled-up feelings.

Although we don't yet know why people sleep or dream, we do know what happens when a person goes without sleep for an extended period of time: he becomes disoriented, starts hallucinating, and can even become physically ill and die.

HOW much sleep does a person need?

In general, kids need more sleep than adults—about nine hours a night. Experts say adults should try to get at least seven or eight hours of sleep every night, but some people are naturally wired to make do with a couple hours less, while others need as many as ten hours of sleep to feel refreshed.

WHY does counting sheep help you sleep?

Like any repetitive task, counting imaginary sheep has a calming effect, distracting you from worries that may be keeping you awake. It's a tried and true technique, but scientists have recently found that it's much more effective to picture a relaxing scene like a park or a waterfall. In fact, counting sheep keeps some people awake!

WHY does warm milk help you sleep?

Warm milk contains a chemical called tryptophan, which (when combined with the calcium and magnesium that's also in milk) is converted by the body into serotonin, a substance that helps you sleep. Roast turkey is also rich in tryptophan, which is why so many people feel drowsy after Thanksgiving dinner.

WHY do we need to breathe?

When an electron (the particle that makes up an electric current) moves from a high-energy state to a low-energy state, it releases energy that can be harnessed by the cells of our body to perform metabolic tasks, like digesting food or synthesizing new kinds of molecules.

Specialized organelles in each of our trillions of cells—called mitochondria—are responsible for this task, using the power of electron gradients to fuel the body's metabolism. However, for this process to work, the low-energy electrons at the end of the cycle need to be absorbed by molecules of oxygen, so the mitochondria can harvest more high-energy electrons and produce more energy.

That, in a nutshell, is why you need to breathe: it brings oxygen into your lungs, from which it's distributed to the cells of your body and used to soak up tired electrons.

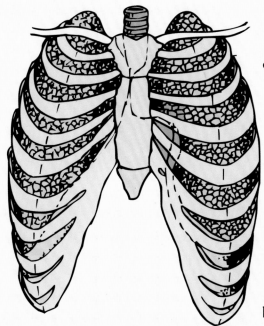

HOW much air can your lungs hold?

If need be, your lungs can hold a little over a gallon of air at one time—which still only provides enough oxygen for a couple of minutes. Normally, every time we breathe, we take in much less than that, about one liter (half a quart) of air. Athletes (who use more oxygen than the rest of us) tend to have slightly higher lung capacities.

HOW long can a person hold his breath?

In extreme situations—say, if he's trapped under a ship—a fit person can hold his breath for about two minutes. Any longer than that, and the body—especially the brain—will begin to shut down from lack of oxygen. By the way, humans are one of the few animals besides dolphins that can deliberately hold their breath for extended periods of time.

WHY does your stomach growl when you're hungry?

If you usually eat lunch or dinner at the same time each day, your stomach "knows" when to expect food, and starts the digestion process (secreting acid and churning its muscular walls) ahead of time. If your meal is delayed, your stomach lets you know how unhappy it is!

WHAT is a calorie?

Technically, a calorie is the amount of heat needed to raise the temperature of one gram of water by one degree Celsius. In diet terms, calories measure the energy content of various foods. For example, a portion of fat contains more calories than an equal portion of protein, and is more likely to cause a person to put on weight.

WHY do people put on weight?

The vast majority of folks put on weight for a very simple reason: they take in more energy (in the form of food) than their bodies burn up in a day. This is why the most effective way to slim down isn't only to eat less food, but to get regular exercise and spend less time watching TV.

However, when you see an overweight person, you shouldn't assume he or she has been eating carelessly. First, some people have a genetic predisposition to heftiness; they can take off pounds by dieting, but the body springs right back to its "natural" weight. Second, women often put on weight while they're pregnant, which can be difficult to lose after they give birth. And third, various medical conditions (like disorders of the thyroid gland) can cause obesity, and are beyond the person's control.

WHAT is cholesterol?

We usually only hear about cholesterol in a bad way, but this chemical is essential to life: it maintains our cell walls, is an essential ingredient of hormones, and helps digest food. Unfortunately, cholesterol can also build up inside blood vessels and cause strokes or heart attacks. That's why it's important to eat healthy, low-fat foods that go easy on the cholesterol!

WHAT is a carb?

If one of your parents is trying to lose weight, you've probably been hearing the word "carb" a lot lately. "Carb" is short for carbohydrate, one of the three essential nutrients in food (the other two are protein and fat). Dietitians have found that excessive carbohydrates (in the form of bread, sugar, or even vegetables) can contribute to weight gain, so counting "carbs" is one popular diet strategy.

HOW many kinds of sugar are there?

The word "sugar" is usually used to describe plain, white table sugar (also known as sucrose). But there are dozens of different kinds of sugars found in foods, plants, and animals—including milk sugar (lactose), corn sugar (dextrose), and fruit sugar (fructose)—and not all of them are sweet. By the way, the word "sugar" comes from the ancient Sanskrit word "sarkara."

WHY do people burp?

When you eat something too quickly, you swallow a lot of air along with your food. If too much gas builds up in your stomach, it needs to get out, quick—and the fastest way out is the same way it came in, via the esophagus and throat. By the way, it's hard to suppress a burp, but it's easy to burp quietly, so try that next time you get the urge!

WHAT are vitamins?

In order to work properly, our cells need certain chemicals that they can't manufacture on their own. These substances, called vitamins, are found in foods, and do everything from improving our vision to keeping our gums healthy (which is why not getting enough of a certain vitamin can make you sick). The body needs at least 13 vitamins, ranging from A to K, though it's possible there are a few varieties that haven't been discovered yet.

To give an example of why vitamins are important, sailors used to go to sea for months at a time without fresh produce, and therefore were prone to develop scurvy—a painful disease marked by rotten gums, difficulty breathing, and disorientation. Scurvy is a condition caused by a lack of vitamin C, which is found in fresh food and vegetables. The problem was solved by a doctor in the early 19th century, when he discovered scurvy could be prevented by adding lime juice to sailors' diets. This is how sailors got the nickname "limeys."

HOW fast can a person run?

A world-class male athlete can run the 100-meter dash in a little under 10 seconds (that's close to 20 miles per hour, or about the speed of a slow car). Because male runners tend to have more muscular bodies than females, the fastest female sprinters are a shade slower, able to complete a 100-meter course in a little under 11 seconds.

Even the best runners can only keep up these blazing speeds for short periods of time. For example, the fastest male athletes can run a 400-meter dash in about 44 seconds, which averages out to 11 seconds per 100 meters. The slowdown is even more apparent during a 1500-meter run, in which the best runners only average 14 or 15 seconds per 100 meters. When you start talking marathons—which are 26 miles long—the fastest runners in the world manage an average speed of only about 12 mph, or a little over two hours for the entire course.

HOW deep can a person scuba-dive?

It's easy to dive deep down into the ocean—the problem is coming back up again, since tiny bubbles of nitrogen in your body (which expand as the water pressure lowers) can kill you if you rise too quickly. Even professional scuba divers rarely go below 130 feet or so, and most recreational divers are happy to swim a few dozen feet below the surface.

HOW many objects can a person juggle at the same time?

Most jugglers only keep three balls or clubs in the air at any given time, but that's small change in the juggling world: the world record is 9 for clubs, and 12 for balls or beanbags. As you might imagine, though, it's hard to juggle a dozen objects for more than a couple of minutes, which is why 3 or 4 clubs or balls is the norm.

HOW long can a person go without eating?

Clearly, a heavy person who stops eating will last longer than a thin person. Unlike water, though—the lack of which will kill you within days—a healthy individual can go without food for weeks or even months before fatally compromising his health.

HOW long can a person live?

Thanks to modern medicine, more and more people are living well into their 100's. The oldest documented person was a 122-year-old French woman who died in 1997. By the way, many folks throughout history have claimed to be incredibly old, but without solid proof (like a birth certificate) it's impossible to tell whether they're telling the truth.

WHY do people live longer now than they used to?

Up until about the 18th century, just a few people had a chance to reach old age. Poor nutrition, lack of sanitation, and the absence of germ-killing antibiotics (which were only discovered in the 20th century) caused many newborn babies to die within a year of birth. Those who survived that long might then die of childhood illnesses (like mumps and measles) that are easily cured today.

Many women died during childbirth in those days, too, and epidemics and infections carried off vast amounts of otherwise healthy adults.

It's not true, however, that nobody before the modern era lived to an advanced age. If people made it safely into their 30's or 40's, they likely had developed an immunity to most common diseases, and were more likely to eventually die of degenerative illnesses like heart disease or cancer. Ancient history is filled with folks who lived well into their 80's or 90's, though not nearly as many as there are today.

WHAT happens if you go without drinking water?

The answer to this has a lot to do with where you are. In the middle of the Sahara desert, where the temperature is over 100 degrees, you can become dehydrated and die within a few hours. But a person can conceivably last over a week without water if he or she is in a cool, dry house.

HOW much can a single person lift?

There's lifting, and then there's lifting. In weightlifting competitions—where an athlete picks up an enormous dumbbell and holds it over his head for a couple of seconds—lifts of a few hundred pounds are common. In real life, there are stories of people briefly lifting one end of 2,000-pound car to save someone trapped underneath, which sure beats any Olympic record!

WHAT is the difference between a dominant and recessive trait?

Every cell in your body contains 46 strands of DNA (the basic molecule of heredity), which are paired up into 23 separate chromosomes. Inside these chromosomes, the strands of DNA are extremely similar, but they do have small differences that can be traced to your parents: one strand comes from your father, and the other strand comes from your mother.

Usually, these strand pairs contain identical genes (the segments of DNA that code for proteins, which perform various functions in the body). However, if the genes are slightly different, they code for different proteins. Usually, one of these genes is "dominant" over the other, meaning that a strand of DNA containing both a dominant and recessive gene will only produce the dominant protein. However, if both genes contain a "recessive" gene, your body will produce that protein.

This is the reason parents with brown eyes can occasionally have a child with blue eyes: the trait for blue eyes is recessive, and the child has inherited both pairs of recessive genes in his DNA.

WHAT is a mutation?

Over the course of billions of years of evolution, our cells have become remarkably good at copying DNA (the basic molecule of heredity) without any errors. However, mistakes occasionally happen, and the DNA is copied with a slight imperfection. Most mutations don't affect an organism one way or the other, but some are instantly fatal to the next generation, and some (once in a long while) produce an amazing innovation that allows the organism's offspring to thrive.

WHAT is cloning?

Normally, a baby inherits genetic material from both its mother and its father, which is why it may have its dad's nose and its mom's ears. Cloning, though, allows scientists (at least theoretically) to make an exact duplicate of a single organism, without having to combine the parents' DNA. But a perfect clone wouldn't be "exactly" like you; any slight differences in the way it was reared would cause it to be a distinct individual.

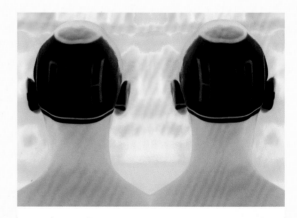

WHAT is the difference between fraternal and identical twins?

Identical twins are the same sex and look almost exactly alike, but fraternal twins don't have to resemble each other and can even be of different sexes. This is because identical twins are conceived from one egg which is fertilized by one sperm, and which then splits in half—so each twin has the identical genetic make-up. However, fraternal twins are conceived from two different eggs that are fertilized at the same time by two separate sperm and then grow in the womb together.

HOW often are twins born?

The gene for multiple births is hereditary, so not all people have it. The odds of a mom having twins are about 1 in 100; triplets are about 1 in 7,000; and the odds against having quadruplets are about 600,000 to 1. That's just for normal births, though. If a woman takes fertility drugs—which make it easier for her to get pregnant—the chances for multiple births become much higher. Most of the triplets, quadruplets, and quintuplets you read about in the news nowadays were conceived because of these medications.

What is DNA?

DNA—the molecule that makes you who you are—is short for "deoxyribonucleic acid." A strand of DNA is made up of an "alphabet" of four smaller molecules called adenine, guanine, cytosine, and thymine, arranged in a double helix. Thanks to this unique structure, a molecule of DNA can be "unzipped" down the middle and faithfully copied, allowing genes to be passed from one generation to the next.

Because it contains so much information, a strand of human DNA is incredibly long: over three billion "base pairs" (the combinations of adenine-thymine and guanine-cytosine that correspond to one another in the helix). If you unfurled a piece of your DNA from end to end, it would be over ten feet long! Fortunately, cells have figured out a way to store this molecule more compactly, bending, folding and stacking it to reduce its size by a factor of ten thousand.

HOW does deodorant work?

Underarm odor happens when bacteria interact with air. Most deodorants don't eliminate the smell from your armpits—they mask the odor with a more pleasant (albeit chemical-derived) scent. Some deodorants have enzymes or minerals in them that keep the bacteria in your sweat from making an odor. Antiperspirants, which are put in many deodorants, contain an aluminum-based compound that inactivates sweat glands.

WHY do kids need to take baths?

Way back in the middle ages, practically nobody took baths—but then again, practically nobody lived past the age of 20. The reason baths are important is because they wash away dirt (which harbors bacteria) from your skin and hair. Also, when dirt builds up and mingles with sweat, it begins to smell—and you don't want to be a smelly kid, do you?

WHY does your skin wrinkle up in the bathtub?

When you soak in the tub, a protein in your skin called keratin absorbs water. Since most of the keratin is in the top layer of skin, it exerts pressure on the bottom layer, which causes your skin to wrinkle up like a prune. The reason this wrinkling is most noticeable in your fingers and toes is because that's where your skin is the thickest.

By the way, if you're the type who likes to lounge and wrinkle in the bathtub for hours at a time, you're doing the environment a favor: a bath uses about 30 gallons of water, while a shower consumes about 3 gallons per minute (so a half-hour shower uses almost 100 gallons of water!) On the other hand, a quick, five-minute shower uses slightly less water than a leisurely bath.

HOW does soap make things clean?

When your hands get sticky, it's usually because of greasy oils and fats that don't mix well with water (which is why plain water won't get them off). Soap works by chemically breaking up the molecules of oil, making it easier for them to dissolve in water.

WHAT is a loofah?

It's almost always mistaken for a sponge, but a loofah--a soft, abrasive, fibery object that's used in the shower to scrub away dead skin--is really the inside of a large fruit called the "dishcloth gourd." Young gourds, which don't have as much spongy material inside, are often eaten in the tropical regions of Asia.

WHY is it dangerous to drink sea water?

"Water, water, all around, and not a drop to drink," reads the famous line in a poem about a stranded sailor. Ocean water isn't just a little salty; it's incredibly salty, so much so that drinking one glassful will put your body into a state of shock (as fluid rushes out of your cells to try to dilute your suddenly salty blood). The result, paradoxically, is that drinking sea water doesn't quench your thirst, but makes you fatally thirsty.

Since only a small percentage of the world's water is fresh, the oceans represent a vast, untapped source of water for drinking and irrigation—if we can figure out a way to remove the salt first. A process called "desalinization" removes salt from ocean water in large quantities, but since desalinization plants are very expensive, and use up a lot of energy, they're generally employed as a last resort.

WHAT is aftershave?

Shaving irritates the skin on the face. Aftershave has two main purposes: first, to kill germs, and second, to soothe and close up the pores of the skin. Most aftershaves contain alcohol, which is why they sting so much when they're applied after a fresh shave.

WHAT is soap made of?

For something that makes you clean, the ingredients of soap are actually pretty yucky: oils, fats, and a dangerous substance (in its pure form) called "lye." When mixed together and "cooked" in just the right way, these substances create a "surfactant," a chemical that loosens dirt particles and allows them to dissolve in water.

WHAT is dandruff?

The skin on your scalp is especially prone to dehydration (drying out), which can cause it to flake off into tiny patches of dead skin called dandruff. Dandruff can usually be treated with medicated shampoo, but it also helps not to scratch your head all the time and make it worse.

WHAT are warts?

They sound icky, but as skin conditions go, warts are pretty harmless. A wart is a small, hard bump on the skin that's caused by a common virus—not by handling toads. Warts will usually go away in about a year, but if you're not willing to wait that long, medications can get rid of them in a few weeks.

WHAT causes bad breath?

Bad breath (or "halitosis," as doctors call it) can have various causes, but the most common is not brushing your teeth as often as you should (which causes a buildup of odor-causing bacteria), and not flossing (which picks up tiny particles of food wedged in your teeth that can decay inside your mouth!). Of course, bad breath can also result from eating garlicky food, but a good brush and gargle with mouthwash will usually eliminate this problem.

WHY do teenagers get pimples?

Pimples are caused by inflamed hair follicles, mostly on the face, though sometimes on the back and neck

as well. When kids become adolescents, they secrete more "sebum" (an oily substance that moisturizes the skin and hair) from these follicles. Bacteria feed on sebum, resulting in a blocked hair follicle, a backup of sebum, and a mild inflammatory response—which is a pimple.

By the way, there's no truth to the belief that eating too much chocolate (or other sweet foods) gives you pimples. The best ways to avoid getting pimples (or to keep from getting more, if you already have them) are washing your face at least twice a day with soap and water, keeping hair sprays or gels away from the skin (because they can clog facial pores), and not overusing anti-acne medications that dry out the skin's sebum, which can cause the skin to become irritated.

WHAT is a concussion?

Your brain isn't wedged tightly inside your skull like a walnut in its shell—it actually floats in a surrounding layer of fluid, so (if you bonk your head under a table, say) it can shift around slightly and absorb the blow. This layer of fluid provides adequate protection against small blows, but more serious accidents (like falling down the stairs or being in a car crash) can cause the brain to rebound sharply against the hard inside of the skull.

When this happens, the result is a concussion—a brief interval during which the brain doesn't function as well as it should. A mild concussion can result in temporary memory loss, dizziness, and a "foggy" feeling, symptoms that usually go away after a couple of days (though you should still see a doctor!). However, a more severe concussion requires a trip to the hospital, because bleeding inside the skull can cause permanent damage to the brain.

WHAT are fallen arches?

A normal human foot has a healthy "arch" on its underside, which is important for maintaining your balance. Because kids' bones are flexible, their feet often flatten out under their weight, a condition that may have to be treated if it persists into elementary school. The best way to treat fallen arches is by wearing orthopedic shoes, which have a pronounced bulge that pushes the arches back into their natural shape.

WHAT causes blisters?

Blisters—raised bumps on the skin filled with clear fluid—are usually caused by burns or friction, which damage the outermost layer of skin. Substances called "histamines" cause the cells under the outer layer to produce fluid, which accumulates under the bubble of dead skin. Blisters usually go away after a few days, but larger ones may need to be treated or lanced by a doctor or nurse.

WHAT is athlete's foot?

Athlete's foot is a fungal infection of the spaces between your toes, a favorite fungal hangout because it's so warm and moist. This itchy condition can easily be treated with medication, and prevented by changing your socks every once in a while.

HOW high a temperature can a person have?

Generally, kids tolerate much worse fevers than adults—some kids can run a temperature as high as 106 degrees Fahrenheit, then be up and running again in a couple of days. If an adult has a fever of 105 or 106 degrees, though, it is very bad news, and may even be fatal if not treated quickly.

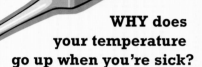

WHY does your temperature go up when you're sick?

Raising its temperature from the normal 98.6 degrees Fahrenheit to 102 or 103 (or more) degrees is the body's natural way of fighting infection. This helps kill the viruses and bacteria that cause disease, without harming the other cells of your body (at least for short periods of time).

WHAT causes stomachaches?

If by "stomachache" you mean the queasy feeling you get right before you throw up, the technical word for that is "nausea," and it can be caused by anything from dizziness to overeating to food poisoning to illness. Other than that, what you think of as a stomachache may not really be in your stomach at all, but lower down in your small intestine. Cramps, for example, can be a warning that you are going to have diarrhea.

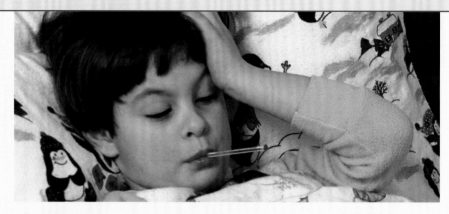

WHAT is the flu?

Flu is short for "influenza," a disease of the respiratory tract (that is, the lungs and throat) caused by a common virus. Most cases of the flu go away after a few days, and cause nothing worse than fever, headache, and coughing. Nowadays the flu is relatively harmless, but as recently as 1918 (before the discovery of effective treatments) a worldwide flu epidemic killed about 20 million people.

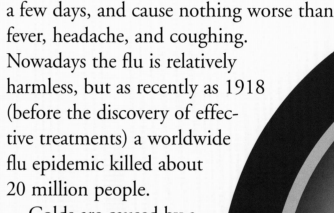

Colds are caused by a different kind of virus that infiltrates the protective lining of the nose and throat. The average kid catches about eight colds every year, and even otherwise healthy adults are prone to three or four.

By the way, despite what your mom says, running around outside and catching a chill doesn't cause you to catch colds. The fact is, by the time you feel a chill, you're usually already sick!

WHAT is a heart attack?

The heart is a big, strong bundle of muscle, which needs a steady supply of blood. This blood is supplied by the heart's blood vessels, which are susceptible to atherosclerosis—a buildup of fatty substances inside the artery that restricts the flow of blood. Severe atherosclerosis can completely block blood flow through the artery, starving the heart of oxygen and causing a heart attack.

WHAT is cancer?

The cells in our bodies are constantly dividing. Ordinarily, a cell is "programmed" by its DNA to divide only a limited number of times, but certain kinds of genetic damage can cause this process to spin out of control. The rapidly dividing cells form a tumor (that is, a collection of diseased cells), which can grow to a dangerous size and then spread to other parts of the body.

Fortunately, doctors today know a lot more about curing (or at least controlling) cancer than they used to. Since the most effective way to treat cancer is to stop the cells from dividing, various drugs have been developed that target cancerous cells while leaving other, normal cells unaffected. And even if a tumor has to be removed, surgery combined with drug treatment adds up to a higher cure rate.

WHAT causes headaches?

There are all different kinds of headaches, but the vast majority have one of two causes: muscle stress (that is, too-tight muscles in your neck or upper back), or dilated (enlarged) blood vessels, which stimulate nearby pain nerves. Most headaches are completely harmless, and usually go away on their own after a few hours.

WHY do we throw up?

People vomit for all sorts of reasons: food poisoning, a bad case of the flu, or sometimes just nerves. When you throw up, the muscles at the top of your stomach loosen (allowing food to escape), while the muscles in your chest and stomach tighten, squeezing your belly and sending its contents out the wrong way.

WHAT is pneumonia?

This serious respiratory disease (marked by fever, pain, and coughing) is caused by a type of virus or bacteria that invades the lungs' air sacs and causes them to swell up and fill with mucus. Before antibiotics were invented, pneumonia killed a lot more people than it does today.

WHY do doctors give shots?

Unlike aspirin, vaccines—preparations of killed or weakened germs that give you immunity from certain diseases—can't be delivered in pill form. The only way to make sure they work is to inject them directly into the bloodstream, and the only way to inject them directly into the bloodstream is with a big needle.

WHY can you only have the chicken pox once?

Chicken pox is one of those diseases that confers "lifelong immunity"—once you've had it, your body knows how to fight it, so you can never come down with it again. In kids, chicken pox is mostly harmless, but it can make adults seriously ill—which is why it's better to have it sooner rather than later.

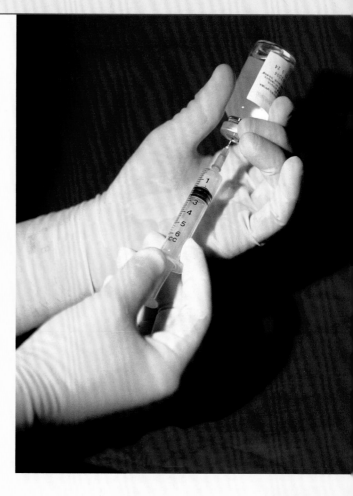

WHY do our bodies need bacteria?

The lining of your large intestine is covered with trillions of good bacteria, which break down and digest foods that your stomach and small intestine can't. The average person is home to about 500 different types of bacteria, some of which create methane and hydrogen sulfide (the kinds of gases that make you fart), and some of which provide the body with nutrients like vitamin K and amino acids (the building blocks of proteins).

Although bacteria can be found in the stomach and small intestine, they're much less prevalent there, because they're usually neutralized by gastric acid (which the stomach uses to break down food). Occasionally, a "bad" version of one of these bacteria can run amok and give you the intestinal flu. Interestingly, babies are born with no bacteria in their large intestines, but develop a full-grown population by the time they're three or four weeks old.

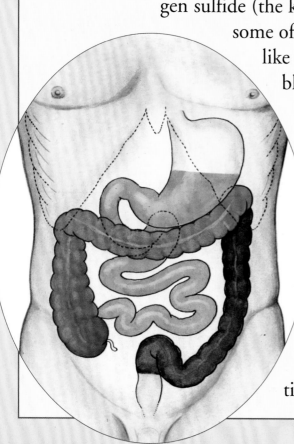

WHY do mosquito bites itch?

A mosquito doesn't just stick its proboscis into your skin and suck out blood; first it injects a small amount of anticoagulant (a chemical that prevents blood from clotting). This foreign protein triggers an immune response in the skin, resulting in that familiar itchy bump.

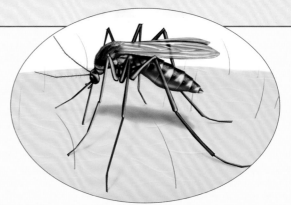

WHY are organs rejected?

Organ transplants aren't as simple as removing a liver from one person and sewing it up inside another. If the proteins in the donated organ don't "match" the proteins in the recipient's body, the result is an immune response (since the body thinks it's being invaded by a foreign organism), and the rejected kidney or liver stops working.

WHAT is AIDS?

Short for Acquired Immune Deficiency Syndrome, AIDS is a disease marked by the gradual destruction of the body's immune system. For this reason, most patients don't die of AIDS per se, but of "opportunistic" infections like pneumonia that the body is no longer able to fight off. Although it still can't be cured, AIDS can now be controlled with carefully calibrated doses of powerful antibiotics.

WHAT is the immune system?

Human beings—or, for that matter, any organisms more complex than a single cell—would never have evolved if they didn't have some way to protect

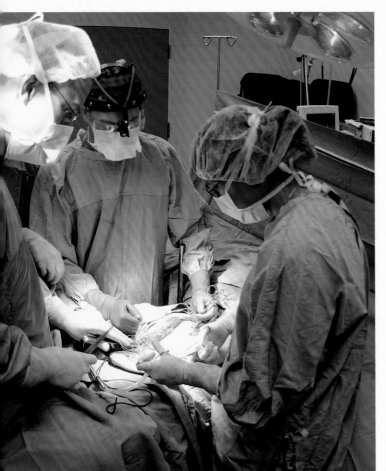

themselves from microscopic organisms like viruses, bacteria, and fungi. That's where the immune system comes in: it's a hugely complex mechanism (involving everything from DNA to white blood cells) that targets and destroys invading microbes, as well as damaged cells in our own bodies.

Because the immune system is so important, a large part of our genetic information goes toward its construction and maintenance. The human body is capable of creating over 10 million different kinds of antibodies (proteins that recognize foreign organisms), compared with the only 30,000 or so basic proteins that help our body day to day.

WHY is a doctor's stethoscope so cold?

It's not that the stethoscope is too cold, it's that your skin is too warm! Remember, the body temperature of a normal person is 98.6 degrees, and room temperature is about 72 degrees. So even if your doctor uses a room-temperature scope, it'll still feel like he's prodding you with a piece of ice.

WHAT is a reflex?

The body can respond to stimuli—say, a sudden tap on the shoulder—in two ways. If a friend does this as he's talking to you, your brain has time to interpret it as a friendly gesture. But if a stranger does it when you're not looking, your body flinches unconsciously in a "startle" reflex.

The reason we have reflexes is that we don't always have the luxury of examining stimuli with our conscious, thinking brains. Imagine if you had to think about the fact that you just laid your hand on a hot stove, and decide if you wanted to pull it away! Since they bypass the conscious brain, reflexes are much quicker, allowing you to jump away from the stove even before you realize you touched it. The human body has many reflexes, including sneezing, coughing, jumping, and the "knee-jerk" response when a doctor taps your knee with a rubber hammer.

WHY do people laugh?

Scientists believe laughter evolved as a way for primitive humans and primates to communicate with each other in a non-threatening manner. When monkeys do it, naturalists call it a "relaxed open-mouth display"—you have to admit that "laughter" sounds like more fun!

WHY do we yawn?

No one really knows, but the best guess is that, when we're not getting enough oxygen deep down into our lungs, a "yawn" signal is triggered in the brain that causes us to open our mouths wide and suck in lots of air. As to why yawns are contagious—that is, why some people start to yawn when they see another person yawn— that's an even bigger mystery than why we yawn in the first place.

WHY do people sweat?

Sweat is the body's natural cooling system. When you exercise, the glands in your skin secrete moisture, which cools you down as it's evaporated by the surrounding air. That's why hot, humid summer days are so uncomfortable: your body produces a lot of sweat, but because the air is already full of moisture, the sweat doesn't evaporate as quickly and you don't cool down as much.

WHY do people sleepwalk?

No one knows, though otherwise this strange phenomenon is fairly well understood. When a person is in the deep, dreaming portion of sleep, the leg muscles "wake up" and prompt the sleepwalker to get up and walk around (or even poke around in the refrigerator). By the way, while it's not true that it's dangerous to wake a sleepwalker, you probably shouldn't do it when he's on the stairs, as it might make him fall.

WHY do we get goose-bumps?

When you're cold or frightened, tiny muscles in your skin cause your hair to stand on end (this is most noticeable on your forearms, because that's where your hairs are the shortest). In other animals, which have thick coats of fur, this "goose-bump" response may be a way of preserving body warmth, but in humans it's just a useless reflex.

WHAT makes people blush?

When people are startled or embarrassed, they experiences a "fight or flight" response—a holdover from prehistoric days, when being surprised often meant you were about to be someone's dinner and had to defend yourself. What we call a blush is caused by a sudden rush of blood to the tiny vessels in the cheeks, and it fades away quickly after the "danger" has passed.

While most people have a naturally tame "fight or flight" response—which only manifests itself in a temporarily heightened heart rate or an occasional blush—some experience a stronger reaction that can cause them to hyperventilate (that is, breathe in and out very quickly) or even faint. People afflicted with these "anxiety attacks" find it difficult to go to shopping malls or give speeches, but this syndrome can usually be treated with medication.

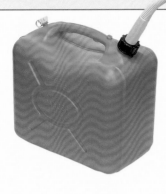

Section 4

Sciences

How do objects become magnetized?
Why can't anything go faster than light?
What is a black hole? This section
ranges across the entire universe,
from the microscopic world of
atoms to the unimaginable
expanses of distant quasars
and galaxies. This is also
the place to find infor-
mation about the earth's
weather, the moon's
craters, and the blaz-
ing hot interior of
the sun.

WHAT is tundra?

Not quite a desert and not quite a sheet of ice, tundra is a vast, frigid landscape where sparse vegetation—such as grass and moss—thrives atop frozen soil (also known as "permafrost.") Although it's a hostile climate, humans can survive in the tundra by hunting such large grazing animals as caribou and reindeer. Most tundra is in the Arctic region, but it can also be found in the Antarctic and at the top of high mountain ranges.

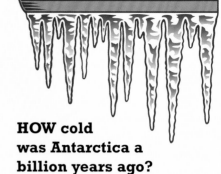

HOW cold was Antarctica a billion years ago?

Today, Antarctica is a huge, barren wasteland, with temperatures so cold that few animals dare to live there. But hundreds of millions of years ago, this continent had mild temperatures and abundant wildlife. In fact, scientists believe that huge amounts of oil (the residue of dead plants and animals) lie under the Antarctic ice sheet, if we can figure out a way to get to it.

HOW did Alaska become part of the U.S.?

In 1867, the cash-strapped country of Russia offered a one-time-only deal to the U.S.: 600,000 square miles of Alaskan territory (which lay to the east of Russia's Siberian provinces) for the asking price of $7.2 million, or about $100 million in today's dollars.

Egged on by U.S. Secretary of State William Seward, the deal squeaked through the U.S. Senate by just one vote—and, when it became public, was immediately criticized by the press as "Seward's Folly." After all, what did our country need with 600,000 square miles of frozen, distant wasteland?

That attitude changed a few decades later, when gold was discovered in the Alaskan territory—and, later, vast reserves of oil and natural gas. Perhaps more important, U.S. possession of Alaska proved crucial during the Cold War, when America was at odds with the Soviet Union (previously Russia). Since it no longer owned the land, the Soviet Union was unable to install missiles in Alaska aimed at the continental U.S., thus decreasing the risk of a nuclear war.

WHAT is the distance between the North and South Poles?

If you could drill a hole straight down into the ice, through the earth's core, and out the other side, the distance would be the diameter of the earth, about 7,900 miles. But, for you to get from one polar ice cap to the other, you would have to journey the long way, over sea and land, so the distance would be half the earth's circumference, or about 12,500 miles.

Between them, the Arctic and Antarctic contain most of the world's ice and fresh water. If all the ice in Antarctica alone were suddenly to melt, it would raise the level of the oceans by about 200 feet—enough to wipe out most of the world's cities, even the ones far inland.

WHAT is a fjord?

No, it's not a type of car. Found in Scandinavian countries like Norway and Sweden, fjords are enormous glaciers (cliffs of ice and rock) that have been penetrated by narrow inlets of sea. You'll have to bring your sweater, but people who've been there say the fjords of Norway are among the most impressive sights in the entire world!

HOW do people stay warm in Iceland?

Iceland isn't as cold as its name implies: the temperature can reach 80 degrees in the summer, and in the winter it's not much colder than New York. In Iceland's capital, Reykjavik, buildings are heated with steam from deep, natural hot springs. Since there's no need to burn oil, Reykjavik is one of the cleanest cities in the world.

HOW did Greenland get its name?

The naming of Greenland is one of the great practical jokes of history. This huge, snow-covered country was discovered by an Icelander named Erik the Red around 1000 A.D., and he dubbed it "Greenland" to encourage more of his countrymen to emigrate there.

WHAT is the world's deepest lake?

Not only is Lake Baikal, on the border of Mongolia in central Asia, the deepest lake in the world—reaching a maximum depth of about one mile—but scientists believe it's the oldest lake as well, scooped out of the earth a whopping 30 million years ago. (Most of the world's more famous lakes, by contrast, are only a few tens of thousands of years old.)

Lake Baikal is notable for two other reasons. First, it contains over 20,000 cubic miles of fresh water, about one-fifth of the world's liquid supply (most fresh water is frozen in glaciers near the north and south poles). And second, as a relatively isolated, self-contained ecosystem, Lake Baikal is home to about 1,500 plant and animal species found nowhere else on the planet—many of which, unfortunately, are endangered.

HOW high is Niagara Falls?

The most famous waterfall in North America isn't very high—only 175 feet, compared to over 3,000 feet for Angel Falls in Venezuela. However, Niagara makes up for its stunted height with its huge volume: every second, over 1.6 million gallons of water tumble over its cliff, the most of any waterfall in the world.

WHAT is the highest waterfall?

Angel Falls, located in a remote part of Venezuela in South America, has Niagara Falls beat by a mile (or, to be accurate, about half a mile)—it's over 3,000 feet high! Amazingly, this waterfall was completely unknown until an American pilot stumbled across it by accident in 1935. His name? Jimmy Angel!

WHAT is the biggest lake?

This is a tough question to answer, because it's a fine line between the world's biggest lake and the world's smallest sea. Some people say the biggest lake is the Caspian Sea in Russia (at over 143,000 square miles), while others say the Caspian is, well, a sea, and the biggest lake is really Lake Superior in the U.S. (at a much smaller 31,000 square miles).

WHAT is the longest river?

The competition is tough, but the Nile river in Africa wins by a hair (or, in this case, 160 miles): it's 4,160 miles long, stretching from central Africa to the Mediterranean Sea. The Amazon river takes a close second, at "only" 4,000 miles, and the Yangtze River in China is just a shade shorter than that. By comparison, the U.S. is only about 3,000 miles wide from coast to coast.

WHY aren't rivers salty?

Rivers flow into oceans and lakes, and not the other way around. As the water streams past, it gradually dissolves the surrounding rocks, which are rich in minerals and salt (though not so much salt that you can taste it in the water). Over hundreds of millions of years, this salt wound up concentrated in the world's oceans and a few lakes, while the rivers have remained comparatively salt-free.

HOW does a dam work?

A dam is a structure that blocks the natural flow of a river. When a dam is built, the portion of river flowing behind it builds up into a lake or reservoir (which often floods the surrounding land), while the portion of river in front dries up. Usually, though, the wall of a dam contains openings that allow a limited amount of water to flow through.

Although some dams are built to irrigate farmland or to prevent flooding downriver, the vast majority are used as a source of hydroelectric power. By blocking up a huge amount of water, and then letting a small amount through at any given time, a hydroelectric dam creates an "energy gradient" by which the rushing water spins mechanical turbines and creates electricity. After the water has expended its energy, it's drained into the river on the near side of the dam.

WHAT is the biggest dam?

The Three Gorges Dam, in China, is one and a half miles long, over 600 feet high, and is capable of creating an artificial lake hundreds of miles in diameter. This dam was built to control flooding on China's Yangtze river.

HOW do mountains form?

The earth's surface is composed of six major "plates" that float—very, very slowly—on a deeper layer of molten rock. The position of these plates accounts for the shapes of the continents, which were very different hundreds of millions of years ago than they are today.

When two plates collide, the result is a kind of slow-motion pileup. Over the course of millions of years, the plates rub and grind against each other, slowly pushing up a mountain range at the point of contact.

This process is most visible in the Himalayan mountain range, which marks the boundary where the Indian subcontintent plowed into central Asia starting about 200 million years ago. Home to some of the world's tallest mountains, the Himalayas are still growing at a rate of about five millimeters a year—so in a million years or so, they'll be three miles higher.

WHAT is the world's tallest mountain?

Most people believe Mount Everest takes the prize, rising to a height of over 29,000 feet (more than five miles) above sea level. But if you measure elevation from below sea level, the record-holder is Mauna Kea in Hawaii, with a combined undersea/oversea height of over 33,000 feet.

WHAT is the difference between a stalactite and a stalagmite?

That's easy: stalactites are the icicle-shaped mineral structures that hang down from the tops of caves. Stalagmites, on the other hand, grow from the ground up. Sometimes, stalactites and stalagmites meet, and form a continuous column that reaches from floor to ceiling.

WHAT is the world's longest mountain range?

The Andes are the only mountains that span an entire continent, running from the southern tip of South America (near the South Pole) all the way up to the equator, for a total distance of 4,200 miles. By comparison, the longest mountain range in North America, the Rockies, measures only 3,000 miles from peak to peak.

WHY do mountains have snow on top?

Even if a mountain is situated in a tropical climate, the air is much thinner and colder near the peak, thousands of feet up. Most of the precipitation on top of the mountain will therefore be in the form of snow, even if there's a tropical thunderstorm raging in the valley below.

WHAT is the earth's core made of?

Based on seismic readings and examinations of the crust, scientists have figured out that the earth's core consists mainly of molten iron, mixed with a smaller amount of nickel. This metallic core is largely responsible for the earth's magnetic field!

WHAT is spelunking?

It's a goofy-sounding word, but spelunking is just a fancy (or not-so-fancy) way of saying "cave exploration." It comes from the old English word "spelunk," meaning "cave," which went out of fashion about 500 years ago.

WHAT is the world's biggest cave?

It depends what you mean by "big." The Mammoth Cave in Kentucky has almost 350 miles of underground passages, meaning you can walk for days and never reach the surface. But the biggest chamber belongs to the Sarawak Cave in Malaysia, which has an interior that's 2,300 feet long, 230 feet high and about 300 feet wide.

WHY do volcanoes erupt?

Beneath its solid crust, the earth is a seething cauldron of super-hot rock and liquid magma (molten rock). Usually, this magma, and the steam it creates, stays safely beneath the surface. Occasionally, though, it'll force its way up through the vent of a volcano, which is basically a mountain the inside of which extends beneath the earth's crust. When this happens, the volcano spews steam, ash, and lava into the sky (or the water, if the eruption happens below the ocean).

Now, you may ask, how did that magma become lava? It didn't, really. What scientists call "magma" is molten rock that's trapped underground; but if it makes its way to the surface (by way of a volcano) it technically becomes "lava." Either way, it's really hot, so keep your distance!

WHAT is an oasis?

Even the driest deserts—like the Sahara in North Africa—are usually punctuated by natural springs or underground aquifers, which attract vegetation. These oases are a valuable resource for travelers and traders, who can rest in the shade and satisfy their thirst. Since oases are so rare, they're often fought over by neighboring tribes and governments!

HOW do deserts form?

There are three different ways deserts can form, over thousands or millions of years: climate patterns caused by nearby mountains, a persistent lack of vegetation, or high elevations.

In the first case, areas downwind of large mountain ranges receive unusually small amounts of rain. This is because the mountains "lift" the nearby air, causing its moisture to condense and precipitate high up in the atmosphere, from which it never manages to reach land.

Second, deserts can form when large areas of land (located far away from lakes or oceans) are stripped of their trees and plants, either by foraging animals or people harvesting wood. This makes it easier for the sun to evaporate the remaining moisture in the soil, which gradually dries up into sand.

Third, deserts can also occur in high elevations, such as the Tibetan plateau. Most people wouldn't consider this ice-covered wasteland a "desert," but it receives very little precipitation, so technically, that's what it is. In this case, the moisture in the air condenses around the surrounding mountains, leaving the plateau high and dry.

HOW is sand made?

Sand is created slowly, over the course of millions of years, by the erosive effects of water as it jostles and tumbles plain, ordinary rocks. It's hard to believe, but most sand grains used to be parts of pebbles, or boulders, or even the sides of cliffs.

HOW fast does a saguaro grow?

Like most other tree-sized plants—including, well, trees—a Saguaro cactus grows slowly over the course of decades or even centuries. For its first 75 years or so, this desert plant grows straight up out of the ground, then slowly develops its distinctive "buds" that look so unnervingly like human arms from a long way away.

WHAT place on earth has the biggest temperature swings?

The widest temperature swings—from way below freezing to well over 100 degrees—occur in the Sahara desert in Northern Africa, although they're a common feature in other hot, dusty deserts, including Death Valley in California.

WHAT is the hottest place on earth?

There's hot, and then there's hot. Death Valley in California regularly reaches temperatures of about 120 degrees Fahrenheit. But the more isolated El Azizia, in Ethiopia on the northeast corner of Africa, has experienced temperatures as high as 136 degrees, making it the clear bake-off winner.

HOW fast is the Sahara desert growing?

Desertification—the process by which a desert slowly expands, turning valuable farmland to dust—has been a serious problem in northern Africa. By some estimates, the Sahara has been expanding southwards at a rate of millions of square meters every year. This is bad news for surrounding farmers, whose crops can't survive the Sahara's lack of precipitation and huge temperature swings (over 100 degrees Fahrenheit during the day and sometimes below freezing at night).

By the way, as big as it is (almost four million square miles), the Sahara hasn't always been a desert. Thousands of years ago, northern Africa was sunny and temperate, with lush vegetation and teeming wildlife.

Another interesting fact about the Sahara desert: the name "Sahara" is derived from the Arabic word for "desert." So when we say the "Sahara desert," we might as well be saying the "desert desert!"

WHAT is the driest place on earth?

The Atacama desert in Chile—which extends about 100 miles inland from the Pacific Ocean and 700 miles down the coast—receives less than an inch of rain per year, making it even drier than the Sahara desert. Oddly, though, the Atacama desert's climate is fairly mild, with temperatures ranging from freezing to about 80 degrees Fahrenheit.

WHAT is the world's biggest desert?

You may be surprised to learn that the answer to this question is the interior of Antarctica—which receives only about an inch of rain per year. But if we're talking traditional, sandy deserts, the Sahara—covering nearly one-third of the African continent—is on top of the list. Next closest is the Arabian desert, which is less than one-third the size of the Sahara.

HOW fast is the Amazon jungle shrinking?

The Amazon rain forest—a vast, teeming jungle in South America—has been shrinking by thousands of square miles every year, as surrounding farmers cut down trees so they can build homes and graze their cattle.

The reason this is bad news is that the world's rain forests help regulate the environment—and the Amazon is, by far, the biggest rain forest in the world. Trees remove carbon dioxide from air, and produce oxygen. If too many trees are cut down, the carbon dioxide levels in the atmosphere build up, which contributes to global warming—and less oxygen means less fresh air for us to breathe.

Also, the Amazon is home to thousands of yet-undiscovered species of plants and animals, some of which may have medicinal uses—and if these species go extinct, we'll never be able to derive their benefits.

WHAT is the greenhouse effect?

The carbon dioxide in the atmosphere has an unusual property: it traps heat emanating from the earth, rather than allowing it to radiate out into space. Burning coal and oil creates excess carbon dioxide, which builds up in the atmosphere and contributes to global warming. If left unchecked, this "greenhouse effect" could wreak havoc on the world's environment.

WHY is the sky blue?

The light of the sun appears to be yellow-white, but in fact it consists of many different colors (which you can see when you refract sunlight through a prism). The sky looks blue because the air molecules in the atmosphere reflect the blue-colored portion of sunlight more efficiently than the red- or orange-colored portion. (That's the same reason the ocean looks blue—just substitute water molecules for air molecules.)

WHY does the wind blow?

Wind is created by differences in air temperature: warm air expands slightly in volume and rises, while colder air has less volume and stays near the earth's surface. These temperature differentials have various causes: sunshine (or the lack of it), the earth's rotation, and the fact that solid ground is better than water at retaining heat, which is why you feel such strong winds at the beach.

WHAT is air made of?

We need air for its oxygen, but oxygen only makes up about 20% of what we breathe—the rest consists of nitrogen (about 80%), argon (about 1%), and various other gases in smaller amounts, including carbon dioxide and helium. By the way, it's a good thing the oxygen content of air isn't any higher, because otherwise things might spontaneously catch on fire!

WHY do cities have smog?

Smog—a mixture of smoke, car and truck exhaust, and fog—is usually found in large, crowded cities with lots of automobiles, and is often visible as a grey or brown haze. Unlike fog, heavy smog can be dangerous to people with breathing problems. The American city that's most famous for its smog is Los Angeles (though this problem has lessened in recent years with stricter car exhaust regulations).

As pesky as smog is, though, it can lead to an even more irritating side effect: acid rain. Although it's not quite as dangerous as it sounds, acid rain is still a serious environmental problem. It's produced when the man-made pollutants in smog mix with rain, snow, or sleet and fall to the ground. Despite its name, acid rain won't melt you into a puddle on the sidewalk, but it can gradually damage statues, buildings, and cars.

WHAT is the ozone layer?

Ozone consists of three atoms of oxygen joined end to end (the oxygen we breathe, by contrast, is made up of two atoms). A thin layer of ozone floats high up in the earth's atmosphere, and blocks harmful ultraviolet rays from the sun. Ozone is easily destroyed by certain man-made substances, which is why governments have tried to cut back on these chemicals before the ozone layer disappears altogether.

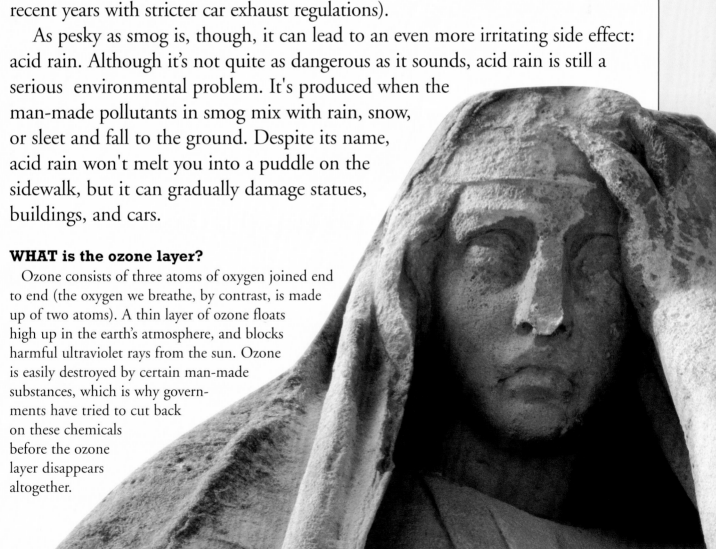

WHY is coal less popular than it used to be?

Back during the industrial revolution, coal (a solid fossil fuel derived from the remains of ancient trees) was the main source of energy. Today, though, most advanced nations prefer to burn oil and gas, which are safer, cleaner, and produce fewer harmful by-products that pollute the atmosphere.

HOW much oil is left in the world?

Oil is what is known as a nonrenewable resource: once it's gone, it's gone for good. For this reason, it's vitally important to know how much oil there is underground, and how soon we're likely to run out.

Different authorities have different estimates of the size of the world's oil reserves. On the low end, there may be as little as 3.5 trillion barrels left, meaning oil production will peak around 2010 and decline steadily thereafter. Other estimates put the reserves at close to 20 trillion barrels, which should supply demand through the middle of the 21st century. (If these sound like enormous numbers, keep in mind that the U.S. alone consumes 20 million barrels of oil every day.)

So what do we do when the oil is gone? One alternative is natural energy sources, like wind and solar power, and another is increased construction of nuclear power plants. In the meantime, though, it is vital for everyone to conserve energy wherever possible, to make the world's oil reserves last as long as they can.

HOW can water catch fire?

Normally, the last thing you'd expect to see burning is a pool of water. By itself, of course, water can't burn, so when you see water on fire (either in real life or in a movie) it's because its surface has been coated with a thin film of oil or gasoline. When the oil slick burns, it looks like the water itself has caught fire!

WHAT is natural gas?

Like crude oil, natural gas is pumped from deep beneath the ground, where it's created from long-decomposed plants and animals. But that's where the similarities end: first, as its name implies, natural gas exists in gaseous form (unlike crude oil, which is liquid), and second, the main ingredient of natural gas is methane—the same compound produced by burping cows!

WHAT is the difference between heating oil and gasoline?

Both heating oil and gasoline are derived from petroleum, which is also known as "crude oil." Petroleum contains a wide variety of hydrocarbons, that is, organic molecules containing hydrogen and carbon atoms. Some of these hydrocarbons are separated out during the distillation process to produce gasoline, while others are used to produce heating oil.

WHY are oil slicks colorful?

A slick is an extremely thin layer of oil (sometimes only one molecule thick!) floating on the surface of water. When sunlight hits an oil slick, it reflects off two boundaries: the one between the slick and the air above, and the one between the slick and the water beneath. Since light travels at different speeds through air, oil, and water, this results in a complicated interference pattern and a swirl of color.

HOW is oil made?

Millions of years ago, the earth was covered with dense populations of plants, bacteria, and animals. When these organisms died, they were gradually buried deep beneath the ground, and the heat and pressure of the surrounding earth "cooked" them into a liquid, carbon-rich substance called oil. (Coal is made a similar way, when the wood of dead trees is subjected to heat and pressure.)

The reason oil and coal are important is because all usable energy on earth ultimately derives from one source: the sun. Photosynthetic organisms like plants and bacteria convert the heat and light of the sun into complex molecules called hydrocarbons. Even after the organisms die, these organic molecules can be combusted with oxygen to produce energy. So by burning "fossil fuels" (as oil and coal are called), we're completing a metabolic chain that began hundreds of millions of years ago!

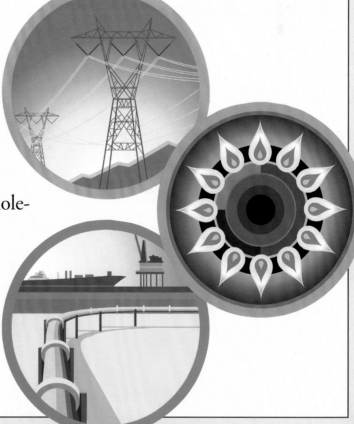

WHY don't hurricanes ever hit the West Coast?

Hurricanes form in the Pacific ocean just as they do in the Atlantic. The difference is that air patterns over the Pacific tend to carry storms further west, away from the west coast of the U.S., while air patterns over the Atlantic carry storms right into the east coast. Also, the water in the Atlantic along the east coast is warmer than in the Pacific along the west coast, giving rise to more destructive and longer-lived hurricanes.

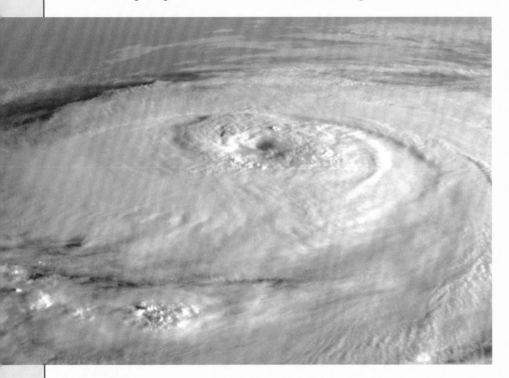

WHAT is the difference between a hurricane and a typhoon?

It's all a matter of location: if a big storm is located east of the International Date Line (an imaginary boundary in the Pacific Ocean) it's called a hurricane, but if it's west of the line it's called a typhoon. Sometimes, a single storm can move back and forth across the line and be classified as both!

WHAT is in the eye of a hurricane?

A hurricane's eye is the empty part of the storm around which the clouds revolve, and is usually 10 to 20 miles wide. Because the eye is so calm and clear, it often gives folks the impression that the hurricane is over—and boy, are they in for a surprise when the second half passes through!

WHAT causes tornados?

Tornadoes occur during thunderstorms or hurricanes, when a layer of cool air suddenly moves over a layer of warm air, which has a tendency to rise. As the warm air rises up through the cooler air, the large difference in temperature causes a vortex to develop, and a narrow funnel reaches down from the thundercloud sporting winds of up to 250 miles per hour—enough to uproot an entire tree or blow down a house.

Part of what makes tornados so dangerous is that they're so unpredictable; these whirling wonders can either stand perfectly still or roar across the ground at 70 miles per hour. They're also unsettlingly common: there are about 1,000 tornadoes a year in the U.S., most in the south or midwest but a few popping up in the west or northeast. Most northern tornadoes occur during the summer, but in the south, they're more common in late winter and spring.

HOW are hurricanes measured?

Hurricanes are classified by the NOAA (National Oceanic and Atmospheric Administration) on a scale of 1 to 5, 1 being the weakest (with maximum winds of "only" about 75 miles per hour) and 5 being the strongest (with maximum winds of over 150 miles per hour). As you might have guessed, level 4 and 5 hurricanes do the most damage, so people along the coasts are usually ordered to evacuate before a level 4 or 5 storm hits land.

No matter how it's measured, a hurricane is dangerous because of how much area it covers—a typical storm is about 300 miles wide, with a calm "eye" at the center that spans 10 or 20 miles. The deadliest part of the hurricane is the area immediately surrounding the eye, which has the strongest winds, while the outer parts, called "spiral rainbands," dump most of the storm's precipitation.

WHY are hurricanes named?

People have a natural desire to "anthropomorphize" things that cause damage—that is, to give them human characteristics. Also, it's easier to refer to, say, "Hurricane Bob" than "the storm system currently developing along the east coast." (By the way, hurricanes used to have exclusively female names, until it occurred to meteorologists that this might be a bit unfair!)

HOW do floods happen?

As you might guess, most floods are caused by an excess of water, such as a sudden, intense rainfall that causes a river to overflow its banks, or excessive melting of ice in the earth's polar regions. Flooding can also be caused by hurricanes, heat waves (which melt mountain snow), and undersea volcanic eruptions.

WHAT is the San Andreas Fault?

The world's most famous (and potentially deadly) fault line, the San Andreas Fault is an 800-mile-long, 10-mile-deep geological formation in California where two of the earth's tectonic plates meet. This fault was responsible for the San Francisco earthquake of 1906, which leveled the city, as well as the less destructive (but almost as powerful) earthquake of 1989. If the San Andreas fault really lets rip, some scientists are worried that the entire state of California could tumble into the sea!

WHAT is the Ring of Fire?

One of the earth's largest tectonic plates encompasses most of the area beneath the Pacific Ocean. At its roughly circular borders—on the east coast of Asia, on the west coast of North America, and across various islands in the southern Pacific—there are an unusual number of earthquakes and volcanos, as the Pacific plate rubs up against surrounding tectonic plates and causes seismic activity.

HOW do forest fires start?

It's true that people can accidentally start forest fires by leaving campfires burning, but the vast majority of fires are caused naturally, by lightning. These fires are ferocious—often whipping up hurricane-force winds and spanning hundreds of acres—but they're also necessary, because they eliminate dead leaves and branches from the forest floor and clear the way for new growth.

WHAT causes earthquakes?

Earthquakes are triggered by movements of the earth's tectonic plates—huge slabs of rock that float miles below the surface on the red-hot liquid mantle. Over the course of thousands or millions of years, these plates can rub up against each other, creating tremendous stress—until eventually one of the plates at this "fault" line break free and lets loose a ground-rattling shock wave.

Most major earthquakes are followed by "aftershocks," smaller quakes caused by the rearrangement of tectonic plates as they settle into their new configuration. Though usually harmless, aftershocks can be very stressful for people who have just experienced a big quake!

Earthquakes are measured according to the Richter scale, in which each succeeding number represents a quake that's 10 times as powerful (for example, a quake measuring 6 on the Richter scale is 10 times more powerful than a quake that measures 5). Most earthquakes are relatively mild, but a level 8 or 9 quake can destroy an entire city.

WHAT causes drought?

A drought is an extended period of time in which the availability of water falls far below demand. It has two major causes: lack of rainfall (due, say, to a change in wind patterns), or excessive use of the water supply by people or crops. If left unchecked, especially in poorer regions of the world, a drought can destroy crops and result in famine—when there is not enough food to sustain the population, and people are at risk of dying of starvation.

HOW dangerous is an avalanche?

Avalanches don't do as much damage as volcanoes or hurricanes, but they take their toll: the worst avalanche in history, in 1962, killed nearly 4,000 people in Peru. By the way, most avalanches occur for natural reasons, and not because someone raised his voice too loud.

WHAT causes tidal waves?

Despite their name, tidal waves have nothing to do with tides. Rather, these enormous waves are caused by undersea earthquakes or volcanic eruptions, or (very, very rarely) the impact of a meteor in the middle of the ocean.

In its early stages, a tidal wave is unimpressive. The undersea quake or eruption spurs the formation of waves hundreds of miles long, but only a few feet high, and traveling extremely fast: about 600 miles per hour. The trouble starts when these waves hit shallow water: their speed suddenly decreases, but the energy they contain remains the same, and they make up for the difference by cresting to a height of up to 100 feet.

However, a tidal wave doesn't have to be enormous to cause severe damage. Some of the most destructive waves measure "only" 15 or 20 feet, which doesn't sound like much unless you happen to live in a house on the beach!

WHY is it called a dandelion?

The name dandelion derives from the old French phrase "dent de lion," meaning "lion's tooth" (which is what this common plant's leaves somewhat resemble). Despite their reputation as harmless weeds, dandelions can be used in salads or even brewed into a concoction called "dandelion wine." Some European cultures also use dandelions as an ingredient in medicines!

WHY are some plants poisonous?

Over the past 500 million years, plants have evolved some nifty tricks to avoid being eaten—and chief among them is the use of poison to ward off pesky insects or grazing animals. Not all the poisons in plants affect all creatures equally, and none of them were developed with people in mind (which you may have a hard time believing if you've ever fallen into a patch of poison ivy).

WHY do potatoes have eyes?

These dark, bumpy spots are actually the buds of yet-to-be-born potatoes. If you cut up a big potato so that each piece has one "eye," each eye will grow into a new potato plant, but if your potato's eyes have started sprouting, you definitely don't want to cook it for dinner.

WHY are four-leaf clovers so rare?

Actually, they're not as rare as they used to be—there are even companies that grow and sell four-leaf clovers! In the wild, four-leaf clovers are mutations of a common plant that normally produces three-leaf clovers, and like any mutation, they're rare enough that you can consider yourself lucky if you find one.

WHAT is the difference between spearmint and peppermint?

The king and queen of the mint family both come from natural sources: spearmint from a plant called *mentha spicata* (spicata is Greek for "spear"), and peppermint from a plant called *menthus piperita*, which is a combination of *mentha spicata* and *mentha aquatica* (aquatica is Greek for "water"). Other kinds of mint—which haven't caught on as chewing gum flavors—include apple mint, orange mint, and curly mint.

By the way, the word "mint" derives from an ancient Greek myth about a nymph called Mentha. As the story goes, Mentha attracted the attention of Hades, the lord of the underworld, and Hades' wife Persephone got mad and turned Mentha into an aromatic herb. (If the name sounds familiar, it's because the flavoring agent "menthol" is derived from concentrated peppermint oil.)

WHAT are weeds?

Grass and the weeds that grow in it are both natural plants, but the weed is what's called an "invasive species"—that is, a tough, fast-growing organism that takes root wherever it can. In lawns and garden, weeds are nothing more than nuisances, but they can damage planted crops like wheat and corn if they're allowed to spread.

WHAT is the difference between soil and mud?

Plain, ordinary mud—the kind you find on the beach during high tide—lacks an essential ingredient of soil: organic matter. In order to grow, plants need not only water and sunlight, but also the teeming bacteria and residues of dead plants that are found in soil. Plant a seed in plain mud, and after a week you'll have a very soggy, probably rotting, seed.

Good farmers and gardeners help their plants and crops grow well by making compost. A compost heap is a mound of fruit and vegetable garbage (carrot tops, lettuce leaves that were too bruised to eat, potato peelings, and the like) that's lumped into a big pile or pit until it rots and turns into compost—a wonderful fertilizer for gardens.

The fermentation process that takes place, caused by trillions of tiny bacteria, generates heat in the compost, which you can actually feel if you're brave enough to touch the compost heap with your hand. On a chilly day, you may even see steam rising from it.

WHY do plants have roots?

If a plant didn't have roots, it would tip over whenever the wind blew. Besides anchoring it into the ground, a plant's roots also collect moisture and nutrients from the soil, and sometimes (as in the case of tubers, such as potatoes, carrots, radishes, etc.) serve as storage areas for food.

WHY do plants have to be watered?

Like any living thing, plants can't survive without water, which drives essential chemical reactions, keeps cells strong and firm, and transports nutrients from the plant's roots to its leaves. Wild plants get their moisture from rainstorms or underground aquifers, but house plants (like house pets) have to be watered by their owners on a regular basis.

HOW fast does bamboo grow?

Some species of bamboo (a species of grass native to Asia) grow at the astonishing rate of over three feet a day—meaning you can actually see it growing if you look hard enough. In about three months, a single strand of bamboo can grow from a tiny seedling to a huge shaft 60 feet high. Oddly enough, though, this super-plant only produces flowers and seeds about once every 100 years.

WHAT is the oldest living thing?

The answer is a tree—not a giant redwood (though that would be a good guess), but a bristlecone pine. Scientists have found a bristlecone near the Sierra Nevada mountains that dates back 5,000 years—meaning it was a young sapling when the Egyptians were building the pyramids.

HOW many acorns can an oak tree make?

Oak trees don't start making acorns until they're 20 to 50 years old, but when they do, it's acorn city—a few thousand over the course of a hundred or so years. The reason an oak produces so many nuts is that it's rare for an acorn to take root in the soil and grow into another oak tree; only about one nut in ten thousand actually manages this feat.

Since oak trees are so ancient and plentiful, you may wonder why more people don't use acorns as food. Although acorns can be eaten when they're thoroughly cooked (and were a staple of various Native American tribes), they're extremely bitter, and botanists have never figured out a way to breed out the "bitter" gene. That, and the long delay before an oak tree produces fruit, has pretty much ruled out acorns as a cash crop.

WHY are bonsai trees so small?

Invented centuries ago in Japan, bonsai trees are scaled-down (one- or two-foot tall) versions of big trees like spruces and palms. Growing a bonsai is a lot of work—it needs to be constantly trimmed, pruned, watered, and fertilized—but after that, you can take care of it like pretty much any house plant.

WHAT is the biggest fruit?

The largest cultivated watermelons can weigh over 250 pounds—as much as a full-grown man. Since watermelons are 90% water, a 250-pound watermelon yields over 200 pounds of water, enough to take a bath in!

As for fruits that naturally grows to a very great size, the jackfruit tree, which grows in India and Southeast Asia, produces giant, pear-shaped fruits weighing about 80 pounds each (or about as much as your average sixth-grader). People in Southeast Asia like to eat dried slices of unripe jackfruit, and sometimes ferment the ripened fruit into a strong liquor.

HOW high can corn grow?

There's a popular saying that, in a bumper crop, the "corn grows as high as an elephant's eye." Unlike most such sayings, that's not far from the truth: some corn stalks can sprout 20 feet into the sky, though the most widely planted varieties reach about eight feet. There's also "dwarf corn," which attains a puny height of only two feet.

WHAT is the world's biggest vegetable?

This is a hard question to answer, because farmers are constantly trying to outdo each other by growing enormous squashes, pumpkins, potatoes, and cabbages. The biggest naturally growing vegetable, though, may be a kind of tropical yam that weighs over 100 pounds.

WHAT is a Venus Flytrap?

Venus Flytraps aren't the only insect-gobbling plants in the world, but they're certainly the most famous. The leaves of the flytrap are hinged like clamshells, and lined with sensitive hairs. Whenever an insect wanders too close and brushes against the hairs, the leaf snaps shut, and a sticky substance keeps the bug from wriggling out. Then it's slowly digested, just like a hamburger!

HOW does a sprouting seed know which way is up?

Imagine you're a tiny seed, buried deep in the ground. When it's time to sprout, how do you know which way to go?

One possibility is that seeds sprout toward the sun, sensing the warmth of sunlight through the soil. The trouble with this theory is that the seeds of forest trees also sprout upward, even though their leaves can't reach the sun until they've grown past the dark canopy of neighboring trees.

Today, scientists believe the answer to this riddle is gravity: a seed's cells, and the water inside them, are pulled down ever so slightly by the earth's gravitational field. This subtle effect allows the seed to "know" which way is up, and climb up toward the sun when it's ready. The details of how it accomplishes this are still a mystery, which may be solved by experiments with weightless seeds in outer space.

WHAT is the worst-smelling flower?

Not only is the Corpse Flower the stinkiest flower in the world, it's also the biggest, growing up to 12 feet high (it looks like a big banana wearing a ballet tutu). The Corpse Flower only blooms a handful of times during its 40-year lifetime, but when it does, watch out—most people find its smell horrible (but not the carrion beetle, which spreads the plant's pollen).

HOW long can a seed survive?

A seed is a self contained survival machine: it can sit dormant for months, years, or (in some cases) centuries, enduring extremes of heat or cold, until conditions are ripe for it to sprout. Scientists believe that some spores—the microscopic "seeds" of fungi or bacteria—can germinate after thousands or even millions of years.

WHY do flowers have petals?

The soft, fragrant petals of a flower attract bugs, which recognize them as a source of nectar. When an insect stops to feed, tiny grains of pollen stick to its body, which wind up fertilizing the next flower down the line. Big, showy petals attract more insects, which spread more pollen, which results in the evolution of even bigger and showier flowers.

However, not all petals are soft and fluffy. Cacti, for example, grow in hot, dry environments where the average lizard or gerbil would be thankful for a quick, juicy meal. That's why, over millions of years, cacti have evolved sharp spines from what used to be flowers, to keep hungry desert critters at a safe distance.

HOW does a sunflower follow the sun?

All plants orient themselves toward the sun, but the sunflower is unique in that it manages to do this despite its enormous size—a full-sized flower has a 10-foot-high stalk and a foot-wide blossom. The sunflower is able to move thanks to the uneven pressure of water in its wide stem, which tilts the heavy plant gradually as the sun travels across the sky.

WHAT is the rarest flower?

All things considered, you probably wouldn't want to wear a rafflesia on your collar. This rarest of all flowers is also one of the biggest and strangest, with a blood-red blossom up to a yard wide and a noxious, un-flowery smell. Oddly, the rafflesia has no roots of its own, but attaches itself to nearby plants and steals their nutrients.

HOW can you tell a tree's age?

When a tree is cut down, you can see a series of concentric circles, called "growth rings," inside the trunk. By counting these, an expert can figure out exactly how old the tree is (or was, since it was just cut down!) It's also possible to count a tree's rings without killing it, by using a "bore bar" to extract a sample from its trunk, then counting the lines on the thin sliver of wood.

HOW deep are a tree's roots?

Since trees tower so high above the ground, you might think they reach just as far below. But in fact, the roots of most ordinary trees spread in a wide circle at a depth of only about a foot and a half. Some species of tree, though, have what are called "tap roots," which extend hundreds of feet below the soil to reach deep sources of water.

WHY do trees have bark?

A tree's bark protects its "cambium"—the delicate, moist layer of cells that allows the tree to grow and sprout leaves—from direct sunlight, bacteria and fungi, and extreme heat and cold. Like human skin, the bark also allows air to pass back and forth, so the cells in the cambium can "breathe."

HOW do trees know when to stop growing?

Scientists haven't quite figured out why trees stop growing after they've reached a certain height. One possibility is that (like human beings and other organisms) their cells simply stop dividing, ending growth at a certain preset limit. Another theory is that a tree stops growing when its transport system—that is, the roots and veins that conduct water to its leaves—can no longer counteract the force of gravity, which grows stronger as the tree grows higher.

This raises the question: why are trees so tall in the first place? All plants survive by collecting sunlight. When trees crowd together in a forest or jungle, they block the sun with their leaves, forming a thick "canopy" that can leave the ground as dark as night. This impels new generations of trees (slowly, over millions of years of evolution) to grow taller and taller so they can harvest the light—kind of a "race to the top."

WHY do coconuts have thick shells?

Coconut trees are native to the Pacific, which is scattered with tiny islands separated by wide stretches of ocean. To spread themselves to new islands, the trees evolved fruits with tough, fibrous shells— coconuts— that could float in the 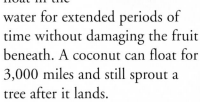 water for extended periods of time without damaging the fruit beneath. A coconut can float for 3,000 miles and still sprout a tree after it lands.

WHY does moss only grow on the north side of a tree?

Moss (a simple plant without leaves or stems) likes to grow in shady areas, so it doesn't get dried out by the sun. In the northern hemisphere, the north sides of trees are shadier than the south sides, so that's where the moss grows. (That's also why, in the southern hemisphere, moss grows on the south side of trees!)

Another thing that grows on shady tree trunks or rock are lichens. These are weird, fuzzy, multicolored growths that can look like dried gray seaweed, or like psychedelic moss dotted with mushrooms. They are actually composed of two very different organisms, fungi and algae. These "compound organisms," as they're known, grow very slowly (sometimes less than a tenth of an inch per year), and some natural varieties may be among the oldest living things on earth.

WHY do leaves change color in the fall?

A leaf's bright green color is caused by chlorophyll, the chemical that converts sunlight into food. In the fall, when there's less sunlight to be gathered, some leaves stop producing chloro-phyll, and other sub-stances that have been in the leaf all along (which have red and yellow colors) become visible.

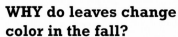

WHAT is lightning?

Electrons (negatively charged particles) tend to accumulate toward the bottom of a thundercloud, giving that part of the cloud a negative electric charge and causing the top of the cloud to take on a positive charge. This creates an electric potential, which is resolved by a sudden bolt of lightning that slices through the cloud and discharges built-up electricity to the ground.

This lightning bolt doesn't flash all at once. Because the air in a storm cloud is so turbulent (and because air isn't a good conductor of electricity in the first place), the bolt's path breaks up every 50 yards or so, creating a jagged-looking chain that conducts electricity all the way down to the earth's surface. This happens so quickly that we don't see the individual "links" in the chain, just the entire, crooked bolt.

WHAT is thunder?

When a lightning bolt knifes down from a thundercloud, it heats up the surrounding air and causes it to expand in a violent shockwave, which reaches our ears as thunder. The reason we hear the thunderclap a few seconds after we see the lightning bolt is that sound travels much more slowly than light: about 5 miles per second compared with 286,000 miles per second.

WHAT is sleet?

Sleet is a weird mixture of all sorts of precipitation: it starts high up in the air as snow, melts partially on the way down, then refreezes into semihard pellets before it hits the windshield of your bus. Although it's a close relative, hail is much more dangerous, consisting of big, irregular lumps of ice formed during strong thunderstorms (even in the summertime).

WHAT is El Nino?

You may have heard a weather person blaming "El Nino" for a drenching thunderstorm in the southern U.S. El Nino isn't a person, but a complicated disruption of wind patterns high up in the atmosphere that causes certain parts of the Pacific Ocean to increase in temperature (with a corresponding effect on the local weather).

WHY are weather forecasts often wrong?

Even though forecasts have become much more accurate over the past few years—thanks to satellites and computers—they're still not foolproof. This is because an approaching hurricane (for instance) is a tremendously complicated system that can go "out of whack" thanks to a sudden shift in wind speed or temperature, which is beyond the ability of science to predict.

HOW much snow is in an inch of rain?

Ever wonder why some places up north are buried three feet deep in snow for much of the winter? It's because an inch of rain in a temperate climate (a good two-hour thunderstorm) translates into about a foot of snow in a cold climate.

WHY are all snowflakes different?

Snowflakes are formed by the crystallization of water, a process so intricate (and so random) that it's been said no two snowflakes are ever alike. But "never" is a big word: although it's nearly impossible to find two identical snowflakes in a single snowstorm, the patterns do occasionally repeat, even if it's only once in a billion billion times.

The more interesting question is how a snowflake "knows" to form a perfectly symmetrical structure. When a substance crystallizes, its atoms arrange themselves into the stablest, lowest-energy state they possibly can, and for most substances, that state happens to be symmetrical.

But why six sides? Scientists believe the unique structure of water molecules—two small hydrogen atoms attached to a larger oxygen atom—causes them to crystallize into shapes with hexagonal (six-sided) symmetry.

WHY do clouds float?

A medium-sized cloud contains tons of water vapor, so you'd think it would crash to the ground like a meteor. However, this water vapor is suspended in a large, diffuse mass of air that's a thousand times as heavy. The tiny water droplets, widely scattered and supported by the surrounding air, are basically unaffected by gravity, which allows the cloud to float.

WHAT is the Great Barrier Reef?

Extending for hundreds of miles along the east coast of Australia, the Great Barrier Reef is a network of thousands of shallow coral reefs (that is, submerged ridges of coral close to the water's surface) that harbors an incredible diversity of colorful wildlife, including thousands of species of fish, mollusks, and birds.

WHAT is the Gulf Stream?

The Gulf Stream is a large, submerged current of warm water that originates in the Gulf of Mexico and travels all the way up the east coast of the U.S. into the icy North Atlantic. It plays an important role in moderating the world's climate, though its most noticeable effect is that it causes the formation of strong hurricanes (since warm water plus cold water equals violent weather!)

HOW long is the equator?

The earth's equator—the "waistline" that divides the planet into north and south latitudes—measures exactly 24,901 miles. But oddly enough, the circumference of the earth from pole to pole—that is, the length of the boundary that divides the planet into the eastern and western hemispheres—is about 40 miles shorter. So the earth isn't a perfect sphere, but a slightly flattened pear.

For most people, the most notable fact about the equator is its tropical climate. The reason nations like Ecuador, Borneo and Uganda have such consistently high temperatures is because they're not tilted toward or away from the sun like the countries of the northern and southern hemispheres, and receive a full 12 hours of sunshine every day.

Since they're situated close to oceans—where tropical air masses soak up tons of humidity—equatorial nations are also very wet and humid, receiving a hundred or more inches of rain per year. That's the equivalent of a good, long, drenching thunderstorm every two or three days (though in practice, the "wet" seasons are incredibly wet and the "dry" seasons are just, well, kind of wet).

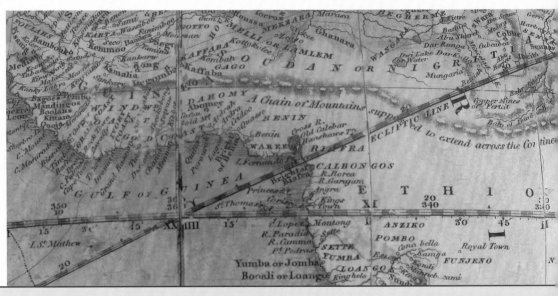

WHY is it foggy in the morning?

Morning fog is caused by lingering moisture in the atmosphere, usually after heavy rainfall the night before. The high humidity keeps the ground wet through the night, and as the sun rises, light winds stir up the water droplets and spread a thin layer of fog a few feet above the ground (which usually burns off in a couple of hours).

WHY is grass wet in the mornings?

"Morning dew" is most common in the spring and fall, when the air is very humid and there's a wide swing in temperature from night to day. Just before dawn, when the air is coldest, some of its moisture precipitates out onto nearby surfaces like grass and windows (the temperature at which this happens is called the "dew point.") As the day progresses and it gets warmer, the dew evaporates.

WHAT is quicksand?

Well, for one thing, it's not very quick! What we call "quicksand" is actually a thick, soupy mix of sand and water, usually the result of sand sitting atop an underground stream. Despite what you see in movies, quicksand isn't very common, and it's usually only a few feet deep—so even if you manage to get sucked in (which isn't as easy as it looks) you can still keep your head above the surface.

By the way, the same process by which quicksand is formed—called "liquefaction"—is also responsible for much of the damage done by earthquakes. Seismic waves can cause moist, solid soil to rearrange itself into a liquid suspension, which causes any buildings perched on top to sink into the ground. This is especially dangerous in coastal cities like San Francisco, which are built on natural sediments prone to liquefaction.

HOW much rain do rain forests get?

They're not called "rain forests" for nothing. These jungle regions—which are most often found near the earth's equator—can receive up to 250 inches of rain per year, and their temperature rarely drops below 70 or 80 degrees Fahrenheit. The heat and constant humidity are the perfect recipe for lush, dense, fast-growing vegetation, which is often so thick that travelers need machetes to hack their way through!

WHAT is dark matter?

When scientists add up all the visible matter in the universe—stars, galaxies, planets, and interstellar dust—they find that the total is much less than theory says it should be. For this reason, physicists believe the majority of matter in the universe is "dark"—that is, composed of an exotic substance that barely interacts with ordinary matter. There's been plenty of debate about what this dark matter consists of, but until we actually find some, we may never know for sure.

WHAT is absolute zero?

An object's temperature reflects how "agitated" its molecules are: for example, molecules of hot water vibrate more rapidly than molecules of cold water. The coldest any object can get is "absolute zero"—minus 459 degrees Fahrenheit—meaning its atoms aren't vibrating at all. (For reasons too complicated to go into here, it's not possible to reach absolute zero, but scientists have gotten to within a few millionths of a degree.)

HOW small is an atom?

Let's put it this way: the human body is made up of about 50 trillion (50,000,000,000,000) cells. Each of these cells is made up of about 100 trillion (100,000,000,000,000) atoms. So a single atom—the smallest possible unit of matter—is about 5,000,000,000,000,000,000,000,000,000,000 (5 nonillion) times smaller than you are. Even so, scientists have been able to see individual atoms using powerful microscopes!

WHAT is radioactivity?

The atoms of some elements have unstable amounts of protons and neutrons in their nuclei. If a nucleus has too many protons, it emits a particle called a positron, changing one of its protons into a neutron; and if it has too many

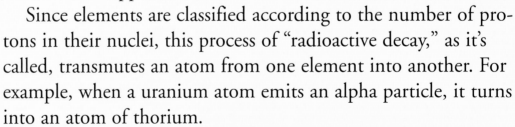

protons and neutrons, it emits an alpha particle (two neutrons and two protons joined together, which also happens to be the nucleus of a helium atom).

Since elements are classified according to the number of protons in their nuclei, this process of "radioactive decay," as it's called, transmutes an atom from one element into another. For example, when a uranium atom emits an alpha particle, it turns into an atom of thorium.

There's a third type of radioactivity that doesn't involve particles: if a nucleus is in a highly energetic state, it may emit a gamma ray to "cool down." Since gamma rays are extremely powerful, this type of radiation is particularly dangerous.

WHAT is a neutrino?

This tiny, virtually undetectable particle is produced when a neutron (one of the basic building blocks in the nucleus of an atom) decays into a proton and electron. Unlike other particles, neutrinos pass right through ordinary matter: if you shot a beam of neutrinos through a slab of solid lead trillions of miles thick, only about half of them would be stopped!

WHAT is antimatter?

Ordinary atoms have three ingredients: protons, neutrons, and electrons. In the atom's central nucleus, protons have a positive electric charge and neutrons have no charge, while the electrons circling the protons and neutrons have a negative charge.

Antimatter consists of atoms in which these charges are reversed: the protons (now called antiprotons) have a negative charge, while the electrons (now called positrons) have a positive charge. Scientists can make antiprotons and positrons fairly easily by colliding atoms at high speeds, but combining them into atoms is another matter: there are only a few thousand atoms of anti-hydrogen (a single positron circling a single antiproton) in the entire world.

It's a good thing there are so few antihydrogen atoms: when an atom of antimatter meets its matter equivalent, the two atoms cancel each other out in an explosion and convert all their mass into energy.

WHAT is heavy water?

A molecule of water consists of two atoms of hydrogen combined with one atom of oxygen. Ordinary hydrogen has one proton in its nucleus and one electron circling around the proton, but the nucleus of a special kind of hydrogen, called "deuterium," contains an extra neutron. When deuterium combines with oxygen to form water, the added weight of all these neutrons makes the water heavier than normal H_2O. (Deuterium, by the way, is an essential component of nuclear bombs.)

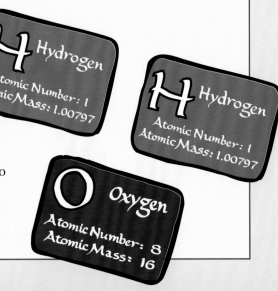

H Hydrogen
Atomic Number: 1
Atomic Mass: 1.00797

H Hydrogen
Atomic Number: 1
Atomic Mass: 1.00797

O Oxygen
Atomic Number: 8
Atomic Mass: 16

WHY do some plugs have three prongs?

Small appliances—like radios and lamps—use two-prong plugs, since their power demands are low. But higher-powered appliances with metal casings—refrigerators, TVs, and computers—require three-prong plugs. The round bottom prong "grounds" the appliance (that is, discharges its excess electricity), preventing you from getting a shock if there's a short-circuit and the metal casing becomes electrified.

WHAT happens to the light in a refrigerator when you close the door?

It goes off. In most refrigerators, when the door is closed, it pushes in a button that switches off the light. When you open the door, the button pops out, and the light goes on. So as hard as you try, you'll never see a refrigerator light actually going off.

Today, lots of freezers have lights, but for a long time this wasn't a standard feature. There are two reasons: first, if you don't take care of your freezer (as many people don't), ice can build up inside and damage the light bulb. Second, since most people don't spend as much time looking inside their freezers as their refrigerators, sticking a light in there wasn't such a high priority.

HOW does a neon light work?

A neon light isn't necessarily filled with neon gas—argon, krypton, or other "noble" gases will also do the trick. The light consists of a gas-filled tube with electrodes at both ends. When the electrodes are turned on, the gas is ionized, causing electrons to flow back and forth and emit colored light. (Neon, by the way, glows bright red, while other gases glow in other colors.)

WHAT is a brownout?

Unlike a blackout—in which the lights goes out completely—a brownout occurs when a utility saves energy by cutting the voltage of its electricity. During a brownout, lights grow dimmer, the size of the picture on your TV shrinks and washing machines and room fans slow down. Although they're less disruptive than blackouts, repeated brownouts can damage some household appliances.

WHAT is static electricity?

Atoms are made of two basic components: protons, which carry a positive charge, and electrons, which carry a negative charge (there are also neutrons, but we'll ignore those for now). When you touch certain materials, like dry fabric, your skin lifts electrons off the outer layer of atoms, giving you a net "negative" charge. If enough electrons build up, they'll discharge with a visible flash (and a painful shock) when you touch a doorknob.

WHAT'S inside a light bulb?

A plain, everyday, 60- or 100-watt light bulb contains a small filament, or coiled wire, of tungsten (a metal closely related to iron) surrounded by inert (that is, noncombustible) gas. When you flick the switch, electric current flows through the filament, heating up the tungsten atoms to about 4,000 degrees Fahrenheit and causing them to emit visible light.

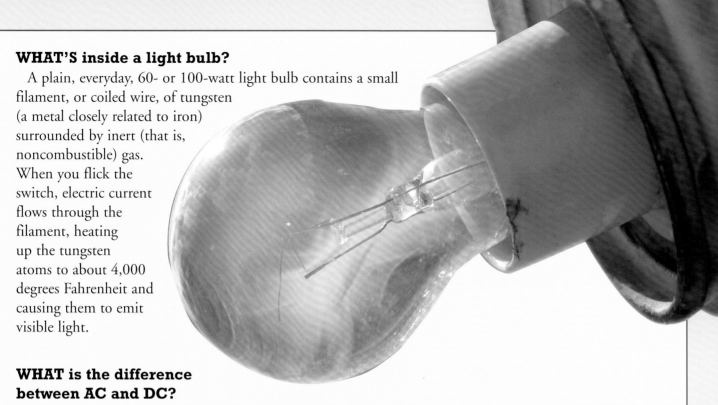

WHAT is the difference between AC and DC?

Most of the electricity that powers your house is AC, which stands for "alternating current." In this type of current, the stream of electrons switches directions millions of times every second. In a DC (direct current) circuit, the electrons stream in only one direction. Most small, battery-powered appliances use a DC current, as does the powerful (and dangerous) third rail of an electric train line.

HOW does a battery work?

A battery has two ends, or "electrodes," one negative (marked with a "–") and one positive (marked with a "+"). Inside the battery, a chemical reaction causes electrons—the particles that make up an electric current—to collect at the negative end. The electrons leave the negative electrode, travel through the device to which the batteries are attached, and flow back through the positive electrode. When the chemical reactions that create the electron flow have been exhausted, the battery stops working and so does your Game Boy.

Batteries use all kinds of chemicals, depending on what kind of work they're being asked to do. Most standard AA batteries have one electrode of carbon and one of zinc, while longer-lasting alkaline batteries contain zinc and manganese oxide and larger and more powerful car batteries contain lead.

HOW powerful is a nuclear bomb?

The first nuclear bomb ever dropped—on Hiroshima, Japan, in 1945—had an explosive force of about 20,000 tons (40 million pounds) of TNT, packed in a missile the size of a small plane. However, this "fission" bomb, as destructive as it was, was only a firecracker compared to what came after: the modern "fusion", or hydrogen, bomb, which can be more than 1,000 times as powerful. One of the first H-bomb tests destroyed an entire island in the Pacific Ocean.

Interestingly, a fission bomb (which produces energy by splitting uranium atoms) is an essential component of a fusion bomb (which produces energy by fusing atoms of hydrogen into atoms of helium). Because it takes a lot of force to fuse hydrogen atoms together, the "fuse" of a fusion bomb is actually a fission bomb.

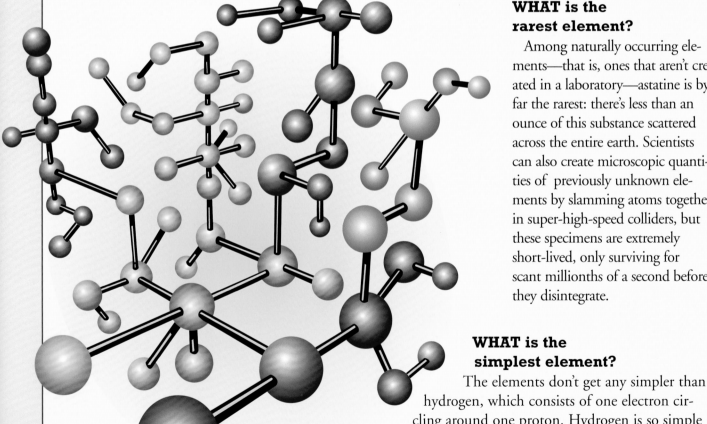

WHAT is the rarest element?

Among naturally occurring elements—that is, ones that aren't created in a laboratory—astatine is by far the rarest: there's less than an ounce of this substance scattered across the entire earth. Scientists can also create microscopic quantities of previously unknown elements by slamming atoms together in super-high-speed colliders, but these specimens are extremely short-lived, only surviving for scant millionths of a second before they disintegrate.

WHAT is the simplest element?

The elements don't get any simpler than hydrogen, which consists of one electron circling around one proton. Hydrogen is so simple and abundant, in fact, that physicists believe it accounted for 93 percent of the composition of the universe right after the Big Bang (with the other seven percent consisting of another simple element, helium).

WHAT is an acid?

In the strict chemical sense, an acid is any molecule that tends to donate one of its protons (the nucleus of a hydrogen atom) to another molecule called a "base."

While we all know about strong, dangerous acids like nitric acid or hydrochloric acid—which can eat through solid metal and cause serious burns—the truth is that most acids are relatively weak and harmless. In fact, without acids, life itself would be impossible: the proteins in our bodies are made up of simple molecules called "amino acids," and we need the acid in our stomachs to digest food.

The strength of acids (and bases) is measured according to the pH scale, in which the number 7 represents pure water. According to this scale, nitric acid has a very strong pH of about 1, while milk (which contains lactic acid) has a mild pH of 6.6.

HOW many elements are there?

This used to be an easy question to answer, until scientists began creating new elements in high-powered laboratory experiments. So far, close to 120 elements have been identified, 102 of which are the more-or-less familiar ones (oxygen, carbon, iron, etc.) and the remainder of which are extremely rare and short-lived radioactive elements like lawrencium and technetium.

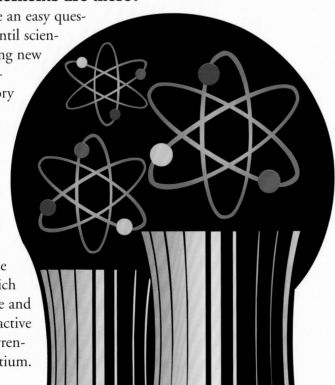

HOW can you store acid?

It's a conundrum nearly as old as chemistry itself: how can you store a powerful acid if it eats through any container you put it in? The fact is, though, that even the strongest acids—like nitric or hydrofluoric acid—only react with certain substances (mostly metals and organic compounds), and usually can be safely contained in a plain glass bottle.

WHAT is dynamite?

Invented in 1866 by Alfred Nobel (who later established the Nobel Prize), dynamite is basically a mixture of sawdust and nitroglycerin (that liquid stuff that explodes if you shake it too hard). Compared to other explosives, dynamite is relatively stable, and will only detonate with the aid of a fuse or blasting cap—which is why it's used by builders and tunnel engineers.

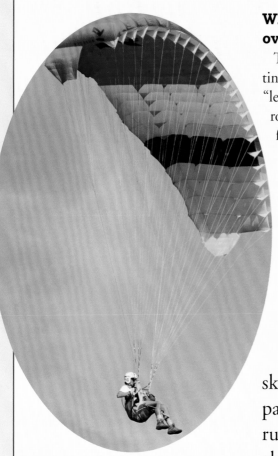

WHY do balloons get smaller overnight?

The gas molecules in a balloon are incredibly tiny—tiny enough, in fact, that they slowly "leak" through microscopic pores in the surrounding walls. Helium balloons deflate faster than regular balloons because helium molecules are smaller than the oxygen, nitrogen, and argon molecules that make up the air, and slip through these pores more easily.

HOW does a parachute work?

When a falling skydiver unfurls his parachute, air rushes into the chute's underside and collects into a high-pressure "bubble" (kind of like the top half of an inflated balloon). This bubble of air pushes up into the parachute, which decreases the speed of the sky-diver's fall. Once he's falling at a reasonable rate, he can land safely on the ground without killing himself.

As you might know if you've ever seen a drag race, parachutes don't only work in a vertical direction—they're also good for slowing down land velocity. By deploying a parachute behind his car to create wind drag, a driver can quickly decelerate from a couple hundred miles per hour to a more reasonable speed, from which he coasts to a smooth stop.

HOW does a boomerang work?

The trick to a boomerang is that it's made of two wings, which are joined together in a slightly curved shape. The wings are rounded on one side and flat on the other, an aerodynamic design that creates lift. As the boomerang flies, its two wings rotate at slightly different speeds, so it eventually returns to the person who threw it (with a lot of practice, of course).

WHY is rubber stretchy?

Rubber is made out of "polymers"—that is, very long strings of molecules joined end to end. When they are in a relaxed state, these polymers bunch up around each other, but when you stretch the piece of rubber they straighten out (almost) to their full length—then snap back to the relaxed state when you let go.

HOW does a gyroscope work?

A gyroscope, a spinning, top-like device that keeps everything from airplanes to space stations pointing up, operates through "precession," a property of spinning objects that makes them resistant to being pushed. Although it may seem like a gyroscope defies gravity, it actually uses the force of gravity to perform this trick.

HOW fast do things fall?

In Earth's gravitational field, objects fall at a rate of 10 meters per second per second—meaning that with each passing second, a falling baseball, or missile, or person goes 10 meters per second faster. That's one of the reasons leaping from a skyscraper is always fatal—by the time you hit the ground, you're zooming earthward at over 100 miles an hour!

The strength of a gravitational field varies with the mass of the body that creates it. On the moon, which is much lighter than the earth, a fall from a high altitude would probably not be fatal (though you wouldn't want to take the risk of damaging your space suit!). The gravitational field of Jupiter, which is much more massive than the Earth, is more than twice as strong—so not only would you fall faster toward its surface, but you'd feel twice as heavy whenever you tried to take a walk.

WHAT makes a stone skip across water?

A surprising number of scientists have investigated this issue. The physics of stone skipping is complicated, but it comes down to the way the sideways velocity of the stone interacts with the upward force exerted by the water. The bottom line (based on experiments) is that you can get the most skips out of your stone by flicking it pondward at a 20-degree angle.

WHY do balls bounce?

A ball can only bounce if it's made of an elastic substance. Rubber balls, which are very elastic, bounce a few feet, while baseballs, which are only slightly elastic, bounce only a couple of inches, and a ball made of solid steel won't bounce at all. Here's how it works: when an elastic ball hits the floor, it flattens slightly, and bounces back up as it rebounds to its normal spherical shape.

WHAT is the biggest object made of solid gold?

King Tut's tomb, which was discovered in an Egyptian pyramid in 1922, is a 2,500-pound casket of solid gold that's worth about $15 million (in addition to its historical value, of course).

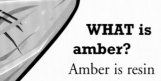

WHAT is amber?

Amber is resin (a natural substance, such as pine pitch) secreted by trees, that has hardened and fossilized over millions of years. Although it is prized for jewelry, amber is also valuable to scientists because it sometimes contains the remains of ancient insects that wandered into the resin all those millennia ago, got stuck, and thus were preserved intact to be studied today.

WHY is gold so valuable?

You might think gold is desirable because it's so rare, but that's not the whole story—there are plenty of elements (and gemstones) that are even rarer.

Gold has been used as money since the beginning of recorded history for three main reasons: first, it looks good; second, it's very malleable, meaning it can be easily shaped into coins or pounded into a very thin sheet; and third, unlike most metals, it's usually found in its natural state (unmixed with other elements) and doesn't need to be refined.

It used to be that industrialized nations kept vast reserves of gold in their central banks as a means of backing their paper currency (which would be worthless if it didn't ultimately represent some "real" value in gold). Nowadays, this "gold standard" has pretty much disappeared, but countries still keep gold reserves as a dependable, and solid, source of wealth.

WHAT is petrified wood?

Petrified wood comes from parts of an ancient tree's structure that have been turned to stone. After they die, most trees decompose completely and return their nutrients to the soil. However, if the tree falls into a lake or river, minerals can seep into the wood over millions of years, gradually infiltrate its cells, and then harden into rock.

HOW are diamonds made?

The recipe for a diamond is simple: take a black, greasy lump of coal (or any other substance made mostly of carbon), bury it a hundred or so miles underground, and let the pressure of the earth slowly cook and compress it over the course of millions of years. The carbon atoms in the coal rearrange themselves into a crystalline lattice, and the result is a clear, sparkling diamond.

Because of its tightly bonded atomic structure, a diamond is the one of the hardest substances on earth: the only thing that can scratch it is another diamond. Although only natural diamonds are prized as jewelry, in the last few decades scientists have perfected the art of creating "artificial" diamonds. This is done by subjecting carbon to extremely high pressures and temperatures in a laboratory setting. Using modern techniques, small, industrial-grade diamonds can be synthesized in a matter of days.

HOW hard is a brick of gold?

Pure gold is actually very soft, and can easily be hammered into a thin sheet (called gold leaf or plate). This is why gold-plated jewelry isn't very expensive—the gold surface is only a tiny fraction of a millimeter thick.

WHY is it called "fool's gold?"

Novice prospectors are often taken in by a common mineral called pyrite, which has a shiny, bright-yellow appearance. This "fool's gold" caused lots of guffaws back in gold-rush California, when clueless newcomers would plunk pretty, but worthless, rocks onto a bank counter and demand to be paid in cash.

WHAT is alchemy?

Centuries ago, people believed there was a way to turn common metals like iron and lead into pure gold. A lot of time and energy went into finding this magic recipe (which usually involved a mysterious substance called the "philosopher's stone"), but the art of alchemy gradually died out as it was supplanted by modern chemistry.

WHAT makes emeralds green and rubies red?

The color of a gemstone is usually related to the type of metal contained in its crystals. Rubies consist of crystals rich in chromium, which gives these gems their characteristic red color. (Rubrum, the word from which "ruby" derives, is Latin for "red.") Emeralds, on the other hand, form from crystals containing beryllium (and traces of other metals), which impart a green tint.

WHAT is cryogenics?

Cryogenics is the practice of freezing a human body after death, in the hopes that doctors of the future will be able to thaw the person out, revive him, and cure his disease. However, since scientists of today haven't yet been able to reliably deep-freeze and revive a mouse, much less a person, it looks doubtful that doctors a hundred years from now (or more) will have any better luck.

WHY does salt cause ice to melt?

Adding salt to plain water lowers its freezing point: pure water freezes at 32 degrees Fahrenheit, but a 10 percent salt solution freezes at 20 degrees, and a 20 percent salt solution freezes at 2 degrees. That's why sprinkling salt on ice makes it melt, as long as the outside temperature isn't too far below freezing.

WHAT are icebergs?

Icebergs are enormous chunks of ice that break off glaciers (ice sheets) in the vicinity of the north and south poles. Scientists keep a close watch on the rate of iceberg formation, since erosion of ice sheets is a sign of global warming (that is, an increase in the world's average temperature).

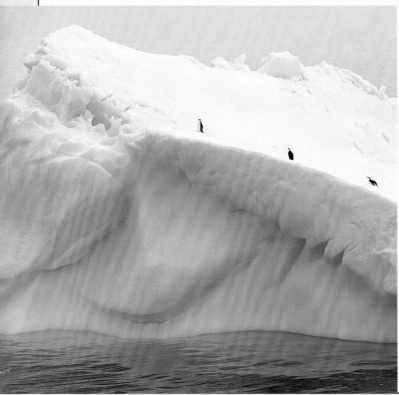

As with most heavy things that float—including oil tankers and passenger liners—about nine-tenths of an iceberg is under water. For this reason, it's not enough to simply steer clear of an iceberg when you're out at sea; you have to give it a wide berth in case any parts jut out below your vessel. In 1912, the ocean liner Titanic sunk after colliding with an iceberg in the north Atlantic, with the loss of over a thousand passengers.

WHY does touching ice make your fingers numb?

Cold substances like ice shrink the capillaries (microscopic blood vessels) in the tips of your fingers, reducing the flow of blood. The lack of blood inhibits the numerous nerves in your fingertips, giving you that "numb" feeling.

WHY doesn't the ice in skating rinks melt?

The ice in a hockey arena doesn't cover a plain wooden floor. It's created on top of a thick slab of concrete containing a large network of pipes, through which flows ice-cold liquid refrigerant. This is why converting an arena from hosting a game of ice hockey to hosting a game of basketball is such an involved process—you can't simply melt the ice and play ball.

WHY does ice float?

In order to float, an object has to be less dense than the liquid it's floating in. When water turns into ice, it expands slightly in volume, because its molecules are arranged in a crystalline structure (the molecules of liquid water are packed together more closely). That's why, even though ice and water are made out of the same substance, the ice floats on top.

Because the cold floating ice is still in contact with the warmer liquid water, some strange physics can result. For instance, when you drop a cold ice cube into warm water, the outside of the ice cube suddenly warms up while the inside remains frozen. This creates stress in the ice cube's structure, which usually relieves itself with a sudden, startling crack.

WHAT is dry ice?

Dry ice isn't technically water at all, but frozen carbon dioxide (which is gaseous in its natural form). The interesting thing about dry ice is that it "sublimates"—that is, it melts directly into carbon dioxide gas, without any liquid state in between. For this reason, dry ice is often used to create "fog" effects on stage and in movies, as the cold evaporating gas becomes visible in the surrounding air. (By the way, you should never, ever touch a piece of dry ice!)

WHAT is ice fishing?

No, it's not a cheap way to get ice cubes. When a lake or pond freezes over during winter, it's possible to drill a hole in the ice (which is usually only a few inches thick) and fish through the opening. There are usually fewer anglers around to compete for available fish, but on the other hand, you have to make sure to put on your long underwear and have lots of patience.

HOW was glass invented?

As with many of the great innovations of history, it's likely that glass was discovered by accident, as a by-product of the pottery-making process. Man-made glass first appeared in Egypt in about 1500 B.C., but it wasn't until the first century B.C. that the art of glass-blowing was perfected, also by the Egyptians. Centuries later, medieval glass-makers discovered that glass could be colored by adding certain minerals, an innovation that resulted in the great stained-glass windows of European cathedrals.

HOW do mirrors work?

A mirror creates a reflection when photons—the tiny particles that make up light—bounce off its surface. Because the mirror is smooth, the photons bounce in a consistent, geometrical way, creating a "mirror image." The reason funhouse mirrors distort your image, making you look fat or thin, is that they're not perfectly smooth.

A one-way mirror is just like an ordinary mirror from one side, but from the other side it's more like a window. The secret is the mirror's "half-silvered" surface, which reflects only half of the incoming light. When the room on one side of the mirror is brightly lit, the people there see an ordinary mirror, but the folks on the other side of the mirror (in a dark room) can see straight through. In dim light, the mirror is semi-transparent to people on either side.

WHAT is a fluorescent light?

Closely related to a neon light, a fluorescent light bulb contains mercury vapor. When the light is switched on, this vapor heats up and radiates ultraviolet light, which then interacts with a substance (called "phosphor") painted onto the inside of the glass. The phosphor absorbs the ultraviolet light and re-radiates it (thanks to a chemical process called "fluorescence") in the form of visible light.

WHY can we see through glass?

Technically, glass is more of a liquid than a solid. Unlike other substances that crystallize as they harden from liquid to solid form, as glass cools its molecules don't arrange themselves in any particular order. Since there's plenty of space between its atoms, hard glass remains transparent to light rays, just like water.

WHAT is a prism?

A prism is a clear, triangular piece of glass or plastic that refracts incoming light (that is, separates light into its individual wavelengths), producing a rainbow pattern on the other side. It accomplishes this trick thanks to the "refractive index" of its molecules, which cause light to bend in a predictable way.

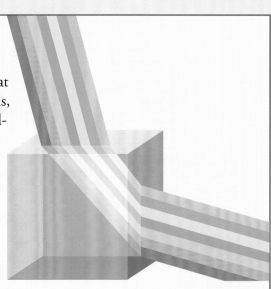

WHAT is safety glass?

Mostly used in the windshields of cars, safety glass is ordinary glass that contains a thin layer of clear, flexible plastic. If the glass is shattered—say, during a head-on collision—shards of glass can't fly into the car and injure the occupants, but remain stuck to the plastic.

WHAT is a rainbow?

Light can be "refracted" (that is, broken up into its constituent colors) by all sorts of things: glass prisms, oil slicks, even raindrops suspended in air. When the sky clears suddenly after a violent storm, the sun shines into these lingering drops, which refract the colorless rays into a colorful rainbow.

The reason a rainbow is curved is that the different colors of light refract at different angles. For example, light toward the red part of the spectrum bends at 42 degrees, but violet light (on the opposite end of the spectrum) bends at only 40 degrees.

By the way, there's a simple way to remember not only the colors of the rainbow, but the order in which they appear. Think of the name "Roy G. Biv." The letters stand for red, orange, yellow, green, blue, indigo (a kind of purple), and violet.

WHAT is an MRI machine?

MRI stands for "magnetic resonance imaging," a painless scanning technique that allows doctors to see the inside of the human body. When a patient is inserted into an MRI machine, the powerful magnetic field tugs on the hydrogen atoms inside the person's body. Since most of the body's hydrogen is in the form of water, and since different tissues of the body have different concentrations of water, this allows the physician to see the patient's internal organs in great detail.

WHAT is a lodestone?

Lodestones are rocks that contain magnetite, a naturally occurring iron ore that possesses a weak magnetic field. Lodestones were used to make the first compasses thousands of years ago (long before people understood the theory of magnetism), and, thanks to their "magical" properties, they've long been employed as lucky charms.

WHAT causes magnetism?

Metals like iron have an abundance of electrons, the tiny particles in an atom that circle the nucleus (and that make up an electric current). Normally, these trillions of electrons "spin" every which way. But in an iron magnet, the electrons all spin in the same direction, creating a magnetic pull that can be felt by other metallic objects of similar composition.

A magnet generates invisible lines of force that "exit" the magnet's north pole and "enter" the south pole, creating a closed loop. This loop must exist for magnetism to exist, so even if you break a bar magnet in half, each piece will generate its own north and south poles. (Scientists speculate that there may be a tiny elementary particle called a "magnetic monopole," with only one pole, but they haven't been able to find it yet.)

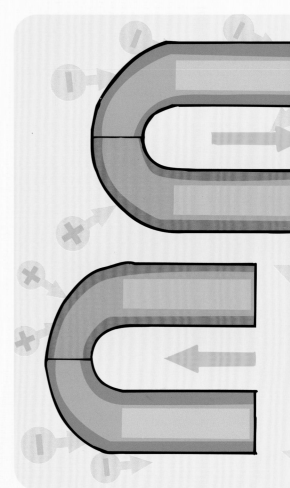

WHY should you never put a magnet near a computer?

The hard disk of a computer—where all its information is stored—is composed of small magnetized regions corresponding to the "1"s and "0"s of binary code. If you wave a bar magnet too near the computer, or stick a magnet on it to hold a piece of paper, it can accidentally erase the hard drive's data (in the best case) or mangle it beyond repair (in the worst case).

WHAT is a superconductor?

Most magnets used for industrial applications aren't the naturally occurring variety; rather, they're "electromagnets," coils of metal (usually copper) that convert an incoming electric current into a magnetic field. A superconductor is a substance that transmits an electric current with virtually no resistance, and thus produces a powerful magnetic field with very little input of energy. Most superconductors have to be cooled to hundreds of degrees below zero, but some produce magnetic fields close to room temperature.

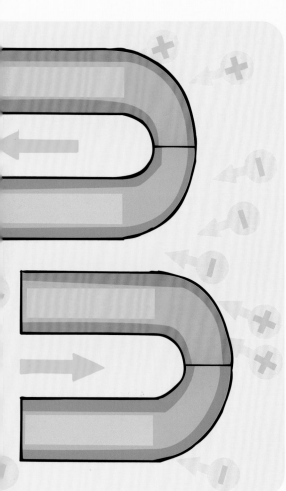

WHY does the earth have a magnetic field?

The earth's core consists mostly of liquid iron. Scientists haven't worked out the details yet, but they believe this iron core sloshes around as the earth rotates, creating a magnetic field in the process. This field is much more intense closer to the core—by the time it reaches the earth's surface, it's barely strong enough to move the needle of a compass.

On a galactic scale, the magnetic field of the earth—and even the sun—is especially puny. Magnetic fields are measured in units called "Gauss," defined as one line of magnetic force per square centimeter of surface. By this measure, the earth's magnetic field has a strength of one Gauss, the sun's magnetic field measures five Gauss, and the magnetic field of a neutron star (in which all the regular components of atoms have been mashed together into neutrons) weighs in at a hefty 1,000,000,000,000 Gauss!

HOW do objects become magnetized?

Whenever you touch a (nonmagnetic) paper clip with a bar magnet, the clip has a weak magnetic field of its own afterward. This is because the more powerful bar magnet temporarily disrupts the "spin" of the paper clip's electrons, which (when the bar magnet is gone) realign themselves with the weak magnetic field of the earth.

WHAT is a real number?

If you envision a number line—say, with 0 on one end and 1 on the other—then any point on that line represents what mathematicians call a "real" number. Since a mathematical point is infinitely small, it follows that there are an infinite amount of real numbers in any line segment, which correspond to decimal expansions that go on into infinity (such as, for instance, .784959424343…..)

WHAT is an imaginary number?

According to the rules of arithmetic, every time you multiply two negative numbers, you get a positive number: for example, minus 2 times minus 2 is positive 4. In other words, you can't multiply two negative numbers to get a negative number. This is where the imaginary number "i" comes in: it's the square root of minus 1 (which is impossible in ordinary arithmetic!), and is used by mathematicians to solve advanced problems.

HOW big is a googol?

Let's put it this way: a thousand is 1 followed by three zeros, a million is 1 followed by 6 zeroes, and a billion (a pretty big number, right?) is 1 followed by 9 zeroes. Well, a googol is 1 followed by 100 zeroes, and it's so big that if you counted every atom in the universe, you wouldn't even get close. There's also the googolplex, which is 1 followed by a googol's worth of zeroes. This number is so enormous that it can't even be written down!

WHY do we count in tens?

For most people, counting to ten is the most natural thing in the world. This isn't because the number 10 has some unique or magical property; it's because human beings have 10 fingers and 10 toes, and thus possessed a "natural" way to count to 10 way back when they were chasing woolly mammoths.

Even so, not all civilizations have used a base 10 counting system. The ancient Babylonians employed a base 60 system, the most important element of which was the number 12 (for the twelve months of the year). This "sexagesimal" system gradually gave way to the "decimal" system of modern times.

So what happens if we encounter an alien race with seven fingers—will there be any way to communicate mathematically? Hopefully, yes: any advanced civilization should know how to communicate using binary notation, which only employs the symbols 1 and 0.

HOW big is infinity?

Infinity isn't a real number in the sense that 1, 2, and 3 are numbers. It is the word used to define something that is endless—it just goes on forever. That's why, if you try to visualize how "big" infinity is, you usually wind up giving yourself a big headache. The symbol for infinity looks like the number 8 lying sideways; if you trace it with a pencil or your finger you just go on and on and on.

The term "infinity" doesn't only mean infinitely big numbers, but infinitely small ones, too. Mathematicians often work with quantities called "infinitesimals," that is, infinitely small numbers that represent the number one divided by infinity. Just as there's no biggest number (since you can always make it even bigger by adding 1), there's no such thing as a smallest infinitesimal, since you can always make it even smaller by dividing it by 10.

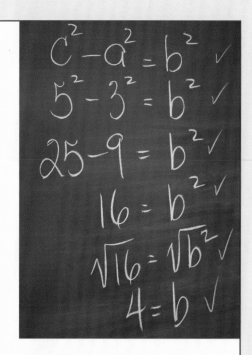

WHAT does "square root" mean?

Any number can be created by multiplying two identical numbers together: for example, 9 is three times three, and 16 is four times four. Square roots are easy for numbers like these, but get trickier with numbers like 2, which can't be expressed as the square of two whole numbers. (For example, the square root of 2 is the fraction 1.41421356…, going on into infinity!)

WHAT is an irrational number?

Most numbers can be expressed as simple fractions: for example, 2 can also be written as $^2/_1$, and we're all familiar with the quantities $^1/_2$ or $^1/_3$. But there are some numbers that can't be written as fractions, no matter how hard you try; you can recognize them because their decimals go on for infinity without any regular pattern (for example, 2.13974295792023…) These are known as the "irrational" numbers.

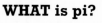

WHAT is pi?

In one way, pi is very simple: it's the ratio between the circumference of a circle (that is, its length all the way around) and its diameter (its length straight across), and comes out to about 3.14. In another way, though, pi is incredibly complicated: it's an infinite, nonrepeating decimal, meaning it can't be calculated exactly. So far, computers have determined the value of pi to about a trillion decimal places!

Why does water swirl counterclockwise when you flush the toilet?

This is an example of the "Coriolis effect." When you flush a toilet, the water on one side of the bowl travels slightly faster than the water on the other side, because the earth is spinning beneath at about 750 miles per hour (we don't feel the earth's rotation, but the water does). The unequal speeds create the familiar spiral. Because of the direction of the earth's spin, toilets flush counterclockwise in the northern hemisphere and clockwise in the southern hemisphere.

While we're on the subject, most toilets use anywhere from five to seven gallons of water per flush—and if you don't think that's a lot, imagine carrying five gallons of milk in a single grocery bag! In the past few years, companies have begun producing low-flush toilets, which only use about two gallons per flush. Not only does this save on your water bill, but it leaves more water around for other people.

WHY do things look crooked when they're dipped in water?

When it hits water, light slows down by about 25 percent (that's still pretty fast, though: the speed of light in a vacuum is 286,000 miles per second!) This "refraction" causes any object dipped into water (like a branch) to look like it's bent, but this is only an illusion caused by light's behavior.

HOW does a well work?

Wells produce water by tapping into aquifers—hidden streams or springs a hundred or so feet deep. Once a well is dug, it's not very efficient to pull up the water by lowering a bucket on a rope, as people did years ago. Instead, modern wells have pumps that draw the water up automatically. Most wells also have filters, which screen out contaminants like pebbles and silt from the underground aquifer.

WHAT is a geyser?

Among the rarest geological phenomena on earth, geysers are jets of hot water and steam that erupt periodically from pools of water or rock formations. Most of the world's geysers are found in Yellowstone Park, including Old Faithful, the most famous of them all. (There are only five major geyser fields besides Yellowstone, in Iceland, New Zealand, Russia, Chile, and Alaska.)

Geysers occur when water seeps down into the ground and comes into contact with magma (molten rock) beneath the earth's surface. As it becomes heated, the water and steam seep back up through a channel of fractured rock and erupt onto the surface.

Flowing water and subterranean magma are common enough; what makes geysers so rare is that they require exactly the right kind of porous rock to funnel the water and steam back to earth. These spurting wonders are also surprisingly delicate; some small geysers have been stopped up by people throwing litter.

WHY do hot liquids get cold, and not the other way around?

You can thank the Second Law of Thermodynamics, which states that heat always flows from a hot substance (say, a cup of tea) to a cold substance (the air surrounding it). An ice cream cone melts for the same reason, as it absorbs heat from the warmer air around it and reaches room temperature.

WHY are there bubbles in boiling water?

When you boil a pot of water, the water at the bottom of the pot (nearer the heat source) heats up faster than the water on top. When this bottom layer reaches the boiling point, the water turns to steam, which floats up in the form of bubbles, (since steam is less dense than liquid water). The steam then evaporates into the air.

HOW is water kept out of a tunnel while it's being dug?

If an underwater tunnel is built properly, there's no need to keep water out at all. The fact is, a tunnel isn't built in the water—it's dug deep into the bedrock below the water. Of course, pumps are on hand to clear out any water that manages to find its way in, but for the most part the construction workers are as dry as you or I.

WHY do teapots whistle?

A teapot whistles because it has a very narrow opening in its spout that funnels rising steam. When a vapor like steam tries to escape from a large area (the inside of the pot) through a smaller one (the narrow hole or slits inside the spout), it "vibrates" at a correspondingly higher pitch, which results in that familiar whistling sound.

WHAT are cosmic rays?

Unlike other rays—such as X-rays and gamma rays—cosmic rays aren't a form of electromagnetic radiation. Rather, these "rays" consist of subatomic particles—mostly protons, electrons, or atomic nuclei—that have been accelerated close to the speed of light.

Cosmic rays strike the earth all the time, from all directions. Some originate in the sun, but the most energetic specimens are created by supernovae (exploding stars) from elsewhere in the Milky Way galaxy.

Although cosmic rays are vanishingly small, they can be extremely powerful (this is because any object, even a single proton, gains mass and energy when it's accelerated close to the speed of light). The most potent cosmic rays yet detected contain about 10 million trillion electron volts of energy, meaning they pack the punch of a baseball thrown 100 miles per hour.

WHAT are gravitational waves?

Einstein's theory of general relativity (the source of the famous equation $E=MC^2$) predicts that massive, compact bodies like black holes can produce ripples in the fabric of space-time that move at the speed of light. These "gravitational waves," as they're called, are extremely difficult to detect, because even the most powerful waves will move the most sensitive detectors yet built by only a microscopic, almost undetectable amount.

WHAT are gamma rays?

As powerful as X-rays are compared to ordinary light, that's how powerful gamma rays are compared to X-rays. The most energetic form of radiation in the universe, gamma rays are created by the most violent events imaginable: say, a star being swallowed by a black hole. Some gamma-ray bursts from distant galaxies contain more energy than our sun will produce in its entire 10-billion-year existence!

WHY is ultraviolet light dangerous?

Ultraviolet light has a very short wavelength, meaning it's more energetic than visible light from the sun. If you're exposed to these rays for extended periods of time, during a hot, sunny day at the beach, they can damage the cells beneath your skin and cause certain types of cancer years later. That's why it's important to use plenty of sunscreen, and not to stay out in the sun for too long.

HOW does a microwave oven cook food?

Microwaves are a form of electromagnetic radiation (like X-waves and radio waves) that interact strongly with the moisture in organic substances and only weakly with paper or plastic. When the water molecules inside food are exposed to microwave radiation, they start vibrating rapidly, heating up your burrito much faster than an ordinary oven.

You may wonder: why doesn't the outside of a microwave oven get hot? The inside of the oven (called the "cooking chamber") is surrounded by a metallic mesh. Microwaves are actually very wide compared to air molecules, so the holes in this mesh are big enough to let air in and out, but small enough to reflect microwaves back so they don't heat up the outside of the oven.

WHAT is a laser?

The word "laser" is an acronym standing for Light Amplification by Stimulated Emission of Radiation. What this means is that lasers produce "coherent" light, that is, a tightly focused beam of photons (particles of light) that all have the same energy and orientation. By contrast, most ordinary light is "incoherent," meaning the photons have different energies and orientations, so they produce a whitish, unfocused blur.

HOW does an electron microscope work?

Rather than light, an electron microscope shoots a beam of electrons (the tiny elementary particles that make up electricity) at the object being magnified. Because electrons are so small, their "wavy" nature causes them to scatter off the object, the way light scatters off objects in a regular microscope. Using an electron microscope, scientists can make out detailed structures in a single human cell!

WHAT is electromagnetic radiation?

Visible light—the kind by which we see everyday objects—makes up only a small part of the electromagnetic spectrum (that is, the wide range of radiation composed of "photons," or particles of light). The parts of this spectrum are classified according to wavelength: high-energy beams (like X-rays) have extremely short wavelengths, low-energy beams (like radio waves) have extremely long wavelengths, and visible light falls somewhere in the middle.

HOW often do meteors strike earth?

Tiny, dust-sized meteors collide with our planet all the time, but they burn up in the atmosphere. Even larger meteorites, which survive this fiery fall and strike the earth fairly often, are not much bigger than pebbles. The meteors to worry about are big, multiton asteroids, which hit the earth every hundred thousand years or so and do a lot of damage.

HOW big is the universe?

Astronomers estimate that the visible portion of the universe stretches for about 15 billion light years in all directions (a light year is about 6 trillion miles), give or take a few billion. As for the invisible portion—the part of the universe whose light hasn't had time to reach us yet—it may well be infinite in volume. As far as scientists can tell, the universe is still expanding, and they don't know when (or if) it will ever stop.

HOW can we find aliens?

No reputable scientists believe that little green men have landed on the earth. However, astronomers have tried to intercept possible radio transmissions from outer space. The trouble is, there are billions of stars in our galaxy where aliens might reside, and we can only search a tiny part of the sky at any given time.

WHAT are comets?

Comets are nothing more than enormous, dirty snowballs (with some ammonia and methane thrown in), ranging in size from a few feet to a few hundred miles. Comets revolve around the sun in extremely wide orbits, which is why the most famous, Halley's Comet, only passes by the Earth once every 76 years!

WHAT is a black hole?

When a cloud of gas in outer space reaches a certain size and temperature, it collapses under its own gravity and a star begins to form in its center. As the star shrinks to a certain size, the pressure in its core becomes equal to the pressure pushing down from the outer layers of gas, and it stops shrinking.

However, if the initial gas cloud is extremely massive, the core of the developing star can't withstand the outer pressure, and the whole thing collapses, or implodes, into an infinitely tiny, infinitely dense point in space, called a "singularity." This weird object is so small and so heavy that it literally warps the space around it, so that not even light can escape. Because of this, astronomers can't observe a black hole directly—they can only see the effects it has on surrounding, normal matter.

WHY don't planets twinkle?

Planets like Venus and Mars reflect the light of the sun, and look extremely bright in the night sky. Because they are so much closer to the earth than stars, their strong reflected light can penetrate the earth's atmosphere without experiencing the "twinkling" effect of distant starlight.

WHY do stars twinkle?

Twinkling is caused by interference from the earth's atmosphere, which scatters and bends starlight every which way. The reason stars appear to twinkle more when they're near the horizon is that you're seeing them through a greater volume of air.

WHAT is a light year?

The gulfs between stars and galaxies are so vast that it doesn't make sense to measure them in feet and inches. Since light is the fastest thing in the universe, scientists find it convenient to state astronomical lengths in light years, the distance light travels in a year—which is about 6 trillion miles.

HOW fast does the earth travel?

The earth moves in so many directions at once it can make you dizzy to think about it. The thing is, the only way we can tell we're moving is when we accelerate (speed up) or decelerate (slow down), and since the earth does all its spinning and rotating at constant speeds, we don't feel any movement at all—for the same reason we don't feel a jet plane moving as it flies at 500 mile per hour.

First, the earth rotates on its axis once every day, which is 24 hours. Its circumference at the equator is about 25,000 miles—and if you divide 25,000 by 24, you'll see that the earth is spinning at just over 1,000 miles an hour. Second, the earth revolves around the sun at about 66,000 miles per hour, third, it moves through space along with the Milky Way galaxy at over 500,000 miles per hour; and fourth, the entire Milky Way galaxy rotates around a bigger group of galaxies at over 600,000 miles per hour.

WHY can't we go back in time?

Actually, scientists haven't ruled out time machines—just the kinds of things you could do with one. For example, you couldn't travel back in time and keep your grandparents from marrying, because then your grandparents wouldn't have had your father, and your father wouldn't have had you (so who traveled back to stop them in the first place?). This is called a "paradox," and it's the main reason most scientists think time travel is impossible.

WHAT are superstrings?

Some physicists believe that all elementary particles—including protons, neutrons, electrons, and photons—represent different vibrations of small, elemental, string-like objects. The problem with this theory is that these strings would be so incredibly tiny (less than a trillion trillion times the size of a single proton) that there's no prospect of our ever actually seeing one!!

WHAT was the Big Bang?

Scientists have known for quite some time that our universe is expanding—and logically, if billions of galaxies are speeding away from each other in the present, there must have been a time in the distant past when all the matter in the universe was compressed into an unimaginably tiny, dense and hot "nugget."

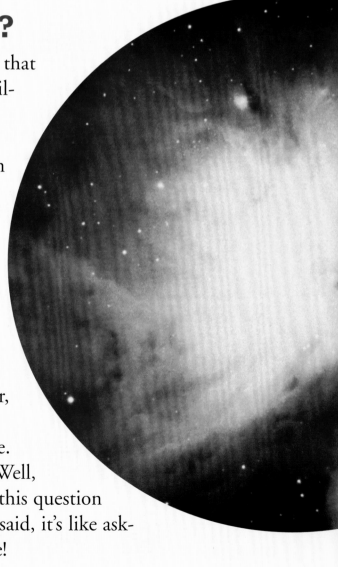

According to the most widely accepted theories, the "Big Bang" that gave birth to the universe occurred about 20 billion years ago. What was truly weird about this unbelievably large explosion was that it didn't occur in a preexisting space and time, like a firecracker going off in an empty room; rather, space and time were created in the explosion itself, along with all the matter of the universe.

So what happened "before" the Big Bang? Well, since the Big Bang created what we call time, this question doesn't really make sense. As one scientist has said, it's like asking what lies 10 miles north of the North Pole!

HOW many parallel universes are there?

The theories involved are very complex, but there is good reason to believe that ours isn't the only universe—there may be trillions upon trillions of "parallel" universes, which contain nearly identical versions of you, your family, and your school. Unfortunately, there's no way to travel to these universes (except in our imaginations), but scientists may one day be able to prove (with subtle experiments) that they really exist.

WHAT is a gravitational lens?

According to the theory of relativity, the gravitational fields of huge, massive objects like quasars, black holes, or large galaxies can "bend" light rays. A gravitational lens occurs when one of these massive objects (which is, say, one billion light-years away) is in the direct path of a more distant galaxy (which is, say, ten billion light-years away). The massive body acts as a "lens" that magnifies the light of the distant object, allowing us to see a galaxy that would otherwise be invisible.

WHAT is quantum physics?

At the level of large, everyday items, like chairs and basketballs, classical physics (the kind discovered by Isaac Newton) works just fine. Among other things, the laws of classical physics state that all bodies fall equally fast in a gravitational field, and that the speed and location of a moving object can be precisely determined.

When dealing with objects the size of atoms, though, a different set of rules come into play, known as quantum physics. Among other odd things, quantum physics states that a single atom can simultaneously behave like a particle and like a "wave" of pure energy, and that the speed and location of this atom can never be determined simultaneously, because of an essential uncertainty about where it really "is."

As scientists learn more and more about quantum physics, they've learned that the microscopic world is much, much weirder than anyone had ever imagined—and that some of these weird phenomena can even affect our own "macroscopic" level!

HOW fast can a rocket ship go?

The fastest speed ever attained by a spacecraft—a solar probe launched in the 1970's—was a little under 200,000 miles per hour. That may sound fast, but let's put it in perspective: the nearest star is about 24 trillion miles from Earth, meaning even a spaceship this fast would take hundreds of thousands of years to make the trip!

WHY doesn't the space shuttle burn up when it enters the atmosphere?

One of the most important components of the space shuttle is its outer tiles, thick, closely fitting slabs of heat-resistant silicon. These slabs are designed to endure the intense heat of re-entry (which is caused by friction from the earth's atmosphere), and if one of them falls off—as happened in 2003 on the space shuttle Columbia—the results can be disastrous.

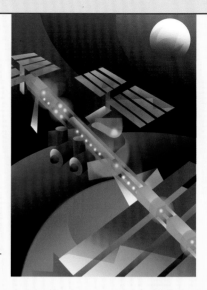

WHY can't a spaceship go faster than light?

Light is made up of particles called photons, which have no mass. According to the laws of physics, these massless particles can only travel at one speed—the speed of light, 186,000 miles per second.

Despite what you see in science-fiction movies, no spaceship can go faster than the speed of light. This is because, as anything made of matter approaches this cosmic speed limit, it becomes heavier and heavier and more and more resistant to acceleration. To boost a rocket to the speed of light, you'd need an infinite amount of energy!

Compared to light, the fastest of our man-made spacecraft are only about as speedy as snails. Some space probes have attained a velocity of about 55 miles per second, which is fast by freeway standards but only a tiny percentage of light speed.

With new technology, though, it's possible that future spacecraft will be considerably faster.

WHY are people weightless in orbit?

When a spacecraft orbits earth, the astronauts inside have escaped the earth's atmosphere, but they haven't escaped its gravitational pull. Weightlessness is equivalent to "free fall," meaning the astronauts are constantly "falling" toward earth but never getting there because of the ship's crosswise motion as it orbits the planet.

WHY can't you hear sounds in space?

Sound is carried by air molecules: when someone talks, it causes a disruption in the air that travels to your ear. Because there's no air in outer space, there's nothing for sound to be "carried" by. So when you see a science-fiction movie filled with loud outer-space laser battles, you know the director hasn't been doing his homework.

HOW many satellites orbit the earth?

The last time a comprehensive survey was made—way back in 1997—scientists estimated that there were about 25,000 man-made objects circling the earth, so that number's bound to be much bigger now. Not all of these are active satellites; in fact, the vast majority are what you would call space junk, satellites that have stopped working but haven't yet dropped out of orbit and burnt up in the atmosphere.

HOW many people have walked on the moon?

A lot fewer than you might think—only an even dozen, starting with Neil Armstrong in 1969 and ending with Eugene Cernan in 1972 (for what it's worth, every moon walker has been American).

Although no one has landed on the moon for over 30 years, there's been talk lately about sending a manned expedition to Mars, a much longer and more expensive trip. Using current technology, a spacecraft would require anywhere from six to nine months to reach Mars, and the same amount of time coming back (compared to the week or so it took to reach the moon back in 1969). With such a long round-trip, a mission wouldn't even make sense if astronauts stayed on Mars for less than a year.

Because a mission to Mars would require so many supplies—not to mention an extra-safe ship that could withstand the long journey—some experts have estimated its cost at well over a trillion dollars.

HOW far can a telescope see?

The very first telescopes could magnify distant objects three or four times, enough to make out details on the moon half a million miles away. The most powerful telescope today, the Hubble Space Telescope, technically has a magnification of about 8,000, but since it peers out over astronomical distances (which span trillions of miles), the concept of "magnification" doesn't make as much sense as it would for an earth-bound scope.

WHAT are quasars?

Quasars are the most powerful objects in the visible universe. When they were first discovered, they looked just like stars, but astronomers quickly realized they were too distant (billions of light-years away) and energetic to be classified that way. Hence the name that was bestowed on them, "quasi-stellar objects," which was soon shortened to "quasar."

Today, scientists have figured out that quasars are extremely young galaxies—formed just a billion years or so after the big bang (compared to 15 billion years for our galaxy)—that have enormous black holes in their centers. A quasar's black hole is so big that it constantly gobbles up nearby stars and dust, a process that releases tremendous amounts of energy.

By the way, since the name "quasar" no longer really makes sense, some astronomers now call these objects "active galactic nuclei."

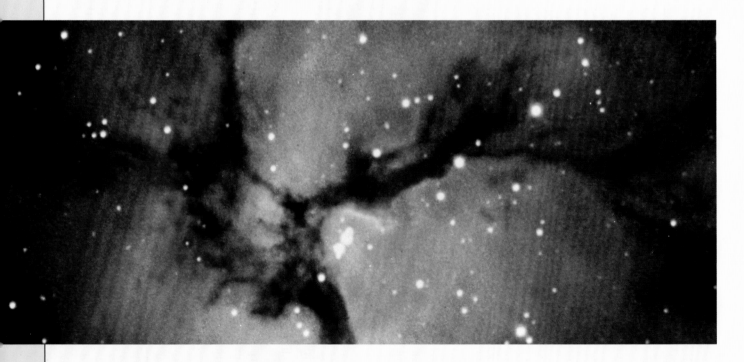

WHAT are galaxies?

Stars don't float out in the middle of space all by themselves—they belong to galaxies, huge collections of a few million to a few hundred billion stars (as well as sizeable portions of gas and dust). The galaxy we live in, the Milky Way, has a spiral shape with curving arms, but smaller, "elliptical" galaxies are basically just spherical blobs of glowing stars.

HOW many stars are in a galaxy?

Galaxies come in all sizes, so naturally, they have different numbers of stars. Our galaxy, the Milky Way, contains about 100 billion (100,000,000,000) stars, while so-called dwarf galaxies may have a few as 100,000. Our galaxy is far from the biggest—the Andromeda Galaxy, our nearest full-sized neighbor, may have as many as 300 billion stars!

HOW far is the closest galaxy?

For years, astronomers thought the closest galaxy to the Milky Way was the Large Magellanic Cloud, about 160,000 light years away (you can see it at night if you live in the southern hemisphere, along with its near companion, the Small Magellani Cloud.) But they've recently discovered a tiny dwarf galaxy, Canis Major ("Big Dog"), that's only 40,000 light years away. This small, faint galaxy is so close that it's actually tangled up with our own Milky Way!

HOW many galaxies are there?

A few decades ago, scientists believed there were only a million or so galaxies, but as astronomers peer deeper and deeper into space, they are discovering more and more galaxies. The latest estimates range anywhere from 100 billion to over a trillion. Not all of these are big, Milky Way–type galaxies, though; many are dwarf galaxies with considerably fewer stars.

WHY isn't the sky blinding white with stars?

This tricky question, also known as "Olber's Paradox," was first posed by a scientist in the nineteenth century: if the universe is infinite, and contains an infinite number of stars, why don't we see them all at the same time, rather than a sprinkle of starlight against a black background?

It took a long time for astronomers to solve this riddle. While the universe may well be infinite in volume, the number of stars we see at night is limited by three factors: the continuing expansion of the universe, the finite (though still extremely fast) speed of light, and the finite life span of the stars themselves.

Because the universe is expanding, we can only see those stars whose light has had time to reach us (since the "big bang" about 20 billion years ago). Also, stars aren't continuously shining: the brightest, most massive stars burn out in tens of millions of years, while more sedate stars like our sun shine for about 10 billion years.

WHAT is the moon made of?

It may be disappointing to all you cheese lovers, but the moon is actually made out of pretty much the same stuff as the earth—rocks and minerals.

Even though it has the same basic ingredients, the surface of the moon looks different from the surface of the earth for two main reasons. First, the moon is much smaller than the earth, with no oceans and a different geographical layout. And second, unlike our planet, the moon has no atmosphere, causing it to reflect light from the sun differently.

So why the myth about the moon being made of cheese? When meteors strike the earth, they usually burn up in the atmosphere before hitting the ground. But the moon, which has no air, is pockmarked by thousands of craters that give it a "swiss cheese" appearance when you see it through a telescope.

WHY does the moon glow?

Although we can usually only see the moon at night—when the sun isn't shining on our half of the earth—that doesn't mean the sun can't be shining on the moon, from a different direction. So the (day-time) moon shines because it's reflecting the light of the sun back to the (night-time) earth.

HOW far away is the moon?

In cosmological terms, the moon is only a stone's throw from earth—about 240,000 miles. That's only an average, though: because of its elliptical (pear-shaped) orbit, the moon can be as close as 225,000 miles or as far away as 252,000 miles at any given time.

HOW does the moon cause the tides?

Although the moon is much smaller than the earth, it still exerts a hefty gravitational pull—and because it's fluid, water responds much more readily to gravity than solid rock! During high tide, the moon is directly over a body of water, lifting it up slightly and drawing it closer to the shoreline. "Low tide," on the other hand, occurs when the moon is all the way on the other side of the planet.

HOW cold is it on the moon?

Because the moon doesn't have an atmosphere to absorb or retain heat, it experiences wild temperature swings, from over 200 degrees Celsius during the day (hotter than a pot of boiling water) to almost 200 degrees below zero at night (colder than the inside of your freezer).

WHAT is a lunar eclipse?

A lunar eclipse occurs when the sun, the earth, and the moon line up, with the earth exactly in the middle. The moon moves into the earth's shadow and is cut off from the light of the sun. In a total lunar eclipse, a full moon passes slowly through the earth's shadow, a process that can take up to two hours. In this respect, a lunar eclipse is a much better show than a solar eclipse, which only lasts for about seven minutes.

WHY does Earth have only one moon?

Our solar system has two kinds of planets: terrestrial planets like Mars and Earth, and gas giants like Jupiter and Saturn. Terrestrial planets are made of rock, while gas giants like Jupiter and Saturn are composed of gases like hydrogen and helium.

After the planets formed, the gas giants had much more extra material circling them, which coalesced into dozens of moons (these young planets may also have captured small satellites from elsewhere in the solar system). By contrast, astronomers believe Earth's moon was created by the impact of a huge meteor hitting the earth billions of years ago.

Although our single moon may seem unimpressive, some scientists think it's responsible for the evolution of life on earth. By causing the tides (which are more extreme than they'd be if there were other moons in orbit elsewhere around our planet), the moon is ultimately responsible for the shallow "tide pools" where organic chemicals may have concentrated and given rise to the very first cells.

WHY can't we see the dark side of the moon?

It takes about as long for the moon to rotate around its axis as it does for it to circle around the earth. That's why, from any given vantage point on earth, we only see the near, familiar side of the moon. The "dark" side of the moon receives an equal share of sunlight, but we're never in a position to see it when it's lit up.

WHY does the moon look bigger when it's near the horizon?

It's an optical illusion! When the moon is close to the horizon, it's easier to judge its size against nearby objects like buildings or mountains, so your brain tells you it's really big. Actually, though, the moon is exactly the same size as when it's high up in the sky, but since there's nothing for your eyes to compare it to it looks much smaller.

HOW often is a "blue moon?"

If you've ever heard the phrase "once in a blue moon," you might be curious how often that is (not to mention what a blue moon is in the first place!). A blue moon is the second full moon in a calendar month, and it happens a little less than once every year. Despite its name, a blue moon is the same color—white—as a regular full moon.

WHAT makes planets round?

When an astronomical object reaches a certain size, its gravity becomes strong enough to pull in equally from all sides and "sculpt" its material into the shape of a sphere (this takes a longer time for rocky planets like the earth than for gas giants like Jupiter). The reason smaller asteroids have irregular shapes is because they don't have enough mass, and therefore enough gravity, to pull off this trick.

HOW many rings does Saturn have?

Astronomers divide Saturn's rings into six main groups, labeled A, B, C, D, E, and F. But within these groups there are thousands of separate "ringlets," too numerous to count, circling the planet. Since Saturn's rings aren't solid—they're made of dust-sized particles—it can be hard to tell where one ring ends and another begins.

WHAT is the Great Red Spot on Jupiter?

Jupiter's famous spot—and "spot" doesn't seem quite like the right word for something 25,000 miles across!—is actually a gigantic storm that's lasted for thousands of years. As big as our planet, this storm packs winds of hundreds (and possibly thousands) of miles an hour, and would completely demolish an earth city in no time flat!

WHY are there canals on Mars?

There aren't, at least not canals as we know them—in the sense of structures created by an intelligent race. In 1876, an Italian astronomer sighted some long, narrow bands on the Martian structure and called them canali ("channels" in Italian). This got translated into English as "canals." No one yet knows what these structures really are, but it's possible they were left by rivers from a billion years ago, when Mars may have had flowing water.

HOW long is a day on Jupiter?

You might think a day on the largest planet in the solar system would last forever, but in fact, Jupiter spins so quickly that its day is only 10 hours long (compared to 24 hours on earth). A year on Jupiter is another matter entirely: the planet takes 4,333 days to revolve around the sun, meaning one Jupiter year is equivalent to a dozen earth years!

HOW many planets are there?

This used to be an easy question to answer: every kid can list Mercury, Venus, Earth, Mars, Jupiter, Saturn, Uranus, Neptune and Pluto. But as with so many things about the solar system, things aren't quite as simple as they seem.

First, there's the matter of Pluto. Scientists have always disagreed about whether this tiny, distant ball of rock qualifies as a planet, since it's about the size of Earth's moon and may well have originated as a satellite of Jupiter or Saturn. Further complicating matters, Pluto was recently discovered to have its own "moon," Charon, which is about half its size. Since Pluto is described as a planet, why not Charon too?

Second, some astronomers believe there may be a huge, Jupiter-sized planet orbiting the sun beyond Pluto and Charon. If so, this planet would be virtually impossible to detect, since it would reflect so little light from the sun.

HOW big is an asteroid?

Like planets and comets, asteroids come in all sizes—ranging from tiny pebbles to huge boulders (the largest asteroid, Ceres, is 578 miles wide). Most asteroids orbit the sun between Mars and Jupiter in what is known as the Asteroid Belt; they might be the remains of a planet that was destroyed millions of years ago!

WHY is Venus so hot?

Mercury may be closer to the sun, but part of the reason the average temperature on Venus is even hotter—about 900 degrees Fahrenheit—is because of the "greenhouse effect." Venus has a lot of carbon dioxide in its atmosphere, which traps heat from the sun and prevents it from radiating back out into space.

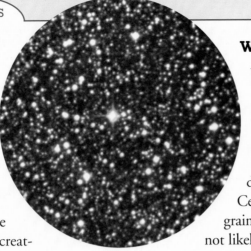

WHAT is a neutron star?

Atoms in the middle of a collapsing star are under enormous pressure. The electrons at the outside of the atom can be "pushed" right into the protons at the center, creating a neutron. Since the outer shell of electrons accounts for most of an atom's size, a star made of neutrons is very, very small and incredibly dense: a single teaspoon of it weighs as much as a billion elephants.

HOW many constellations are there?

A constellation isn't an astronomical object, like a planet or a galaxy; rather, it's a connect-the-dots picture imagined in ancient times by people looking up at stars in the night sky. There are 88 official constellations, ranging from familiar ones like Ursa Major—better known as the Big Dipper—and Orion, to obscure ones like Mensa and Microscopium.

WHY don't stars ever collide?

Stars are actually quite small compared to the vast distances separating them. Proxima Centauri, the closest star to the sun, is 4.3 light years away—which doesn't sound like much, until you realize that's over 25 trillion miles. If you scaled that down so the distance was one mile, the sun and Proxima Centauri would each be the size of sand grains—and two grains of sand a mile apart are not likely to have a collision.

WHAT is a white dwarf?

Not all stars end their lives as supernovas. When a star the size of our sun runs out of fuel, it gradually sheds most of its outer layers, and the remaining core shrinks into a small, dense, glowing remnant. Over billions of years, this "white dwarf" gradually cools down until it is an invisible cinder floating in space.

WHY do stars have different colors?

Just as they vary in size, stars have different colors and temperatures. Our own star, the sun, is fairly small as stars go, and produces light in the orange-yellow part of the spectrum (which is a good thing, since this is the perfect kind of radiation to support life). Smaller, hotter stars have a blue-white appearance, while giant, cooler stars have a distinct reddish color.

This leads to an interesting question: if there are red stars and blue stars, why aren't there green stars? In fact, some stars do radiate green light, but they also glow strongly in the colors surrounding green in the spectrum, like yellow and blue. By the time the light of these stars reaches earth, all of these colors have mixed together, and the result is a plain, white dot in the sky.

WHAT is the biggest star in our galaxy?

Not only is Eta Carinae, which is about 7,500 light years away, over 100 times bigger than the sun, but it's one of the most spectacular objects in the universe. This star is so gigantic and so unstable that it's on the verge of exploding. It has already ejected two gigantic lobes of expanding dust and gas, each of which is hundreds of times bigger than our own solar system. Scientists predict that Eta Carinae may become a supernova within the next ten or twenty thousand years.

WHAT is a supernova?

When a massive star—one that's at least five or ten times bigger than the sun—nears the end of its life, it exhausts the nuclear fuel in its core and starts to contract. At some point, the core becomes so incredibly dense that it can't be squeezed any further. The outer layers of the star, which had been rushing inward at incredible speeds, suddenly bounce back, creating a huge shock wave. In its first few seconds, a supernova radiates as much energy as a hundred billion stars!

After supernovas explode, some leave behind small, rapidly spinning neutron stars, while the cores of more massive stars can collapse into invisible black holes. Whatever the case, a huge cloud (called a nebula) of gas and dust surrounds the stellar remnant, visible for all to see. The Crab Nebula, for example, is all that's left of a supernova that exploded in our galaxy back in the 11th century.

WHAT is a solar eclipse?

A solar eclipse occurs when the moon passes between the earth and the sun. Because the moon is small compared to the earth—and because its orbit around the earth is tilted at a slight incline from the earth's orbit around the sun—partial eclipses (in which the moon only blocks out a part of the sun) are much more common than full eclipses.

During a full solar eclipse—a very rare event where the moon completely blocks out the sun over a certain part of the world—it gets as dark as night for three our four minutes. This darkness is so convincing, in fact, that it can completely fool local animals. During one daytime eclipse in Africa, bats and owls came out of their caves and trees convinced that the sun had gone down and it was time to hunt!

HOW far away is the sun?

The sun is about 93 million miles away from earth, and that's a good thing—any closer and our planet would be too hot to support life, and any farther away and it'd be too cold. At this distance, the light from the sun takes eight minutes to reach earth (or, as astronomers might put it, the sun is eight light-minutes away).

WHY are days hotter in summer and colder in winter?

It's not colder in the winter because the earth is farther away from the sun. It's because the earth revolves around the sun on a tilted axis, meaning the northern hemisphere is inclined toward the sun for half the year and inclined away from the sun for the other half. Since the sun's rays are less "direct" in winter, the temperature drops accordingly. The exact opposite thing happens in the southern hemisphere, which is why Christmas in Australia takes place during the summer.

HOW hot is the sun?

On its surface, the sun is a relatively cool 5,000 degrees Celsius, but in its center, where hydrogen atoms fuse into helium to create energy, the temperature is 15 million degrees—hotter than an exploding nuclear bomb.

HOW big is the sun?

The sun's diameter is about 100 times that of our planet, meaning the space it takes up could be occupied by one million earths. But the sun isn't even the biggest star around; there are plenty of stars in our own Milky Way galaxy that make it seem puny by comparison.

WHAT makes the sun shine?

You may have heard of Albert Einstein's famous equation, $E=MC^2$. What these deceptively simple symbols mean is that E (energy) is equal to mass (M) multiplied by the speed of light squared (C^2). In plain language, a tiny bit of mass contains an enormous amount of energy.

In the sun's core, hydrogen atoms are constantly being fused into helium atoms, a process that takes place at a staggering temperature of 15 million degrees. However, the weight of the resulting helium atoms is a tiny bit less than the weight of the hydrogen atoms that produced them. This missing percentage is converted into energy, which radiates out into space as light and heat.

The sun converts 600 million tons of hydrogen into helium every second. Amazingly, our star is massive enough that it can sustain this output for 10 billion years!

WHY does the sun turn red when it sets?

As the sun nears the horizon, its light travels through more of the earth's atmosphere than when it's high up in the sky. Since the air in the atmosphere scatters short-wavelength light (that is, light in the blue part of the spectrum), the light that reaches your eyes from the setting sun has longer wavelengths, in the red and orange part of the spectrum.

WHY do planets orbit the sun?

Technically, planets move in straight lines—it's the space around them that's curved! Because the sun is so massive, it "warps" the space around it into a roughly spherical shape (this is what we experience as gravity). As far as a planet knows, it's moving in a perfectly straight line, but because it's trapped in this "gravitational well" it orbits the sun like a marble circling the rim of a soup bowl.

Index